A Model of Macroeconomic Activity

Volume I:
The Theoretical Model

A Model of Macroeconomic Activity

Volume I:
The Theoretical Model

Ray C. Fair

Ballinger Publishing Company ● Cambridge, Mass.
A Subsidiary of J. B. Lippincott Company

International Standard Book Number: 0-88410-268-8

Library of Congress Catalog Card Number: 74-12199

Printed in the United States of America

Library of Congress Cataloging in Publication Data

Fair, Ray C
        A model of macroeconomic activity.
        Bibliography: v. 1, p.
        Contents: v. 1. The theoretical model.
        1. Macroeconomics—Mathematical models. I. Title.
HB171.F24   339   74-12199
ISBN 0-88410-268-8

Table of Contents

List of Tables

Preface

The work in this volume grew out of both my dissatisfaction with the standard static-equilibrium model that is found in most macroeconomic textbooks and my interest in the problem of basing macroeconomic theory on more solid microeconomic foundations. I was also interested in trying to incorporate into a general model of macroeconomic activity the recent work in economic theory that has been done on relaxing the assumptions of perfect information and the existence of tâtonnement processes that clear markets every period.

It soon became apparent as I began working on this project that the model that I had in mind would not be capable of being analyzed by standard analytic methods. I wanted to develop a macroeconomic model that was general, was based on solid microeconomic foundations, and was not based on the assumptions of perfect information and the existence of tâtonnement processes. I also wanted the model to account for wealth effects, capital gains effects, and all flow-of-funds constraints. Because of the likely complexity of any model of this sort, I decided at an early stage of the project to use computer simulation techniques to help analyze the properties of the model. The methodology that I followed is described in section 1.3.

One of the main dangers in building a model that is only feasible to analyze using computer simulation techniques is that the model becomes too detailed or complex for anyone other than the model builder to want to spend the time that it takes to understand the model. I clearly face this danger in the present case. However, I have tried to write this volume to make the model as intelligible as possible in as simple a way as possible. First, I have constructed a "condensed" version of the basic model, with the aim of making the model easier to understand. Second, I have constructed a "static-equilibrium" version of the model, with the hope that this will put the basic model in a better perspective. Third, I have organized the discussion so that the different sectors are each discussed individually before the overall model is put together. The discussion of each sector is fairly self-contained, so that the reader can concentrate at first on the properties of each sector without having to comprehend the complete model. (I have, however, given a brief outline of the overall model in Chapter One.) Finally, I have relied heavily on the use of tables to present the model and have tried to make the tables fairly self-contained from the discussion in the text. One should be able to get a good picture of the overall model from a careful reading of the tables. The tables should also be useful for reference purposes.

There are, as discussed in Chapter Eight, many ways in which the present model might be extended. In many cases these extensions were not carried out here because of the desire not to increase the complexity of the model anymore than already existed. In future work, if the model does not turn out to be too unwieldy to comprehend, it would be of interest to carry out many of the extensions.

This volume is one of two. In Volume II an empirical model will be developed that is based on the theoretical model found in this volume. Because there is no unique way to specify an empirical version of the theoretical model, it seemed best to present the theoretical and empirical models in two separate volumes. The present volume can be read without reference to Volume II.

Neither volume has been written specifically as a textbook. It is possible, however, that either or both volumes could be used as texts in a graduate level macroeconomics course. Because of my unhappiness with the standard textbook model, I have used for the past two years parts of the present volume in a graduate level macroeconomics course that I have taught at Princeton.

I would like to thank a number of people for their helpful comments on an earlier draft of this volume. These include Alan S. Blinder, Gregory C. Chow, Robert W. Clower, Kenneth D. Garbade, Herschel I. Grossman, Edwin Kuh, and Michael Rothschild. I am also grateful to the National Science Foundation for financial support.

Ray C. Fair
May 1974

A Model of Macroeconomic Activity

Volume 1:
The Theoretical Model

Chapter One

Introduction

1.1 THE PURPOSE OF THE STUDY

Much of the work in economic theory in the past few years has been concerned with relaxing two important assumptions of classical economic theory: perfect information and the existence of tâtonnement processes to clear markets. One group of studies has followed from the work of Patinkin [43, Chapter 13] and Clower [10].[a] Some of the studies in this group have been concerned with the question of whether standard, textbook Keynesian theory is different from what Keynes [30] actually had in mind. Clower [10] and particularly Leijonhujvud [32] have argued that it is, whereas Grossman [25] has argued that it is not. Although the question of what Keynes meant is primarily of historical interest, the studies of Clower and others have made important advances in macroeconomic theory. By relaxing the assumption that markets are always in equilibrium, these studies have provided a more solid theoretical basis for the existence of the Keynesian consumption function and for the existence of unemployment. The existence of excess supply in the labor market is a justification for including income as an explanatory variable in the consumption function, and the existence of excess supply in the commodity market is a justification for the existence of unemployment.

Another group of studies concerned with relaxing the assumption of perfect information has followed from the work of Stigler [52].[b] The most prominent studies in this group are the studies in Phelps et al. [44]. Many of the studies in this group have been concerned with the mechanism by which prices or wages are determined.[c] In most cases prices or wages are postulated as being set by firms, as opposed to, say, by customers or workers. The price- or wage-setting activities of firms are usually assumed to be guided by profit-maximizing considerations. In particular, Phelps has emphasized with respect to

1

the studies in Phelps et al. [44] that ". . . [the theory] sticks doggedly to the neoclassical postulates of lifetime expected utility maximization and net worth maximization. . ."[45, p. 3].

Although important progress has been made in relaxing the assumptions of perfect information and tâtonnement processes, no general theoretical model has been developed with these assumptions relaxed. In the disequilibrium model of Barro and Grossman [5], for example, only output and employment are determined. All other variables, including prices and wages, are taken as given. There are no financial and investment sectors in the model. In the further study of Grossman[26], only investment is determined, and no attempt is made to integrate the investment model with the earlier output and employment model.

In the Solow and Stiglitz model [51], output, employment, prices, and wages are determined, but there are no financial and investment sectors. Also, as Barro and Grossman point out,[d] the Solow and Stiglitz model is not constructed on a choice-theoretic basis. Likewise, the Korliras model [31], which is similar to the Solow and Stiglitz model but does include financial and investment sectors, is not constructed on a choice-theoretic basis. The model of Tucker [55] is concerned with short run fluctuations in output and employment, and prices and wages are taken as given. In the group of studies concerned with price-setting behavior,[e] the price- or wage-setting activities of firms have also not been considered within the context of a general theoretical model. In the Maccini model [36], for example, which is one of the more general models in this group, only prices, output, and inventories are determined. There are no employment, investment, and financial sectors in the model.

The studies cited above, with the possible exception of the study of Korliras [31], could be characterized as "partial equilibrium" studies if they were equilibrium studies, but given that the studies are concerned with disequilibrium phenomena, they can perhaps best be characterized as "partial disequilibrium" studies. The partial nature of these studies is particularly restrictive in a disequilibrium context because of the possible effects that disequilibrium in one market may have on other markets. For example, models in which there is no financial sector rule out any effects that disequilibrium in financial markets may have on labor and goods markets. The Korliras model, while being more general in certain respects than the other models, is particularly restrictive with respect to the effects of one market on another. The model rules out any cross-market effects of disequilibrium and concentrates only on within-market disequilibrium effects. Tucker's discussion [56] of Korliras's model emphasizes this point.

In addition to the partial nature of the studies cited above, it is also the case that the price-setting behavior postulated by the second group of studies, in particular that firms set prices and/or wages to maximize profits, has not been integrated into the first group of studies. Only in the models of Solow and Stiglitz and Korliras are prices and wages determined, and these models are not choice-theoretic. The treatment of prices and wages as exogenous or in an ad hoc manner is again particularly restrictive in a disequilibrium context because disequilibrium questions are inherently concerned with the problem that prices somehow do not get set in such a way as always to clear markets. It is thus particularly important in a disequilibrium context to determine how prices are set and why it is that prices may not always clear markets.

The purpose of this study is to develop a theoretical model of macroeconomic activity with the following characteristics.

1. The model should be general enough to incorporate most of the variables of interest in a macroeconomic context.
2. The model should be based on solid microeconomic foundations in the sense that the decisions of the main behavioral units in the model should be derived from the assumption of maximizing behavior.
3. The behavioral units in the model should not be assumed to have perfect foresight, but instead should be assumed to have to make decisions on the basis of expectations that may not always turn out to be correct.
4. Tâtonnement processes that clear markets every period should not be postulated.

Regarding point 1, the endogenous variables in the present model include sales, production, employment, investment, prices, wages, interest rates, and loans. The model also accounts for wealth effects, capital gains effects, all flow-of-funds constraints, and the government budget constraint. The general nature of the model allows cross-market disequilibrium effects to be analyzed, allows one to consider why prices, wages, and interest rates may not always be set in such a way that clears markets every period, and allows the effects of various aggregate constraints, like the flow-of-funds constraints, to be analyzed.

The rest of this chapter provides an outline of the model and discusses various methodological and computational issues. The individual behavioral units are discussed in detail in Chapters Two through Five. The dynamic properties of the overall model are discussed in Chapter Six. A static-equilibrium version of the dynamic model is presented in Chapter Seven, and this version is compared to the standard static-equilibrium model found in most macroeconomic textbooks. Chapter Eight contains a brief summary of the model and its properties, a discussion of how the model might be changed or extended, and a discussion of some of the empirical implications of the model.

1.2 AN OUTLINE OF THE MODEL

There are five basic behavioral units in the model: banks, firms, households, a bond dealer, and the government. Banks are meant here to include all financial intermediaries, not just commercial banks. At the beginning of each period each bank, firm, and household, knowing last period's values, receiving in some cases information from others regarding certain current-period values, and forming expectations of future values, solves an optimal control problem.

The objective function of banks and firms is the present discounted value of expected future after-tax profits, and the objective function of households is the present discounted value of expected future utility. The fact that the decisions of the main behavioral units are derived by solving optimal control problems places the model on a respectable microeconomic foundation, thus meeting the requirement of point 2 above. Point 3 is also met in the sense that the decisions are based on *expectations* of future values, rather than on the actual future values. None of the behavioral units in the model has perfect foresight.

The model is recursive in the sense that information flows in one direction from the bond dealer, to banks, to firms, to households. Banks, for example, are not given an opportunity to change their decisions for the current period once firms and households have made theirs. After all decisions have been made at the beginning of the period, transactions take place throughout the rest of the period. The recursive nature of the model meets the requirement of point 4 above in the sense that recontracting is not allowed. Banks, for example, only find out what the decisions of firms and households are in the current period by the transactions that take place during the period. Likewise, firms only find out what the decisions of households are by the transactions that take place.

There is one good in the economy, which can be used either for consumption or investment purposes. There are no consumer durables: all goods that are used for consumption purposes are consumed in the current period. All labor is homogenous. Bank loans are one-period loans, government bills are one-period securities, and government bonds are consols. There is no currency in the system.

The decision variables of the government are the various tax rates in the system, the reserve requirement ratio, the number of goods to purchase, the number of worker hours to pay for, the value of bills to issue, and the number of bonds to have outstanding. The government is subject to the constraint each period that expenditures less revenues must equal the change in the value of bills plus bonds plus bank reserves (high powered money).[f] The government's decisions are treated as exogenous in the model.

Banks receive money from households in the form of savings deposits, on which interest is paid, and from households, firms, and the bond dealer in the form of demand deposits, on which no interest is paid. Banks lend money to households and firms and buy government bills and bonds. Banks are assumed not to compete for savings deposits, and the rate paid on all savings deposits is assumed to be the bill rate. Banks hold reserves in the form of deposits with the government. Banks do not hire labor and do not buy goods.

At the beginning of the period, banks receive information from the government on the tax rates and the reserve requirement ratio for the current period and from the bond dealer on the bill and bond rates for the current period. However, at this time banks do not know the values of their demand and savings deposits for the current period, and do not know the demand schedules for their loans. Banks must form expectations of these variables for the current period, as well as for the future periods, when making their decisions at the beginning of the period.

The three main decision variables of each bank are its loan rate, the value of bills and bonds to buy, and the maximum amount of money that it will lend in the period. Once a bank makes its decision on the value of bills and bonds to buy, the bank is assumed to have to buy this amount in the period. A bank needs to set a maximum on the amount of money that it will lend in the period in order to prepare for the possibility that it either overestimates the supply of funds available to it in the period or underestimates the demand for its loans at the loan rate that it set. Because of these two possibilities, a bank may end up with the actual demand for its loans at the loan rate that it set being greater than the amount that it can supply. A bank is assumed to prepare for this by setting the maximum amount of money that it will lend in the period low enough so that the bank is assured, based on its past expectation errors, that it will end up in the period with at least this much money to lend.

Firms borrow money from banks, hire labor from households, buy goods from other firms for investment purposes, and produce and sell goods to other firms, households, and the government. At the beginning of the period each firm receives information from the government on the profit tax rate for the current period, and from banks on the loan rate that it will be charged for the period and on the maximum amount of money that it will be able to borrow in the period. (Since in general each bank sets a different loan rate, it is not obvious which loan rate any particular firm faces. It also is not obvious how the loan constraints from the banks are translated into the loan constraint facing any particular firm. Problems of this sort are discussed in section 1.3.) Firms do not know at this time the demand schedules for their goods for the current period and the supply schedules of labor for the current period.

The seven main decision variables of a firm are: (1) its price, (2) its production, (3) its investment, (4) its wage rate, (5) its loans from banks, (6) the maximum number of worker hours that it will pay for in the period, and (7) the maximum number of goods that it will sell in the period. Regarding the latter two variables, firms, like banks, must prepare for the possibility that their expectations are incorrect. A firm is assumed not to want to hire more labor in the period than it plans at the beginning of the period to hire. Since a firm may underestimate the supply of labor facing it at the wage rate that it set, it prepares for this possibility by setting a maximum on the amount of labor that it will hire in the period. This maximum is assumed to be the amount that the firm plans at the beginning of the period to hire. A firm is also assumed to set a maximum on the number of goods it will sell in the period, since it cannot sell more goods in the period than the sum of what it produces and has in inventories. The maximum is assumed to be set low enough so that the firm is assured, based on its past expectation errors, that it will end up in the period with at least this many goods to sell.

Households receive wage income from firms and the government, purchase goods from firms, and pay taxes to the government. A household either has a positive amount of savings or is in debt. It it has savings, the savings can take the form of demand deposits, savings deposits, or stocks. If it is in debt, the debt takes the form of loans from banks. A household does not both borrow from banks and have savings deposits or stocks at the same time. At the beginning of the period each household receives eight items of information for the current period: (1) the tax rates, (2) the rate it will be paid on its savings deposits (the bill rate), (3) the loan rate it will be charged, (4) the maximum amount of money it will be allowed to borrow, (5) the price it will be charged for goods, (6) the wage rate it will be paid, (7) the maximum number of hours it will be allowed to work, and (8) the maximum number of goods it will be allowed to purchase. (The question of how this information gets translated to each particular household is discussed in section 1.3.) The two main decision variables of a household are the number of hours to work and the number of goods to purchase.

The bond dealer represents in the model both the bill and bond market and the stock market. The bond dealer does not hire labor and does not buy goods. The decision variables of the bond dealer are the bill rate, the bond rate, and the average stock price. The bond dealer is not a profit maximizer; rather, its tries to set the bill and bond rates for the next period so as to equate the demand for bills and bonds in that period to the supply of bills and bonds in the period. The bond dealer holds an inventory of bills and bonds, and it absorbs in each period any difference between the supply of bills and bonds from the government and the demand for bills and bonds from the banks.

Households own the stock of the banks, the firms, and the bond dealer. All after-tax profits of the banks, firms, and bond dealer are paid to the households in the form of dividends. Banks, firms, and the bond dealer are assumed not to issue any new stocks. The bond dealer sets the average stock price equal to the present discounted value of expected future dividend levels, the discount rates being expected future bill rates. The expectations of the future dividend levels and bill rates are formed by households and are communicated to the bond dealer. All households are assumed to have the same expectations regarding these variables.

Because of the way the bond dealer sets the stock price, households expect the before-tax, one-period rate of return on stocks, including capital gains and losses, to be the same for a given period as the expected bill rate for that period. The bill rate is the rate paid on savings deposits. Now, capital gains and losses are assumed to be recorded each period and to be taxed as regular income, which means that households also expect the *after-tax* rates of return on stocks and savings deposits to be the same. Households can therefore be assumed to be indifferent between holding their assets in the form of stocks or in the form of savings deposits. This assumption greatly simplifies the model.

Banks are similarly assumed to be indifferent between holding the nonloan part of their assets in the form of bills or in the form of bonds. The bond dealer sets the price of a bond, each bond yielding one dollar per period forever, equal to the present discounted value of a perpetual stream of one-dollar payments, the discount rates being the current bill rate and expected future bill rates. These expectations of the bill rates are formed by banks and are communicated to the bond dealer. All banks are assumed to have the same expectations regarding the future bill rates. The bond rate is equal to the reciprocal of the bond price.

Because of the way that the price of a bond is set, banks expect the before-tax, one-period rate of return on bonds, including capital gains and losses, to be the same for a given period as the expected bill rate for that period. Since capital gains and losses are recorded each period and taxed as regular income, banks also expect the *after-tax* rates of return on bills and bonds to be the same, which means that they can be assumed to be indifferent between the two.

The discussion in the last three paragraphs can be summarized to say that stocks and savings deposits are assumed to be perfect substitutes and that bills and bonds are assumed to be perfect substitutes. These assumptions have the effect of decreasing the number of decision variables of both households and banks by one each, and they obviously simplify the model. As will be seen in section 1.3, distributional issues are generally ignored in this study, and the above assumptions are in a sense just another example of the ignoring of distributional issues. The reason that stocks and bonds were included in the model at all was so that the effects of capital gains and losses on the economy could be analyzed.

The bond dealer is assumed to set the bond price and the stock price for the next period at the end of the current period, but before all transactions for the current period have been completed. This is assumed to be done so that capital gains and losses for the current period can be recorded during the current period. All stocks in the model are end-of-period stocks. The model is discrete, and no consideration is given to the rate of change of the stock variables during the period.

In a nontâtonnement model the order in which information flows and transactions take place is obviously quite important. In a tâtonnement model the order is not important because recontracting is allowed and no transactions take place until the equilibrium prices and quantities have been determined. One must also be concerned in a nontâtonnement model with what determines the actual quantities traded when the quantities demanded do not necessarily equal the quantities supplied. In the present case the order of the flow of information has been specified in a way that makes it easy to determine the actual quantities traded. The important property of the model that allows this to be done is that firms make their decisions subject to the loan constraints from the banks and that households make their decisions subject to the loan constraints from the banks and the hours and goods constraints from the firms.

It will be useful for purposes of describing the determination of the actual quantities traded to define a firm's *unconstrained* demand for loans to be the firm's demand for loans if it were not subject to a loan constraint.[h] This demand can be computed by solving the optimal control problem of the firm with no loan constraint imposed. A firm's *constrained* demand for loans will be defined as the firm's demand for loans when it is subject to the loan constraint. When the loan constraint is not binding, the firm's unconstrained and constrained demands are the same. Otherwise, the constrained demand is less than the unconstrained demand. The constrained demand will sometimes be referred to as the "actual" demand, since, as discussed below, the constrained demand is always the actual value of loans taken out in the period.

It will likewise be useful to define a household's unconstrained demand for goods and supply of labor to be the household's demand and supply if it were subject to none of the three possible constraints. The constrained demand and supply are the demand and supply that result when the three constraints are imposed on the household. The constrained demand is the actual quantity of goods bought in the period, and the constrained supply is the actual quantity of labor sold in the period. Using these definitions, the determination of the actual quantities traded in the model can now be described.

Since firms and households make their decisions knowing the loan constraints from banks, the constrained-maximization processes of firms and households will always result in the constrained demand for loans being less than or equal to the maximum set by the banks. Since banks are assumed to set the maximum low enough so that they are assured of ending up with this much money to lend, the constrained demand for loans will always be the actual value of loans taken out in the period. If the actual value of loans in the period turns out to be less than the amount of money the banks end up with to lend, the difference is assumed to take the form of excess reserves.

In the case in which banks receive more money in the period to lend that they expected, they are assumed not to receive this information quickly enough in the period to be able to pass it along to firms and households in the form of less restrictive loan constraints. Banks will, of course, end up with excess reserves not only if they underestimate the supply of funds available to them in the period, but also if they overestimate the demand for loans. In other words, the loan constraints may not be binding on firms and households, and firms and households may choose, unconstrained, to borrow less money at the given loan rates than the banks had expected.

Households make their decisions knowing the hours constraints from firms and the government, thus the constrained maximization processes of households will always result in the constrained supply of labor being less than or equal to the sum of the government's demand and the maximum set by the firms. The constrained supply of labor will thus always be the actual quantity of labor sold in the period. If the hours constraints are not binding on the households, so that the unconstrained and constrained supplies of labor are the same, then the supply of labor will be less than the sum of the government's demand and the maximum set by the firms. In this case the government is assumed to get all the labor that it demanded, so that the firms are the ones who end up with less labor than they expected. (Remember that the maximum set by a firm is its expected supply.) In this case the firms may be forced to produce less output than they had planned, depending on how much excess labor they had planned for. (The concept of "excess labor" is discussed at the end of this section.)

Because households make their decisions knowing the goods constraints from firms, the constrained maximization processes of households will always result in the constrained demand for goods being less than or equal to the maximum set by the firms. The demand for goods includes the demand by households, the demand by the government, and the demand by firms (in the form of investment). Firms and the government are assumed always to get the number of goods that they want, so that households are the ones who are subject to a goods constraint.

Since firms are assumed to set the maximum low enough so that they are assured of having this many goods to sell in the period, it will always be the case that the constrained demand for goods is less than or equal to the available supply. Any difference between the number of goods produced and sold by the firms results in a change in inventories. If it happens that the actual demand for a firm's goods exceeds the demand the firm expected,[i] the firm is assumed not to receive this information quickly enough for it to be able to increase its production and employment plans for the period.

This completes the discussion of some of the main transactions in the model. It is obvious that the particular order of information flows and transactions postulated in the model is somewhat arbitrary and that other orders could be postulated. The particular order chosen here was designed to try to capture possible credit rationing effects from the financial sector to the real sector and possible employment constraints from the business sector to the household sector. This order seemed to be the most natural one, although in future work it would be of interest to see how sensitive the conclusions of this study are to the postulation of different orders.

The assumptions that firms do not retain any earnings and do not issue any bonds and new stocks are not as restrictive in the present context as one might think. What the model is trying to capture are aggregate financial restrictions facing the firm sector, and if in practice at least some firms are constrained at times from being able to borrow as much money as they would like at the current interest rates (i.e., either constrained in their borrowing from financial intermediaries, in their issuing of bonds, or in their issuing of new stocks), the specification of the model may not be too unrealistic. In the aggregate, only so much money is available in any given period to borrow, and if interest rates do not get set in such a way as to clear the financial markets every period, then in periods of too-low interest rates some potential borrowers must go unsatisfied.

   The model does account for all aggregate flow-of-funds constraints, and so the most important financial restrictions in a macroeconomic context have been taken into account. It should also be emphasized that "banks" in the model are meant to include commercial banks, savings and loan associations, mutual savings banks, life insurance companies, and other financial interme-diaries, which makes it less unrealistic to assume that all borrowing takes place from the "banks." Also, many corporate bond issues are in practice privately placed—mostly to life insurance companies—and this again lessens the restrictive-ness of the assumption that all borrowing in the model takes place from the banks.

   Before concluding this section, it will be useful to describe the model of firm behavior in somewhat more detail. It is usually the case that the price, production, investment, and employment decisions of a firm are analyzed separately rather than within the context of a complete behavioral model. A few studies have analyzed two of the decisions at a time. Holt, Modigliani, Muth, and Simon[29], for example, have considered the joint determination of production and employment decisions within the context of a quadratic cost minimizing model. Lucas [34] has recently postulated a general stock adjustment model in which the stock of one input may influence the demand for another input, and Nadiri and Rosen [41] have used this basic model in an empirical study of employment and investment decisions. Coen and Hickman[11] have worked with a model that takes into account the interrelationship of employment and investment decisions. Mills [38], Hay [27], and Maccini [36] have considered the joint determination of price and production decisions. In the model of firm behavior in this study, all four of the decisions are determined simultaneously.[j]

   The underlying technology of a firm is assumed to be of a "putty-clay" type, where at any one time there are a number of different types of machines that can be purchased. The machines differ in price, in the number of workers that must be used with each machine per unit of time, and in the amount of output that can be produced per machine per unit of time. The worker-machine ratio is assumed to be fixed for each type of machine.

   One important premise of this study regarding the production, employment, and investment decisions of a firm is that there are costs involved in changing the size of the work force and in changing the size of the capital stock. Because of these costs, a firm is likely to choose to operate some of the time below capacity and off its production function. This means that some of the time the number of worker hours paid for may be greater than the number of hours that the workers are effectively working. Similarly, some of the time the number of machine hours available for use may be greater than the number of machine hours actually used.

The evidence presented in Fair [14, Chapter 3] rather strongly indicates that firms do spend some of the time off of their production functions, and the model of employment decisions developed in [14] was based on the distinction between hours paid for and hours worked. The difference between hours paid for by a firm and hours worked will be referred to as "excess labor."[k] Similarly, the difference between the number of machines on hand and the number of machines required to produce the output will be referred to as "excess capital." Two important constraints facing a firm are that the number of worker hours paid for must be greater than or equal to the number of worker hours worked and that the number of machine hours used must be less than or equal to the number available for use.

Another important premise of this study concerns the firm's price decision. A firm is assumed to have a certain amount of monopoly power in the short run in the sense that raising its price above prices charged by other firms will not result in an immediate loss of all its customers and lowering its price below prices charged by other firms will not result in an immediate gain of everyone else's customers. There is assumed, however, to be a tendency in the system for a high price firm to lose customers over time and for a low price firm to gain customers. This assumption—that a firm's market share is a function of its price relative to the prices of other firms—is common to the studies of Mortensen [39], Phelps [46], Phelps and Winter [47], and Maccini [36]. The model developed here, however, differs from or expands on the models in these studies by postulating that a firm also expects that the future prices of other firms are in part a function of its own past prices. As will be seen in Chapters Two and Three, this postulate has an important influence on the final properties of the model.

The tendency for firms to lose or gain customers depending on whether their prices are high or low can be justified by assuming that customers search. If during each period some customers search, and if each customer who searches buys from the lowest price firm that he or she finds, then there will be a tendency for high price firms to lose customers and vice versa. Although this tendency can be justified by assuming that customers do search, in the present case the search activities of customers are not explained within the model. In the specification of the behavior of households, for example, the possible gains and costs of search are not considered, and search is not considered a decision variable of households. If search were treated as a decision variable, it would be necessary to specify a much more complicated model than has been done. Such an undertaking is beyond the scope of the present study.

A firm's market share of labor supplied to it is treated in a manner similar to its market share of goods sold: a firm's market share of labor is assumed to be a function of its wage rate relative to the wage rates of other firms. Also, a firm is assumed to expect that the future wage rates of other firms are in part a function of its own past wage rates.

Finally, a bank's market share of loans is treated in a manner similar to a firm's market share of goods: a bank's market share of loans is assumed to be a function of its loan rate relative to the loan rates of other banks. Likewise, a bank is assumed to expect that the future loan rates of other banks are in part a function of its own past loan rates.

1.3   THE METHODOLOGY OF THE STUDY

The methodology of this study is unusual enough to require some discussion. The most important aspect of the methodology is the use of computer simulation to analyze the behavior of the banks, firms, and households and to analyze the properties of the overall model. The behavior of each bank, firm, and household was analyzed in the following way.

1. The basic equations were specified and the optimal control problem was formulated for the behavioral unit.
2. Assumptions regarding the formation of expectations were made.
3. Using the information from 1 and 2, algorithms were written to solve the optimal control problem of the behavioral unit.
4. Particular values for the parameters and initial conditions were chosen, and a "base run" was obtained by using the algorithms to solve the optimal control problem for these particular values. The parameter values and initial conditions were chosen so that the optimal paths of the decision variables for the base run would be roughly flat.
5. Various changes in the initial conditions from those used for the base run were made, and for each change the control problem was resolved to obtain the optimal paths of the decision variables corresponding to the change. These new paths were then compared to the base run paths to see how the behavioral unit modified its decisions as a result of the change. A "flat" base run was chosen in 4 to make it easier to compare the behavioral unit's modified decisions to its original decisions.

The results in 5 are analogous to partial-derivative results in analytic work in the sense that one obtains the change in one variable corresponding to a change in some other variable. In Chapters Two, Three, and Four, tables of results of carrying out the procedure in 5 are presented for banks, firms, and households, and from these tables one can get an understanding of how each unit behaves.

After the behavior of each unit was analyzed separately, the entire model was put together and solved. One solution of the overall model for one time period corresponds to the solution of an optimal control problem for each behavioral unit and to the computation of the transactions that take place after all the decisions have been made. After the transactions have all been computed, time switches to the beginning of the next period, and the behavioral units solve their control problems again, the new solutions being based on the new information that has resulted from the previous period's transactions. After the new solutions have been obtained, the new transactions based on these solutions are computed, and then time switches to the next period. This process can be repeated for as many periods as one is interested in.

One important point to keep in mind about the solution of the overall model is that although the solution of the optimal control problem for each behavioral unit corresponds to optimal *time paths* of the decision variables being computed, only the values for the current period are used in computing the transactions that take place. Each period new time paths are computed for each decision variable, and so the optimal values of the decision variables for periods other than the current period are of importance only insofar as they affect the optimal values for the current period.

The optimal control problem of each behavioral unit is stochastic, nonlinear, and subject to equality and inequality constraints. In order to simplify the problem somewhat, each behavioral unit was assumed to convert its stochastic control problem into a deterministic control problem by setting all of the values of the stochastic variables equal to their expected values before solving. This is a common procedure in the control literature (see, for example, Athans [3]). The solution values that result from such a procedure must, of course, be interpreted as being only approximations to the true solution values of the complete stochastic control problem. Only in the linear case would the decision values for the current period that result from this procedure be the same as the decision values that result from solving the complete stochastic control problem.

There is also another source of inaccuracy in this study regarding the solutions of the control problems. Cost considerations prevented the writing of highly accurate algorithms to solve the deterministic control problems, and there is no guarantee that the optima found by the algorithms are in fact the true optima of the deterministic control problems. Particular attention was concentrated, however, on searching over values of the decision variables for the first few periods of the horizon, so that some confidence could be placed on the assumption that the values chosen for the current period are close to the true solution values of the deterministic control problem for the current period. The algorithms that have been used to solve each particular control problem are discussed in the following chapters. The length of the decision horizon for each behavioral unit was always assumed to be 30 periods in the programming of the model.

Because of the assumption that the behavioral units replace stochastic variables with their expected values, the model is presented in the text using expected values directly rather than density functions. A superscript "e" on a variable is always used to denote the expected value of the variable.

Another important aspect of the methodology of this study is the treatment of the aggregation problem. There are at least two basic ways in which one might put a model of the sort developed in this study together. One way would be to specify a number of different banks, firms, and households; have each one solve its control problem; and then have them trade with each other in some way. To do this, one would have to specify mechanisms for deciding who trades with whom and would have to keep track of each individual trade in the model. Questions of search behavior invariably arise in this context, as do distributional questions. This way of putting the model together is considerably beyond the scope of the present study.

The other basic way of putting the model together is to ignore search and distributional questions. Even within this context, however, there are at least two ways in which search and distributional questions can be ignored. One way would be to postulate only one bank and one firm and treat the two as monopolists. The other way is to postulate more than one bank and one firm, but treat all banks as identical and all firms as identical. This second way is the approach taken in this study. The advantage of postulating more than one bank and one firm is that models can be specified in which the behavior of an individual bank or firm is influenced by its expectations of the behavior of other banks or firms. Models of this type, in which market share considerations can play an important role, seem more reasonable in a macroeconomic context than do models of pure monopoly behavior.

An apparent disadvantage of postulating more than one bank and firm and yet treating all banks and firms as identical is that whenever, say, a firm expects other firms to behave differently than it plans to behave, the firm is always wrong. If all firms are identical, they obviously always behave in the same way, even though they almost always *expect* that they will not all behave in the same way. Firms never learn, in other words, that they are all identical. Fortunately, this disadvantage is more apparent than real. If one is ignoring search and distributional questions anyway, there is no real difference (as far as ignoring these questions is concerned) whether one postulates only one firm or many identical firms. Both postulates are of the same order of approximation, namely the complete ignoring of search and distributional questions, and if one feels that a richer model can be specified by postulating more than one firm, one might as well do so. One will gain the added richness without losing any more regarding search and distributional issues than is already lost in the monopoly model.

The fact that distributional issues are ignored in the model makes the treatment of stock prices and shares of stock much easier than it otherwise would be. The economy can be treated as if there were only one share of stock in existence, of which individual creditor households own certain fractions. The price of this share of stock is set by the bond dealer. The bond dealer uses expectations of future aggregate dividend levels in setting the price, where the aggregate dividend level in any period is the sum of all of the dividends from the firms, the banks, and the bond dealer. The households are, of course, the ones who form the expectations of the future aggregate dividend levels, which then get communicated to the bond dealer.

Two versions of the overall model have actually been used in this study, one called the "non-condensed" version and one called the "condensed" version. The non-condensed version postulates two identical banks, two identical firms, and two households. The two households are not identical; one is a creditor and one is a debtor. This version is solved in exactly the manner described above. Since the non-condensed version is large, costly to solve, and somewhat difficult to comprehend in its entirety, an alternative and smaller version was also specified. This "condensed" version was specified as follows.

1. The behavior of the banks, firms, and households was examined by looking at the tables of results obtained by the procedure described in 1 through 5 above (p. 12).
2. Using the results in these tables and a general knowledge of the optimal control problems of the behavioral units, the behavior of the banks, firms, and households was approximated either by equations in closed form or by simple algorithms. In the process of making these approximations, the banks were aggregated and the firms were aggregated, so that one ended up with equations or algorithms pertaining only to a "bank sector" and a "firm sector."
3. The transactions equations for the non-condensed model were then modified appropriately to correspond to the more simplified nature of the condensed model.

The advantage of the condensed version is that one can see more directly what influences the decisions of the behavioral units. In the non-condensed version the influences are buried in the optimal control problems of the behavioral units, and many times one cannot see directly what affects what. No optimal control problems have to be solved in computing the solution of the condensed version each period since the optimal control problems have in effect been approximated by equations in closed form or by simple algorithms.

For the analysis of the properties of the overall model in Chapter Six, the condensed version has been used. The analysis of the non-condensed version is relegated to the Appendix. Since the properties of the two versions are virtually the same—one merely being an approximation of the other—it seemed best to concentrate on the simpler version in the text. The Appendix contains the results of a few runs and enough discussion to show how the non-condensed version is solved.

There is also a "static-equilibrium" version of the model, and this version should not be confused with either the condensed or non-condensed versions, which are both dynamic. The static-equilibrium version is discussed in Chapter Seven. The Gauss-Seidel algorithm is used to solve the static-equilibrium version in Chapter Seven, and again this algorithm should not be confused with either the algorithms used to solve the optimal control problems or the algorithms used in the condensed version of the dynamic model.

The advantage of using computer simulation techniques over standard analytic methods to analyze models is that one can deal with much larger and more complete models. More than merely one or two decision variables of a behavioral unit can be considered at the same time, multiperiod decision problems can be considered, and in general one can get by with making less restrictive assumptions. It should be stressed, however, that the simulation work in this study is not meant to be a "test" of the validity of the model, but only an aid to understanding its properties. The parameter values and initial conditions have all been made up and have not been estimated from any data.

It should be obvious by now that the model developed in this study is based on numerous assumptions that can in no way be verified or refuted directly. As with most economic models, the model is highly abstract. The philosophy that underlies the construction of the present model goes something as follows. The author looks on a theoretical model of the sort developed in this study as not so much true or false as useful or not useful. The model is useful if it aids in the specification of empirical relationships that one would not already have thought of from a simpler model and that are in turn confirmed by the data. It is not useful if it either does not aid in the specification of empirical relationships that one would not have thought of from a simpler model or aids in the specification of empirical relationships that are in turn refuted by the data.

As discussed in Chapter Eight, the present model does imply that macroeconometric models ought to be specified quite differently from the way they now are. The model does appear, therefore, to meet the requirement that it lead to new empirical specifications, and so it does appear to be possible, according to the above philosophy, to decide whether the model is more useful than other theoretical models. (Volume II will carry out such an analysis.)

1.4   SUGGESTIONS TO THE READER

Because of the model's size and the reliance on computer simulation to analyze its properties, the overall model is not particularly easy to comprehend. The reader should have a good understanding of the behavior of the individual units in the model from the discussion in Chapters Two through Five before proceeding to the discussion of the complete model in Chapters Six through

Eight and in the Appendix. Of particular importance in Chapters Two, Three, and Four are the tables of simulation results (Tables 2-3, 3-3, 4-3, and 4-4), where one can see how the behavioral units respond to various changes in the initial conditions. The tables presenting the equations of the condensed model for each behavioral unit (Tables 2-4, 3-4, and 4-6) should also help one to understand the behavior of each unit.

The two most important tables in the book are Table 6-2 and Table A-2, where the complete sets of equations for the condensed and non-condensed models are presented, respectively. Since the condensed model is a close approximation to the non-condensed model and is easier to comprehend, it is advisable for most purposes to study Table 6-2 rather than Table A-2. After having studied Table 6-2 carefully, the simulation results for the complete model in Table 6-6 and the related discussion should be understandable. In general, the discussion in the text relies heavily on the use of tables, and in most cases it is necessary to study the tables carefully in order to follow the discussion in the text. In order to make Chapters Two through Five a little more self-contained, some of the discussion of the behavioral units in section 1.2 in this chapter is repeated in the following chapters.

NOTES

aExamples of these studies are the studies of Leijonhujvud [32], [33], Tucker [53], [54], [55], Barro and Grossman [5], and Grossman [24], [25], [26]. See also the studies of Solow and Stiglitz [51] and Korliras [31].

bSee Rothschild [50] for a survey of some of the more recent studies, and see also Nordhaus [42].

cSee, for example, Alchian [1], Diamond [12], Fisher [18], [19], Gepts [20], Gordon and Hynes [22], Lucas and Rapping [35], Maccini [36], Mortensen [39], [40], Phelps [46], Phelps and Winter [47], and Rothschild [49]. See also an early paper by Clower [9], in which an attempt is made to provide a general theory of price determination that is applicable to all types of market structures.

dBarro and Grossman [5], pp. 83–84, fn. 6.

eSee footnote c.

fSee, for example, Christ [8] for a discussion of the government budget constraint.

gThe bond dealer will be referred to as an it, rather than as a he or a she.

hUnless otherwise stated, the phrase "demand for" or "supply of" in the text is meant to refer to the quantity demanded or supplied, not to a demand or a supply schedule.

iSince in general a firm plans to end up with a positive level of inventories at the end of the period, the firm's expected demand for its goods is usually less than the maximum number of goods that it is willing to sell.

jA firm's "employment" decision in the present context corresponds to its wage-rate decision and its decision on the maximum amount of labor to hire.

k"Excess labor" was defined in a slightly different way in [14] as the difference between standard hours and hours worked. Under this definition excess labor can be negative if hours worked exceed standard hours. For purposes of the present study it is more convenient to refer to the difference between hours paid for and hours worked as "excess labor."

Chapter Two

Banks

2.1 THE BASIC EQUATIONS

In Table 2-1 the important symbols used in this chapter are listed in alphabetic order. The first half of the table presents the notation for the non-condensed model, and the second half presents the notation for the condensed model. The notation for the condensed model pertains only to the discussion in Section 2.6.

Each bank, say bank i, receives money from households in the form of savings deposits (SDB_{it}), on which interest is paid, and from firms, households, and the bond dealer in the form of demand deposits $(DDBit)$, on which no interest is paid. Each bank lends money to firms and households (LB_{it}) and buys government bills $(VBILLB_{it})$ and bonds $(BONDB_{it})$. Bank loans are one-period loans, bills are one-period securities, and bonds are consols. Each bank holds reserves in the form of deposits with the government (BR_{it}). Each bank sets its own loan rate (RB_{it}). The three main decision variables of each bank are its loan rate, the value of bills and bonds to purchase (VBB_{it}), and the maximum amount of money that it will lend in the period $(LBMAX_{it})$. Banks are assumed not to compete for savings deposits, and the rate paid on all savings deposits is assumed to be the bill rate (r_t).

Table 2-1.   Notation for Banks in Alphabetic Order

Non-Condensed Model

Subscript i denotes variable for bank i. Subscript j denotes variable for bank j. Subscript t denotes variable for period t. An e superscript in the text denotes an expected value of the variable.

$BONDB_{it}$	= number of bonds held, each bond yielding one dollar per period
BR_{it}	= actual reserves
BR^*_{it}	= required reserves
d_1	= profit tax rate
d_2	= penalty tax rate on the composition of banks' portfolios
DDB_{it}	= demand deposits
$DIVB_{it}$	= dividends paid
$EMAXDD_i$	= largest error the bank expects to make in overestimating its demand deposits for any period
$EMAXSD_i$	= largest error the bank expects to make in overestimating its savings deposits for any period
$FUNDS^e_{it}$	= amount that the bank knows it will have available to lend to households and firms and to buy bills and bonds even if it overestimates its demand and savings deposits by the maximum amounts
g_1	= reserve requirement ratio
g_2	= no-tax proportion of banks' portfolios held in bills and bonds
L_t	= total value of loans of the bank sector
LB_{it}	= value of loans
$LBMAX_{it}$	= maximum value of loans that the bank will make
LUN_t	= total unconstrained demand for loans
r_t	= bill rate
R_t	= bond rate
RB_{it}	= loan rate (of bank i)
RB_{jt}	= loan rate (of bank j)
$\overline{RB}_t$	= average loan rate in the economy
SDB_{it}	= savings deposits
$TAXB_{it}$	= taxes paid
$T+1$	= length of decision horizon
VBB_{it}	= value of bills and bonds that the bank chooses to purchase $[VBILLB_{it} + BONDB_{it}/R_t]$
$VBILLB_{it}$	= value of bills held
ΠB_{it}	= before-tax profits

Condensed Model (For equations in Table 2-4 only.)

Subscript t denotes variable for period t. Only notation that differs from the notation for the non-condensed model is presented here.

$EMAXDD$	= largest error the bank sector expects to make in overestimating its demand deposits for any period
$EMAXSD$	= largest error the bank sector expects to make in overestimating its savings deposits for any period
$FUNDS^e_t$	= amount the bank sector knows it will have available to lend to households and firms and to buy bills and bonds even if it overestimates its demand and savings deposits by the maximum amounts
$LBMAX_t$	= maximum value of loans that the bank sector will make
RL_t	= loan rate of the bank sector
SD_t	= savings deposits of the bank sector
$TAXB_t$	= taxes paid by the bank sector
VBB_t	= value of bills and bonds that the bank sector chooses to purchase $[VBILLB_t + BONDB_t/R_t]$
$VBILLB_t$	= value of bills held by the bank sector
ΠB_t	= before-tax profits of the bank sector

The basic equations for bank i for period t are the following:

$$VBB_{it} = VBILLB_{it} + BONDB_{it}/R_t, \text{ [value of bills and bonds held]} \tag{2.1}$$

$$\Pi B_{it} = RB_{it}LB_{it} + r_t VBILLB_{it} + BONDB_{it} - r_t SDB_{it}$$
$$+ (BONDB_{it}/R_{t+1} - BONDB_{it}/R_t), \text{ [before-tax profits]} \tag{2.2}$$

$$TAXB_{it} = d_1 \Pi B_{it} + d_2 [VBB_{it} - g_2(VBB_{it} + LB_{it})]^2, \text{ [taxes paid]} \tag{2.3}$$

$$DIVB_{it} = \Pi B_{it} - TAXB_{it}, \text{ [dividends paid]} \tag{2.4}$$

$$BR_{it} = DDB_{it} + SDB_{it} - LB_{it} - VBB_{it} - (BONDB_{it}/R_{t+1} - BONDB_{it}/R_t)$$
$$= DDB_{it} + SDB_{it} - LB_{it} - VBILLB_{it} - BONDB_{it}/R_{t+1}, \text{ [actual reserves]} \tag{2.5}$$

$$BR^*_{it} = g_1 DDB_{it}, \text{ [required reserves]} \tag{2.6}$$

$$BR_{it} \geq BR^*_{it} . \text{ [actual reserves must be greater than or equal to required reserves]} \tag{2.7}$$

Equation (2.1) merely defines the value of bills and bonds held. Since bonds are consols and since each bond is assumed to yield one dollar each period, the value of bonds held is merely the number held divided by the bond rate, $BONDB_{it}/R_t$. Equation (2.2) defines before-tax profits. The first three terms on the right-hand side of the equation are the interest revenue received on loans, bills, and bonds, respectively.[a] The fourth term is the interest paid on savings deposits. The last term is the capital gain or loss made on bonds held in period t.

Taxes are defined in Equation (2.3), where d_1 is the profit tax rate. With respect to the second term on the right-hand-side of the equation, the government is assumed through its taxing policy to try to induce banks to hold a certain proportion, g_2, of their assets in bills and bonds. In practice, commercial banks and other financial intermediaries are under certain pressures to hold particular kinds of securities, and here these pressures are assumed to take the form of government taxing policy. If, in the model, banks were not induced in some way to hold bills and bonds, they would never want to hold bills and bonds as long as their loan rates were higher than the bill rate. The introduction of government taxing policy is a simple way of explaining why banks hold more than one kind of asset.

In Equation (2.3), bank i is assumed to be taxed at rate d_2 on the square of the difference between the value of bills and bonds held and g_2 times the value of loans issued plus bills and bonds held. Since capital gains and losses are included in the definition of profits, Equation (2.3) also reflects the assumption that capital gains and losses are taxed as regular income. Bank i is assumed not to retain any earnings, so that the level of dividends, as defined in Equation (2.4), is merely the difference between before-tax profits and taxes.

Bank reserves are defined in Equation (2.5). Since bank i pays out in the form of taxes and dividends any capital gains made in the period (and conversely for capital losses), and yet does not receive any actual cash flow from the capital gains, capital gains take away from (and conversely capital losses add to) bank reserves, as specified in (2.5). Required reserves are defined in Equation (2.6). For simplicity, no reserve requirements are placed on savings deposits. Actual reserves must be greater than or equal to required reserves, as indicated in (2.7).

2.2   THE FORMATION OF EXPECTATIONS

Let $T+1$ be the length of the decision horizon. In order for the bank to solve its control problem at the beginning of period t, it must form expectations of a number of variables for periods t through $t+T$. Bank i is assumed to form the following expectations.[b]

$$\frac{RB^e_{jt}}{RB_{jt-1}} = \left(\frac{RB_{it-1}}{RB_{jt-1}}\right)^{\alpha_1} \left(\frac{r_t}{r_{t-1}}\right)^{\alpha_2}, \; \alpha_1 > 0, \, \alpha_2 > 0, \; \text{[expected loan rate of bank } j \text{ for period } t]} \tag{2.8}$$

$$\frac{RB^e_{jt+k}}{RB^e_{jt+k-1}} = \left(\frac{RB_{it+k-1}}{RB^e_{jt+k-1}}\right)^{\alpha_1}, \; \text{[expected loan rate of bank } j \text{ for period } t+k \\ (k = 1, 2, \ldots, T)] \tag{2.9}$$

$$\overline{RB}^e_{t+k} = (RB_{it+k} \cdot RB^e_{jt+k})^{\frac{1}{2}}, \; \text{[expected average loan rate for period } t+k \\ (k = 0, 1, \ldots, T)] \tag{2.10}$$

$$LUN^e_t = LUN_{t-1} \left(\frac{\overline{RB}_{t-1}}{\overline{RB}^e_t}\right)^{\alpha_3}, \; \alpha_3 > 0, \; \text{[expected aggregate unconstrained} \\ \text{demand for loans for period } t] \tag{2.11}$$

$$LUN^e_{t+k} = LUN^e_{t+k-1} \left(\frac{\overline{RB}^e_{t+k-1}}{\overline{RB}^e_{t+k}}\right)^{\alpha_3}, \; \text{[expected aggregate unconstrained} \\ \text{demand for loans for period } t+k \\ (k = 1, 2, \ldots, T)] \tag{2.12}$$

$$L^e_{t+k} = LUN^e_{t+k}, \; \text{[expected aggregate constrained demand for loans for period} \\ t+k \; (k = 0, 1, \ldots, T)] \tag{2.13}$$

$$\frac{LB^e_{it}}{L^e_t} = \frac{LB_{it-1}}{L_{t-1}} \left(\frac{RB_{it}}{RB^e_{jt}}\right)^{\alpha_4}, \; \alpha_4 < 0, \; \text{[expected market share of loans for period } t] \tag{2.14}$$

$$\frac{LB_{it+k}^e}{L_{t+k}^e} = \frac{LB_{it+k-1}^e}{L_{t+k-1}^e} \left(\frac{RB_{it+k}}{RB_{jt+k}^e}\right)^{\alpha_4} , \text{ [expected market share of loans for period}$$
$$t+k \ (k=1,2,\ldots,T)] \tag{2.15}$$

$$DDB_{it+k}^e = DDB_{it-1}, \text{ [expected level of demand deposits for period } t+k$$
$$(k=0,1,\ldots,T)] \tag{2.16}$$

$$SDB_{it+k}^e = SDB_{it-1}, \text{ [expected level of savings deposits for period } t+k$$
$$(k=0,1,\ldots,T)] \tag{2.17}$$

$$r_{t+k}^e = r_t, \text{ [expected bill rate for period } t+k \ (k=1,2,\ldots)] \tag{2.18}$$

$$\frac{1}{R_{t+k}^e} = \frac{1}{(1+r_{t+k}^e)} + \frac{1}{(1+r_{t+k}^e)(1+r_{t+k+1}^e)} + \frac{1}{(1+r_{t+k}^e)(1+r_{t+k+1}^e)(1+r_{t+k+2}^e)} + \ldots$$
$$= \frac{1}{r_t}. \text{ [equation determining expected bond rate for period } t+k$$
$$(k=0,1,\ldots,T+1)] \tag{2.19}$$

The first term on the right-hand side of Equation (2.8) reflects the fact that bank i expects its rate setting behavior in period $t-1$ to have an effect on bank j's rate setting behavior in period t. The second term is designed to represent the effect of general market conditions on bank i's expectation of bank j's rate. The bond dealer sets the bill rate for period t at the end of period $t-1$, and bank i knows the bill rate for period t at the time that it makes its decisions for period t. If the bill rate for period t has changed, then bank i is assumed to expect that this change will have an effect in the same direction on the rate that bank j sets in period t.

Bank i must also form expectations of bank j's rate for periods $t+1$ and beyond. These expectations are specified in Equation (2.9), which is the same as Equation (2.8) without the final term. Equation (2.9) means that bank i expects that bank j is always adjusting its rate toward bank i's rate. If bank i's rate is constant over time, then bank i expects that bank j's rate will gradually approach this value.

In Equation (2.10) bank i's expectation of the average loan rate is taken to be the geometric average of its rate and its expectation of bank j's rate. Without loss of generality, there is assumed to be only one other bank, bank j, in existence. It should be obvious how the number of other banks in existence can be generalized to be more than one. There is nothing inconsistent in the model with there being a relatively large number of other banks in existence. The geometric average is used in (2.10) rather than the arithmetic average to make the solution of the model easier. Bank i expects that the aggregate unconstrained demand for loans is a function of the average loan rate, as specified in Equations (2.11) and (2.12).[c] The aggregate unconstrained demand for loans in, say, period

$t-1$ (LUN_{t-1}) is what would have been the demand for loans on the part of firms and households had they not been subject to any constraints. Each bank is assumed to be aware of this demand. The aggregate constrained demand for loans (L_{t-1}) is the actual value of loans made in period $t-1$. Equation (2.13) states that bank i expects that firms and households will not be constrained in their borrowing behavior in periods t and beyond. The expected aggregate constrained demand for loans is assumed in Equation (2.13) to be equal to the expected aggregate unconstrained demand for loans for each period. As will be seen below, bank i does not itself expect to turn any customers away, and so Equation (2.13) merely states that bank i also does not expect any customers in the aggregate to be turned away.

Equation (2.14) determines bank i's expectation of its market share for period t and reflects the assumption that a bank expects that its market share is a function of its rate relative to the rates of other banks. The equation states that bank i's expected market share for period t is equal to last period's market share times a function of the ratio of bank i's rate for period t to the expected rate of bank j for period t. Equation (2.15) is a similar equation for periods $t+1$ through $t+T$.

It should be noted that the market share for period $t-1$ on the right-hand side of Equation (2.14) is the ratio of the actual value of loans of bank i in period $t-1$ to the *actual* value of aggregate loans in period $t-1$ (LB_{it-1}/L_{t-1}) and is not the ratio of the actual value of bank i's loans to the aggregate *unconstrained* demand for loans (LB_{it-1}/LUN_{t-1}). Since bank i is assumed to know both L_{t-1} and LUN_{t-1}, the latter specification is a possibility.

The justification for the use of LB_{it-1}/L_{t-1} is as follows. L_t^e is bank i's expectation of the aggregate unconstrained (and constrained) demand for loans for period t. Of the potential customers represented by this amount, some will come to bank i during the period. How many come depends on how large a part bank i is of the market in period $t-1$ and on the relative loan rates. Now, a good measure of how large a part bank i is of the market in period $t-1$ is its actual market share in period $t-1$. This measure is a better measure than LB_{it-1}/LUN_{t-1}, since the latter does not represent in any direct sense bank i's participation in the market. If LUN_{t-1} is greater than L_{t-1}, only a part of the unsatisfied customers represented by this amount are likely to have been turned away by bank i. The rest of the customers would not have sampled bank i in the period. Therefore, it seems more in the spirit of the search literature to use the actual market share on the right-hand side of Equation (2.14).

As should be evident from the discussion in the next section, Equations (2.8)-(2.15) are quite important in determining the rate setting behavior of bank i. Two similar sets of equations are also postulated in Chapter Three regarding the price setting and wage setting behavior of a firm. The two most important assumptions underlying Equations (2.8)-(2.15) are that bank i expects that its rate setting behavior has an effect on bank j's rate setting behavior and that bank i expects that its market share is a function of its rate relative to bank j's rate. The equations can be easily modified if there is more than just one other bank in existence. Equations (2.8) and (2.9) would hold for each bank. Equation (2.10) would be the geometric average over all banks. Equations (2.11)–(2.13) would remain the same, and Equations (2.14) and (2.15) would be changed either to include all the ratios of bank i's rate to the other banks' rates, or to include the ratio of bank i's rate to the average of the other banks' rates.

In Equations (2.16)–(2.18) bank i is assumed to expect that the values of demand deposits, savings deposits, and the bill rate for all future periods will be the same as the last observed values of these variables. Equation (2.19) determines the expected bond rate. The right-hand side of the equation is the present discounted value of a perpetual stream of one-dollar payments, the discount rates being the expected future bill rates. The right-hand side of the equation can thus be considered to be the expected price of a bond for period $t+k$, and so the reciprocal of this expression can be considered to be the expected bond rate for period $t+k$. This assumption, of course, ignores the fact that the expected value of a ratio is not equal to the ratio of the expected values, but this type of problem is ignored all the way through this study by the converting of stochastic control problems into deterministic control problems in the manner discussed in Section 1.3.

The assumptions in (2.16) and (2.17), that bank i expects no change in its demand and savings deposits from the last observed values, are important and typical of many expectational assumptions made in the model. Whenever an expectational assumption had to be made that was either not concerned with market share situations or for which no obvious assumption was available, the simple assumption of no change from the last observed value was made. The aim was not to complicate the model any more than seemed necessary to capture important expectational issues.

As long as lagged values have some effect on expectations of current and future values, assumptions like (2.16) and (2.17) should not be too unrealistic. It should also be noted that because of the assumption in (2.18), that bank i expects no change in the future bill rates from the last observed rate, the expected bond rates in (2.19) are simply equal to the current bill rate. It was mentioned in Section 1.2 that the only reason bonds were included in the model at all was to account for the effects of capital gains and losses, and so nothing is really lost in the model by having the bill rate and bond rate always be equal.

2.3 BEHAVIORAL ASSUMPTIONS

The objective of a bank is to maximize the present discounted value of expected future after-tax profits. The discount rate is assumed to be the bill rate. The objective function of bank i at the beginning of period t is:

$$OBJB_{it} = \frac{\Pi B_{it}^e - TAXB_{it}^e}{(1+r_t)} + \frac{\Pi B_{it+1}^e - TAXB_{it+1}^e}{(1+r_t)(1+r_{t+1}^e)} + \dots$$

$$+ \frac{\Pi B_{it+T}^e - TAXB_{it+T}^e}{(1+r_t)(1+r_{t+1}^e)\dots(1+r_{t+T}^e)} \, , \qquad (2.20)$$

where $\Pi B_{it+k}^e - TAXB_{it+k}^e$ is the expected value of after-tax profits for period $t+k$ $(k=0,1,\dots,T)$.

Three of the decision variables of bank i are its loan rate, RB_{it+k}, the value of bills to purchase, $VBILLB_{it+k}$, and the number of bonds to purchase, $BONDB_{it+k}$ $(k=0,1,\dots,T)$. Given paths of these three variables, the corresponding value of the objective function can be computed as follows.

1. Given bank i's rate path, bank i's expectation of bank j's rate path can be computed from (2.8) and (2.9). The path of the expected average loan rate can then be computed from (2.10), followed by the path of the expected aggregate unconstrained demand for loans from (2.11) and (2.12). The path of the expected aggregate constrained demand for loans can then be computed from (2.13), followed by bank i's expectation of the demand for its own loans from (2.14) and (2.15).

2. The paths of expected demand deposits, savings deposits, the bill rate, and the bond rate are determined in Equations (2.16)–(2.19). Given these four paths and given the paths discussed in 1, the paths of expected profits and taxes can be computed from (2.2) and (2.3),[d] which then means that the value of the objective function can be computed.

A few general remarks can now be made regarding the control problem of a bank. A bank expects that it will gain customers by lowering its rate relative to the expected rates of other banks. The main expected cost to a bank from doing this, in addition to the lower price it is charging per loan, is that it will have to pay more and more taxes the further it deviates from holding proportion g_2 of its portfolio in bills and bonds. It is also the case that a bank expects that other banks will follow it if it lowers its rate, so that it does not expect to be able to capture an ever increasing share of the market without further and further rate reductions.

A bank expects that it will lose customers by raising its rate relative to the expected rates of other banks. Again, the main cost from doing this, in addition to the lost customers, is the higher taxes that must be paid from not holding proportion g_2 of its portfolio in bills and bonds. On the plus side, a bank expects that other banks will follow it if it raises its rate, so that it will not lose an ever increasing share of the market without further and further rate increases.

With respect to a bank's decision regarding bills and bonds, equation (2.19) means that a bank expects that the before-tax, one-period rate of return on bonds, including capital gains and losses, for a given period will be the same as the expected bill rate for that period. Since capital gains and losses are taxed at the same rate as other income, the expected after-tax rates of return on bills and bonds are also the same. Because of this, banks are assumed to be indifferent between holding bills and bonds, and so instead of determining two variables, $VBILLB_{it}$ and $BONDB_{it}$, a bank can be considered, given R_t, as determining only VBB_{it}.

The main constraint facing a bank is the reserve requirement constraint (2.7). A bank expects to receive in funds in period $t+k$, $DDB^e_{it+k} + SDB^e_{it+k}$, of which $g_1 DDB^e_{it+k}$ is needed to meet the reserve requirement. Therefore, $(1-g_1)DDB^e_{it+k} + SDB^e_{it+k}$ is the expected amount available for period $t+k$ to lend to households and firms and to buy bills and bonds. A bank is assumed, however, to have to prepare for the possibility that it overestimates its demand and savings deposits. A bank is assumed from past experience to have a good idea of the largest error it is likely to make in overestimating its demand and savings deposits. Call the error for demand deposits $EMAXDD_i$ and the error for savings deposits $EMAXSD_i$. For simplicity, these expected maximum errors are assumed not to change over time. The quantity $(1-g_1)(DDB^e_{it+k} - EMAXDD_i) + (SDB^e_{it+k} - EMAXSD_i)$ is the amount that bank i knows it will have available in period $t+k$ to lend to households and firms and to buy bills and bonds even if it overestimates its demand and savings deposits by the maximum amounts. Denote this quantity as $FUNDS^e_{it+k}$:

$$FUNDS^e_{it+k} = (1-g_1)(DDB^e_{it+k} - EMAXDD_i) + (SDB^e_{it+k} - EMAXSD_i). \quad (2.21)$$

Now, given a path of bank i's loan rate, it was seen from 1 above that bank i can compute the path of its expected loans $(LB^e_{it+k}, k=0,1,\ldots,T)$. In order to make sure of meeting the reserve requirement constraint, bank i is assumed to behave by choosing the path of its loan rate and the path of the value of bills and bonds to buy $(VBB_{it+k}, k = 0,1,\ldots,T)$ so as to satisfy the constraint that

$$LB^e_{it+k} + VBB_{it+k} = FUNDS^e_{it+k}, \quad k=0,1,\ldots,T. \quad (2.22)$$

By satisfying equation (2.22), bank i is assured that it will have enough funds to meet the expected loan demand each period, given its path of the value of bills and bonds to buy. Once a bank decides at the beginning of period t the value of bills and bonds to purchase in the period, it is assumed that the bank must purchase this value.

This is still not the end of the story, however, for bank i must also prepare for the possibility that it underestimates the demand for its loans at the loan rate path that it has chosen. Bank i is assumed to prepare for this possibility by announcing to households and firms the maximum amount of money that it will lend in each period, in addition to announcing the loan rate. The maximum amount each period ($LBMAX_{it+k}$, $k = 0,1, \ldots ,T$) is assumed to be equal to the expected loan demand for that period:

$$LBMAX_{it+k} = LB^e_{it+k}, \ k=0,1,\ldots,T. \tag{2.23}$$

Bank i is now assured of meeting its reserve requirement. It will always have at least amount $FUNDS^e_{it+k}$ at its disposal, and it will never use more than this amount to lend to households and firms and to buy bills and bonds. The procedure just described means, of course, that a bank expects to hold some amount of excess reserves most of the time. Only in the extreme case where it overestimates its demand and savings deposits by the full amounts $EMAXDD_i$ and $EMAXSD_i$, and also lends to households and firms the maximum amount of money that it set, will it end up with zero excess reserves.

Although in practice commercial banks and some other kinds of financial intermediaries can usually meet unexpected situations by borrowing from a monetary authority, the procedure just described by which banks account for unexpected situations in the model is not necessarily unrealistic. Commercial banks and other financial intermediaries are under basic constraints of the kind considered above, and it is not unreasonable to assume that these constraints play an important role in their decision making processes. Also, if a bank can hold negative excess reserves in the short run by borrowing from a monetary authority, all this really means in the present context is that the bank would maximize (2.20) subject to the constraint that $LB^e_{it+k} + VBB_{it+k}$ in (2.22) be equal to $FUNDS^e_{it+k}$ *plus* some positive number. The positive number might be, for example, the maximum that the bank could expect to borrow from the monetary authority in an emergency situation.

It is likewise not necessarily unrealistic to assume that banks must buy in the period the value of bills and bonds that they chose to buy at the beginning of the period. Although in practice one bank can sell bills and bonds to another bank to get more funds to lend to households and firms, in the aggregate this cannot be done. In the aggregate the government determines the number of bills and bonds to have outstanding, and the private sector must behave within this constraint. In the model the bond dealer absorbs each period the difference between the supply of bills and bonds from the government and the demand from the banks, so the assumption that banks cannot change their decisions on the value of bills and bonds to buy during the period merely simplifies the specification of the way that transaction takes place during the period. Any discrepancy between the supply from the government and the demand from the banks in the current period affects the bill and bonds rates set by the bond dealer for the next period.

2.4 THE SOLUTION OF THE CONTROL PROBLEM

It was seen in the last section that given the paths of the loan rate and the value of bills and bonds to buy, the corresponding value of the objective function can be computed. In order to solve the control problem of bank i, an algorithm was written to search over various loan rate paths. The base path, from which other paths were tried, was taken to be the path in which the proportion of bills and bonds held each period was equal to the no-penalty-tax proportion g_2. The loan rate path corresponding to this situation is computed as follows.

First, VBB_{it+k} is set equal to $g_2 FUNDS_{it+k}^e$, and LB_{it+k}^e is set equal to $FUNDS_{it+k}^e - VBB_{it+k}$ $(k=0,1,\ldots,T)$. Now, for period t, given the values for period $t-1$, Equations (2.8), (2.10), (2.11), (2.13), and (2.14) form a system of five equations in six unknowns: RB_{jt}^e, $\overline{RB}_t^e$, LUN_t^e, L_t^e, LB_{it}^e, and RB_{it}. Given a value for LB_{it}^e, the system reduces to a system of five equations in five unknowns, which can be solved recursively to obtain a value for RB_{it}. For period $t+1$, given the values for period t, Equations (2.9), (2.10), (2.12), (2.13), and (2.15) likewise form a system of five equations in six unknowns. Given a value for LB_{it+1}^e, a value for RB_{it+1} can be obtained. This process can then be repeated for periods $t+2,\ldots,t+T$ to obtain the base loan rate path.

Given the base loan rate path, it is straightforward to search over alternative paths. Given a value of RB_{it} and given values for period $t-1$, equations (2.8), (2.10), (2.11), (2.13), and (2.14) can be solved for RB_{jt}^e, $\overline{RB}_t^e$, LUN_t^e, L_t^e, and LB_{it}^e. Once LB_{it}^e has been determined in this way, the value of VBB_{it} is merely the difference between $FUNDS_{it}^e$ and LB_{it}^e. Values for periods $t+1$ and beyond can be obtained in the same way by solving Equations (2.9), (2.10), (2.12), (2.13), and (2.15). The algorithm was programmed to search in one direction until the value of the objective function decreased and then to try other directions. Particular importance was attached to searching over values of RB_{it}, since this is the value actually used in the solution of the overall model.

2.5 SOME EXAMPLES OF SOLVING THE CONTROL PROBLEM OF BANK i

PARAMETER VALUES AND INITIAL CONDITIONS

The parameter values and initial conditions that were used for the first example are presented in Table 2-2. The most important parameters are d_2, the penalty tax rate on portfolio composition, α_1, the measure of the extent to which bank i

Table 2-2.   Parameter Values and Initial Conditions for the
Control Problem of Bank i

Parameter	Value	
$T+1$	30	
g_1	0.1667	
g_2	0.2956	
d_1	0.5	
d_2	0.0028	
α_1	0.5	
α_2	0.4	
α_3	0.2	
α_4	-3.6	
$EMAXDD_i$	1.9	
$EMAXSD_i$	10.1	

Variable	Value	
DDB_{it-1}	96.1	
SDB_{it-1}	506.7	
LB_{it-1}	405.1	
L_{t-1}	810.2	
LUN_{t-1}	810.2	
RB_{it-1}	0.0750	
RB_{jt-1}	0.0750	
r_t	0.0650	
r_{t-1}	0.0650	
$FUNDS^e_{it}$	575.1	$= (1-g_1)(DDB_{it-1}-EMAXDD_i)+(SDB_{it-1}-EMAXSD_i)$
VBB_{it}	170.0	$= FUNDS^e_{it} - LB_{it-1}$
$\dfrac{VBB_{it-1}}{LB_{it-1}+VBB_{it-1}}$	0.2956	$= g_2$

expects bank j to respond to bank i's rate setting behavior, α_2, the measure of the extent to which bank i expects bank j to change its rate for period t as a result of a change in the bill rate, and α_4, the measure of the extent to which bank i loses or gains market share as its rate deviates from bank j's rate. The market share parameter, α_4, is more important than the parameter α_3, which is the measure of the extent to which bank i expects the aggregate demand for loans to change as a function of the average loan rate in the economy. More will be said about this in Chapter Six.

The parameter values and initial conditions were chosen, after some experimentation, so that the optimum values of each control variable for periods t through $t+T$ would be essentially the same as the initial value for period $t-1$. This was done to make it easier to analyze the effects on the behavior of the bank of changing various initial conditions. As can be seen from Table 2-2, the initial conditions for the first example correspond to bank i's having half of the loans in period $t-1$. The loan rates of bank i and bank j in period $t-1$ are the same. The bill rate is one percentage point lower than the loan rates. The ratio of bills and bonds to loans plus bills and bonds in period $t-1$ is equal to the no-tax ratio g_2. The aggregate unconstrained demand for loans in period $t-1$ is the same as the constrained demand. The length of the decision horizon is 30 periods.

THE RESULTS

The results of solving the control problem of bank i for the parameter values and initial conditions in Table 2-2 are presented in the first row of Table 2-3. Only a small subset of the results is presented in Table 2-3, as it is not feasible to present all 30 values for each variable. Values for the first two periods are presented for bank i's loan rate, its expectation of bank j's loan rate, its expectation of the aggregate demand for loans, its expectation of the demand for its own loans, its expectation of its market share, the value of bills and bonds to purchase, and its expectation of the ratio of the value of bills and bonds held to the value of loans plus bills and bonds held. The values in the first row of Table 2-3 for each variable are equal to the corresponding initial value in Table 2-2, which reflects the way the parameter values and initial conditions were chosen.

One important reaction of a bank is how the bank responds to a change in its demand or savings deposits. For the results in row 2 in Table 2-3, $FUNDS_{it}^e$ was increased by 5.0 percent. An increase in $FUNDS_{it}^e$ can come about by an increase in period $t-1$ of either demand deposits or savings deposits or by a decrease in the reserve requirement ratio. Because of the expectational assumptions regarding demand and savings deposits, a 5.0 percent increase in $FUNDS_{it}^e$ means that bank i expects all future values of this variable to be 5.0 percent higher as well.

From the results in row 2 it can be seen that this change caused bank i to lower its loan rate for periods t and beyond in an attempt to increase the demand for its loans. Since bank i expected that bank j's rate would not respond to this change in bank i's rate until period $t+1$, bank i expected to increase its share of the market from 0.5000 to 0.5241 in period t. The aggregate demand for loans was expected to increase slightly in period t from 810.2 to 811.3 because of the lower average loan rate caused by bank i lowering its rate. Bank i also chose to raise its ratio of bills and bonds to loans plus bills and bonds from 0.2956 to 0.2960. This slight substitution into bills and bonds from the no-tax amount was caused in effect by the lower loan rate relative to the bill rate.

The values of all of the variables for period $t+1$ were essentially the same as the values for period t except for the value of the loan rate. Bank i found it to its advantage to lower its loan rate by ten basis points for period t and then to raise the rate back by five basis points for period $t+1$. This move enabled bank i to increase its expected market share by enough to absorb the extra loanable funds it expected to have at its disposal for periods t and beyond.

For the results in row 3 in Table 2-3, $FUNDS_{it}^e$ was decreased by 5.0 percent. The results in this case were essentially the opposite to those in row 2.

Table 2-3.　Results of Solving the Control Problem of Bank i

Initial Conditions from Table 2-2 except:	RB_{it}	RB_{it+1}	RB_{jt}^e	RB_{jt+1}^e	L_t^e	L_{t+1}^e	LB_{it}^e ($LBMAX_{it}$)	LB_{it+1}^e ($LBMAX_{it+1}$)
1. No exceptions	0.0750	0.0750	0.0750	0.0750	810.2	810.2	405.1	405.1
2. $FUNDS_{it}^e$ = 603.9 (+5.0%)	0.0740 (−1.3%)	0.0745	0.0750	0.0745	811.3	811.3	425.1	425.3
3. $FUNDS_{it}^e$ = 546.3 (−5.0%)	0.0761 (+1.5%)	0.0755	0.0750	0.0755	809.1	809.1	384.8	384.8
4. a	0.0760 (+1.3%)	0.0755	0.0750	0.0755	849.6	849.6	405.1	405.1
5. b	0.0740 (−1.3%)	0.0745	0.0750	0.0745	770.8	770.8	404.9	405.0
6. r_t = 0.0683 (+5.0%)	0.0764 (+1.9%)	0.0764	0.0765	0.0764	807.1	807.1	404.9	405.0
7. r_t = 0.0618 (−5.0%)	0.0736 (−1.9%)	0.0735	0.0735	0.0735	813.4	813.5	405.3	405.2
8. RB_{jt-1} = 0.0788 (+5.0%)	0.0768 (+2.4%)	0.0769	0.0769	0.0769	810.2	810.2	405.3	405.2
9. RB_{jt-1} = 0.0713 (−5.0%)	0.0731 (−2.5%)	0.0731	0.0731	0.0731	810.2	810.2	404.9	405.0
10. g_2 = 0.3104 (+5.0%)	0.0754 (+0.5%)	0.0752	0.0750	0.0752	809.7	809.7	396.6	396.6
11. g_2 = 0.2808 (−0.5%)	0.0746 (−0.5%)	0.0748	0.0750	0.0748	810.7	810.7	413.4	413.5

Table 2-3. (continued)

Initial Conditions from Table 2-2 except:	$\dfrac{LB^e_{it}}{L^e_t}$	$\dfrac{LB^e_{it+1}}{L^e_{t+1}}$	VBB_{it}	VBB_{it+1}	$\dfrac{VBB_{it}}{LB^e_{it}+VBB_{it}}$	$\dfrac{VBB_{it+1}}{LB^e_{it+1}+VBB_{it+1}}$
1. No exceptions	0.5000	0.5000	170.0	170.0	0.2956	0.2956
2. $FUNDS^e_{it}$ = 603.9 (+5.0%)	0.5241	0.5242	178.7 (+5.1%)	178.6	0.2960	0.2958
3. $FUNDS^e_{it}$ = 546.3 (−5.0%)	0.4757	0.4757	161.5 (−5.0%)	161.5	0.2956	0.2956
4. a	0.4768	0.4768	170.0 (+0.0%)	170.0	0.2956	0.2956
5. b	0.5253	0.5255	170.2 (+0.1%)	170.1	0.2960	0.2958
6. r_t = 0.0683 (+5.0%)	0.5017	0.5018	170.2 (+0.1%)	170.1	0.2959	0.2958
7. r_t = 0.0618 (−5.0%)	0.4983	0.4981	169.8 (−0.1%)	169.9	0.2952	0.2954
8. $RB_{jt−1}$ = 0.0788 (+5.0%)	0.5002	0.5001	169.8 (−0.1%)	169.9	0.2953	0.2954
9. $RB_{jt−1}$ = 0.0713 (−5.0%)	0.4998	0.4999	170.2 (+0.1%)	170.1	0.2960	0.2958
10. g_2 = 0.3104 (+5.0%)	0.4898	0.4898	178.5 (+5.0%)	178.5	0.3104	0.3104
11. g_2 = 0.2808 (−5.0%)	0.5100	0.5101	161.7 (−4.9%)	161.6	0.2812	0.2810

[a] $LB_{it−1}$ = 425.4 (+5.0%), $L_{t−1}$ = 850.7 (+5.0%), $LUN_{t−1}$ = 850.7 (+5.0%)

[b] $LB_{it−1}$ = 384.8 (−5.0%), $L_{t−1}$ = 769.7 (−5.0%), $LUN_{t−1}$ = 769.7 (−5.0%)

The bank increased its loan rate to lower its expected market share, decreased the value of bills and bonds to purchase, and decreased the maximum amount of money that it will lend to firms and households. In this case, however, the bank did not choose to substitute away from bills and bonds as a result of the higher loan rate relative to the bill rate.

For the results in row 4 in Table 2-3, the value of bank i's loans in period $t-1$ was increased by 5.0 percent, along with a 5.0 percent increase in the aggregate unconstrained and constrained demands for loans. This change caused bank i to increase its loan rate for periods t and beyond. The loan rate was increased to lower the bank's market share to the point where the expected demand for its loans was equal to what the demand was in row 1. This meant that the value of bills and bonds to purchase was not changed. Since $FUNDS_{it}^e$ was not changed for this run, the sum of the value of bills and bonds to purchase (VBB_{it}) and bank i's expected loans (LB_{it}^e) could not be changed, and so with LB_{it}^e remaining unchanged, VBB_{it} must remain unchanged. The results in row 5 in Table 2-3, based on a 5.0 decrease in loans, are essentially the opposite to those in row 4. For the results in row 5, however, the bank chose to substitute into bills and bonds slightly as a result of the lower loan rate relative to the bill rate. The sum of LB_{it}^e and VBB_{it}^e was still, of course, unchanged, which meant that LB_{it}^e was decreased slightly.

For the results in row 6 in Table 2-3, the bill rate for period t was increased by 5.0 percent. This caused bank i to increase its expectation of bank j's rate for period t from 0.0750 to 0.0765. Bank i was led to increase its loan rate one basis point less than this and thus increase its share of the market slightly. The proportion of bills and bonds to loans plus bills and bonds was increased from 0.2956 to 0.2959. Bank i's expectation of the aggregate demand for loans for period t decreased from 810.2 to 807.1 due to the higher loan rates. The results in row 6 thus show that there is some slight substitution into bills and bonds from loans when the bill rate rises. Since $FUNDS_{it}^e$ was not changed, the slightly higher value of VBB_{it} implied a slightly lower value of LB_{it}^e. The results in row 7 in Table 2-3, based on a 5.0 decrease in the bill rate, are opposite to those in row 6.

For the results in row 8 in Table 2-3, bank j's loan rate for period $t-1$ was increased by 5.0 percent to 0.0788. This caused bank i to increase its expectation of bank j's rate for period t to 0.0769 from the 0.0750 in row 1. Bank i increased its loan rate one basis point less than this and thus increased its share of the market slightly. The proportion of bills and bonds to loans plus bills and bonds was decreased from 0.2956 to 0.2953, which meant that there was some substitution into loans from bills and bonds because of the higher loan rate relative to the bill rate. The results in row 9, based on a 5.0 percent decrease in bank j's rate, are opposite to those in row 8.

For the results in row 10 in Table 2-3, the no-tax proportion of bills and bonds, g_2, was increased by 5.0 percent. This caused bank i to increase its loan rate and thus lower its market share. The bank chose to hold 5.0 percent more in bills and bonds (8.5 more in value), which, with $FUNDS_{it}^e$ unchanged, caused LB_{it}^e to decrease by 8.5. The higher loan rate was the rate necessary to lead to a decrease in the expected demand for the bank's loans of this amount. The results in row 11, based on a 5.0 percent decrease in g_2, are essentially the opposite to those in row 10. In this case the bank chose to hold a slightly higher proportion of bills and bonds than the no-tax proportion as a result of the lower loan rate relative to the bill rate.

The results in Table 2-3 can be summarized briefly as follows. A bank is constrained in how much it can lend to households and firms (LB_{it}^e) and in the value of bills and bonds that it can purchase (VBB_{it}) by its expected level of funds ($FUNDS_{it}^e$). When $FUNDS_{it}^e$ increases, bank i lowers its loan rate, thus increasing LB_{it}^e, and increases VBB_{it}. The opposite happens when $FUNDS_{it}^e$ decreases. When either the bill rate for the current period increases or bank j's rate of the previous period increases, bank i increases its loan rate for the current period because it expects that bank j's loan rate for the current period will be higher than otherwise. The opposite happens when the rates decrease. When the demand for loans of the previous period increases, with no change in $FUNDS_{it}^e$, this also causes bank i to increase its loan rate for the current period in order to lower its expected market share. The opposite happens when the demand for loans of the previous period decreases. Because of the restriction that $VBB_{it} + LB_{it}^e$ equals $FUNDS_{it}^e$, LB_{it}^e can increase, with $FUNDS_{it}^e$ unchanged, only at the expense of VBB_{it}, and vice versa. When the bill rate decreases relative to the loan rate, there is a tendency for the bank to substitute away from bills and bonds into expected loans, and vice versa.

2.6 THE CONDENSED MODEL FOR BANKS

The bank behavioral equations for the condensed model are presented in Table 2-4. In terms of notation, all i subscripts have been dropped from the variables, since for the condensed model there is only a bank sector rather than individual banks. Also, the loan rate for period t is now denoted RL_t rather than RB_{it}, and the level of savings deposits is denoted SD_t rather than SDB_{it}. Otherwise, the notation is the same for both the non-condensed and condensed models.

In Equation (1) in Table 2-4, $FUNDS_t^e$ is defined in exactly the same way as it is for the non-condensed model. Equation (2) determines the loan rate and is based on the results in Table 2-3. The coefficients were chosen to be consistent with the size of the reactions in Table 2-3. For example, a 5.0 percent increase in $FUNDS_{it}^e$ led to a 1.3 percent decrease in the loan rate in Table 2-3, and a 5.0 percent decrease in $FUNDS_{it}^e$ led to a 1.5 percent increase in the loan

Table 2-4. Bank Equations for the Condensed Model

(1) $FUNDS_t^e = (1-g_1)(DDB_{t-1} - EMAXDD) + (SD_{t-1} - EMAXSD),$

(2) $RL_t = 1.102(RL_{t-1})^{0.50}(FUNDS_t^e)^{-0.28}(g_2)^{0.10}(r_t)^{0.38}(LUN_{t-1})^{0.26},$

(3) $VBB_t = 1.003\, g_2\, FUNDS_t^e\, (r_t)^{0.02}(RL_{t-1})^{-0.02},$

(4) $LBMAX_t = FUNDS_t^e - VBB_t.$

---

rate. The average response was thus -1.4 percent, so that the elasticity of the loan rate with respect to $FUNDS_{it}^e$ is $-1.4/5.0 = -0.28$, which is the coefficient used for $FUNDS_t^e$ in Equation (2) in Table 2-4. The other coefficients were determined in a similar manner. The loan rate is a negative function of $FUNDS_t^e$ and a positive function of last period's loan rate, of g_2, of the bill rate, and of last period's unconstrained demand for loans.

Equation (3) determines the value of bills and bonds purchased by the bank sector. The equation is based on the results in Table 2-3 and states that the value of bills and bonds purchased deviates from the expected no-tax proportion $(g_2 FUNDS_t^e)$ as a positive function of the bill rate and a negative function of last period's loan rate. The choice for the values of the constant terms in Equations (2) and (3) (1.102 and 1.003) will be discussed in Chapter Six.

Equation (4) is the same as for the non-condensed model. The bank sector is assumed to set the maximum value of loans that it will make in the period equal to the difference between its expected funds and the value of bills and bonds that it chooses to purchase.

NOTES

[a]Whenever an interest rate multiplies a stock in the model, the resulting interest revenue or interest payment, a flow, is assumed to be received or paid during the current period. For example, $RB_{it}LB_{it}$ in equation (2.2) is assumed to be the interest revenue received by bank i on its loans during period t.

[b]Since all expectations are made by bank i, no i subscript or superscript has been added to the relevant symbols to denote the fact that it is bank i making the expectation. The same procedure will be followed for firms and households below.

[c]In the programming for the non-condensed model, bank i was assumed to estimate the parameter α_3 in Equations (2.11) and (2.12) on the basis of its past observations of the correlation between changes in the aggregate unconstrained demand for loans and changes in the average loan rate. The exact procedure by which bank i was assumed to estimate α_3 is described in the Appendix. No t subscript is added to α_3 in the text, even though for the non-condensed model bank i's estimate of α_3 will in general be changing from one decision period to the next.

[d]Although Equations (2.1) – (2.7) are written only for period t, they are also meant to hold for periods $t+1, \ldots, t+T$ as well. In addition, an e superscript should be added to a variable when bank i only has an expectation of that variable. For example, Equation (2.2) should be written

$$\Pi B_{it}^e = RB_{tt}LB_{it}^e + r_t VBILLB_{it} + BONDB_{it} - r_t SDB_{it}^e$$

$$+ (BONDB_{it}/R_{t+1}^e - BONDB_{it}/R_t), \qquad (2.2)'$$

$$\Pi B_{it+k}^e = RB_{it+k}LB_{it+k}^e + r_{t+k}^e VBILLB_{it+k} + BONDB_{it+k}$$

$$- r_{t+k}^e SDB_{it+k}^e + (BONDB_{it+k}/R_{t+k+1}^e - BONDB_{it+k}/R_{t+k}^e), k=1,2,\ldots,T. \qquad (2.2)''$$

To conserve space, Equations $(2.1) - (2.7)$ will not be written out in this expanded way, but the expansion in each case is straightforward.

Because Equations $(2.1) - (2.7)$ are meant to hold for periods $t+1$ through $t+T$, some assumption has to be made about bank i's expectations of the future values of the tax parameters, d_1, d_2, and g_2, and the reserve requirement ratio, g_1. As is consistent with the practice in this study, bank i is assumed to expect the values of these parameters to remain unchanged over time. Similarly, firms and households are assumed to expect the values of the government tax parameters to remain unchanged over time. Because of these assumptions, t subscripts have not been added to the tax parameters and the reserve requirement ratio, although the government is, of course, free to change these parameters if it so desires.

Chapter Three

Firms

3.1 THE BASIC EQUATIONS

INTRODUCTION

In Table 3-1 the important symbols used in this chapter are listed in alphabetic order. Each firm, say firm i, borrows money from banks (LF_{it}), hires labor from households (HPF_{it}), buys goods for investment purposes from other firms (INV_{it}), produces goods (Y_{it}), and sells goods to households and the government (XF_{it}). The seven main decision variables of a firm are its price (PF_{it}), its production, its investment, its wage rate (WF_{it}), the amount of money to borrow from the banks, the maximum number of hours that it will pay for $(HPFMAX_{it})$, and the maximum number of goods that it will sell $(XFMAX_{it})$. Firm i receives at the beginning of period t information from the banks on the loan rate it will be charged in the period (RF_{it}) and on the maximum amount of money that it will be able to borrow $(LFMAX_{it})$. The underlying technology of a firm is assumed to be of a "putty-clay" type, where at any one time different types of machines with differing worker-machine ratios can be purchased. The worker-machine ratio is assumed to be fixed for each type of machine.

Table 3-1.   Notation for Firms in Alphabetic Order

Non-Condensed Model

Subscript i denotes variable for firm i. Subscript j denotes variable for firm j. Subscript t denotes variable for period t. A p superscript in the text denotes a planned value of the variable, and an e superscript denotes an expected value of the variable.

CF_{it}	= cash flow before taxes and dividends
$\overline{CF}_{it}$	= cash flow net of taxes and dividends
d_1	= profit tax rate
DDF_{it}	= actual demand deposits
DDF_{1it}	= demand deposits set aside for transaction purposes
DDF_{2i}	= demand deposits set aside to be used as a buffer to meet unexpected decreases in cash flow
DEP_{it}	= depreciation
$DIVF_{it}$	= dividends paid
$EMAXHP_i$	= largest error the firm expects to make in overestimating the supply of labor available to it for any period
$EMAXMH_i$	= largest error the firm expects to make in underestimating its worker hour requirements for any period
$\overline{H}$	= maximum number of hours that each machine can be used each period
HP_t	= total number of worker hours paid for in the economy
HPF_{it}	= number of worker hours paid for (by firm i)
HPF_{jt}	= number of worker hours paid for (by firm j)
$HPFMAX_{it}$	= maximum number of worker hours that the firm will pay for
$HPUN_t$	= total unconstrained supply of hours in the economy
I_{nit}	= number of machines of type n purchased ($n=1,2$)
INV_{it}	= number of goods purchased for investment purposes
$\overline{K}$	= minimum number of machines required to be held in each of the last m periods of the decision horizon
K^a_{nit}	= actual number of machines of type n held ($n=1,2$)
KH_{nit}	= actual number of machine hours worked on machines of type n ($n=1,2$)
$KMIN_{nit}$	= minimum number of machines of type n required to produce Y_{nit} ($n=1,2$)
LF_{it}	= value of loans taken out
$LFMAX_{it}$	= maximum value of loans that the firm can take out
m	= length of life of one machine
MH_{nit}	= number of worker hours worked on machines of type n ($n=1,2$)
MH_{3it}	= number of worker hours required to handle deviations of inventories from β_1 times sales
MH_{4it}	= number of worker hours required to handle fluctuations in sales
MH_{5it}	= number of worker hours required to handle fluctuations in worker hours paid for
MH_{6it}	= number of worker hours required to handle fluctuations in net investment
MH_{it}	= total number of worker hours required
PF_{it}	= price set (by firm i)
PF_{jt}	= price set (by firm j)
$\overline{PF}_t$	= average price level in the economy

Table 3-1. (continued)

PFF_{it}	= price paid for investment goods
RF_{it}	= loan rate paid
$T+1$	= length of decision horizon
$TAXF_{it}$	= taxes paid
V_{it}	= stock of inventories (of firm i)
V_{jt}	= stock of inventories (of firm j)
WF_{it}	= wage rate (of firm i)
WF_{jt}	= wage rate (of firm j)
$\overline{WF}_t$	= average wage rate in the economy
X_t	= total number of goods sold in the economy
XF_{it}	= number of goods sold (by firm i)
XF_{jt}	= number of goods sold (by firm j)
$XFMAX_{it}$	= maximum number of goods that the firm will sell
Y_{nit}	= number of goods produced on machines of type n $(n=1,2)$
Y_{it}	= total number of goods produced
δ_n	= number of goods it takes to create a machine of type n $(n=1,2)$
λ_n	= amount of output produced per worker hour on machines of type n $(n=1,2)$
μ_n	= amount of output produced per machine hour on machines of type n $(n=1,2)$
ΠF_{it}	= before-tax profits

Condensed Model (For equations in Table 3-4 only.)

Subscript t denotes variable for period t. Superscripts p and pp in Table 3-4 denote a planned value of the variable, and superscript e denotes an expected value of the variable. Unless otherwise stated, the variables refer to the firm sector. Only the notation that differs from the notation for the non-condensed model is presented here.

CF_t	= cash flow before taxes and dividends
$\overline{CF}_t$	= cash flow net of taxes and dividends
DDF_t	= actual demand deposits
DDF_{1t}	= demand deposits set aside for transactions purposes
DDF_2	= demand deposits set aside to be used as a buffer to meet unexpected decreases in cash flow
DEP_t	= depreciation
$EMAXHP$	= largest error the firm sector expects to make in overestimating the supply of labor available to it for any period
$EMAXMH$	= largest error the firm sector expects to make in underestimating its worker hour requirements for any period
HPF_t	= number of worker hours paid for by the firm sector
$HPFMAX_t$	= maximum number of worker hours that the firm sector will pay for
$HPFMAXUN_t$	= maximum number of worker hours that the firm sector would pay for if it were not constrained
INV_t	= number of goods purchased for investment purposes (one good = one machine)
$INVUN_t$	= unconstrained investment demand of the firm sector
K_t^a	= actual number of machines held
KH_t	= number of machine hours worked

Table 3-1.   (continued)

$KMIN_t$	= minimum number of machines required to produce Y_t
LF_t	= value of loans taken out
$LFMAX_t$	= maximum value of loans that the firm sector can take out
$LFUN_t$	= unconstrained demand for loans of the firm sector
MH_{1t}	= number of worker hours worked on the machines
MH_{3t}	= number of worker hours required to handle deviations of inventories from β_1 times sales
MH_{4t}	= number of worker hours required to handle fluctuations in sales
MH_{5t}	= number of worker hours required to handle fluctuations in worker hours paid for
MH_{6t}	= number of worker hours required to handle fluctuations in net investment
MH_t	= total number of worker hours required
P_t	= price level
PUN_t	= price level that the firm sector would set if it were not constrained
RL_t	= loan rate
V_t	= stock of inventories
W_t	= wage rate
WUN_t	= wage rate that the firm sector would set if it were not constrained
$XFMAX_t$	= maximum number of goods that the firm sector will sell
Y_t	= total number of goods produced
Y^pUN_t	= number of goods that the firm sector would plan to produce if it were not constrained
λ_1	= amount of output produced per worker hour
μ_1	= amount of output produced per machine hour
ΠF_{it}	= before-tax profits

EQUATIONS REGARDING THE TECHNOLOGY AND CAPITAL AND LABOR REQUIREMENTS

$$MH_{nit} = \frac{Y_{nit}}{\lambda_n}, \ n = 1, 2, \ [\text{worker hours required to produce } Y_{nit}] \tag{3.1}$$

$$KH_{nit} = \frac{Y_{nit}}{\mu_n}, \ n = 1, 2, \ [\text{machine hours required to produce } Y_{nit}] \tag{3.2}$$

$$KMIN_{nit} = \frac{KH_{nit}}{\bar{H}}, \ n = 1,2, \ [\text{minimum number of machines required to produce } Y_{nit}] \tag{3.3}$$

$$K^a_{nit} = K^a_{nit-1} + I_{nit} - I_{nit-m}, \ n = 1,2, \ [\text{actual number of machines of type } n \text{ on hand}] \tag{3.4}$$

$$INV_{it} = \sum_{n=1}^{2} \delta_n I_{nit}, \ n = 1,2, \ [\text{number of goods purchased for investment purposes}] \tag{3.5}$$

$$Y_{it} = \sum_{n=1}^{2} Y_{nit}, \text{ [total level of output]} \tag{3.6}$$

$$V_{it} = V_{it-1} + Y_{it} - XF_{it}, \text{ [level of inventories]} \tag{3.7}$$

$$MH_{3it} = \beta_2(V_{it} - \beta_1 XF_{it})^2, \beta_1 > 0, \beta_2 > 0, \text{ [worker hours required to maintain}$$
$$\text{deviations of inventories from } \beta_1$$
$$\text{times sales]} \tag{3.8}$$

$$MH_{4it} = \beta_3(XF_{it} - XF_{it-1})^2, \beta_3 > 0, \text{ [worker hours required to handle fluctua-}$$
$$\text{tions in sales]} \tag{3.9}$$

$$MH_{5it} = \beta_4(HPF_{it-1} - HPF_{it-2})^2, \beta_4 > 0, \text{ [worker hours required to handle}$$
$$\text{fluctuations in hours paid for]} \tag{3.10}$$

$$MH_{6it} = \beta_5 \left[\sum_{n=1}^{2} K^a_{nit} - \sum_{n=1}^{2} K^a_{nit-1} \right]^2, \beta_5 > 0, \text{ [worker hours required to}$$
$$\text{handle fluctuations in net}$$
$$\text{investment]} \tag{3.11}$$

$$MH_{it} = MH_{1it} + MH_{2it} + MH_{3it} + MH_{4it} + MH_{5it} + MH_{6it}, \text{ [total worker hours}$$
$$\text{required]} \tag{3.12}$$

$$K^a_{nit} \geqslant KMIN_{nit}, n=1,2, \text{ [number of machines of type } n \text{ on hand must be}$$
$$\text{greater than or equal to minimum number required]} \tag{3.13}$$

$$HPF_{it} \geqslant MH_{it}. \text{ [worker hours paid for must be greater than or equal to worker}$$
$$\text{hours required]} \tag{3.14}$$

Equation (3.1) defines the number of worker hours required to product output Y_{nit} on machines of type n, and Equation (3.2) defines the number of machine hours required. These two equations reflect the putty-clay nature of the technology. Without loss of generality, the number of different types of machines is taken to be 2.[a] There is assumed to be no technical progress, so that λ_n and μ_n ($n = 1,2$) are not functions of time. Machines are also assumed not to be subject to physical depreciation, so that λ_n and μ_n ($n = 1,2$) are not a function of the age of the machines. The machines are assumed to wear out completely after m periods.

Equation (3.3) defines the minimum number of machines of type n required to produce Y_{nit}. It is assumed that $\bar{H}$, the maximum number of hours that each machine can be used each period, is constant over time. Equation (3.4) defines the actual number of machines of each type on hand in period t. Machines purchased in a period are assumed to be able to be used in the production process in that period. In Equation (3.4), I_{nit} is the number of machines of type n purchased in period t and I_{nit-m} is the number of machines of type n that wear out at the end of period $t-1$ and so cannot be used in the production process in period t. The firm is subject to the restriction (3.13), which says that the actual number of machines of type n on hand must be greater than or equal to the minimum number required.

There is assumed to be only one good in the system, which can be used either for consumption or investment purposes. δ_n is the number of goods it takes to create a machine of type n. In Equation (3.5) the number of machines purchased in period t is translated into the equivalent number of goods purchased. To rule out the possibility of one type of machine completely dominating the other in efficiency, it was assumed for the simulation work that $\mu_1 = \mu_2$, so that the types differ from each other only in terms of the λ coefficients. Machines of type 1 were assumed to have a lower worker-machine ratio, $\lambda_1 > \lambda_2$, and to require more goods to create one machine, $\delta_1 > \delta_2$. Equation (3.6) defines the total level of output, and equation (3.7) defines the stock of inventories.

Equations (3.8) through (3.11) define various adjustment costs facing the firm, the costs taking the form of increased worker hour requirements. Equation (3.8) reflects the assumption that there are costs involved in having inventories be either greater than or less than a certain proportion of sales. It is possible that inventory costs are asymmetrical in the sense that negative deviations may be more costly than positive deviations, but for simplicity this possibility was not incorporated into the model. Any positive stock of inventories is, of course, costly to the firm in the sense that the stock must be financed. Equations (3.9)–(3.11) reflect the assumptions that there are costs involved in having sales, worker hours paid for, and net investment fluctuate. The use of the lagged change in worker hours paid for in equation (3.10) is made for computational convenience and is not a critical assumption of the model. Equation (3.12) defines total worker hour requirements. The firm is subject to the restriction (3.14), which says that worker hours paid for must be greater than or equal to worker hour requirements.

EQUATIONS REGARDING FINANCIAL VARIABLES

$$DEP_{it} = \frac{1}{m}(PFF_{it}INV_{it} + PFF_{it-1}INV_{it-1} + \ldots + PFF_{it-m+1}INV_{it-m+1}),$$

$$\text{[depreciation]} \quad (3.15)$$

$$\Pi F_{it} = PF_{it}Y_{it} - WF_{it}HPF_{it} - DEP_{it} - RF_{it}LF_{it} + (PF_{it} - PF_{it-1})V_{it-1},$$

$$\text{[before-tax profits]} \quad (3.16)$$

$$TAXF_{it} = d_1 \, \Pi F_{it}, \quad \text{[taxes paid]} \tag{3.17}$$

$$DIVF_{it} = \Pi F_{it} - TAXF_{it}, \quad \text{[dividends paid]} \tag{3.18}$$

$$CF_{it} = PF_{it}XF_{it} - WF_{it}HPF_{it} - PFF_{it}INV_{it} - RF_{it}LF_{it}, \quad \text{[cash flow before taxes and dividends]} \tag{3.19}$$

$$\overline{CF}_{it} = CF_{it} - TAXF_{it} - DIVF_{it} \quad \text{[cash flow net of taxes and dividends]}$$
$$= DEP_{it} - PFF_{it}INV_{it} + PF_{it-1}V_{it-1} - PF_{it}V_{it}, \tag{3.20}$$

$$DDF_{it} = DDF_{it-1} + LF_{it} - LF_{it-1} + \overline{CF}_{it}, \quad \text{[demand deposits]} \tag{3.21}$$

$$LF_{it} \leqslant LFMAX_{it}. \quad \text{[loan constraint]} \tag{3.22}$$

The government is assumed to allow for tax purposes straight line depreciation, which is reflected in Equation (3.15). Equation (3.16) defines before-tax profits on an accounting basis, which is equal to price times output less wage costs, depreciation, and interest costs and plus any gains or losses on the stock of inventories due to price changes. Taxes are defined in Equation (3.17), where d_1 is the profit tax rate.

The firm is assumed not to retain any earnings, so that the level of dividends, as defined in Equation (3.18), is merely the difference between before-tax profits and taxes. Equation (3.19) defines cash flow gross of taxes and dividends, and Equation (3.20) defines cash flow net of taxes and dividends. The level of demand deposits, defined in Equation (3.21), is a residual in the model, given the loans of the firm and its cash flow net of taxes and dividends. The firm's level of loans is a decision variable, and its determination is discussed in Section 3.3. The firm is subject to the loan constraint (3.22).

3.2 THE FORMATION OF EXPECTATIONS

As was the case for banks, let $T+1$ be the length of the decision horizon. In order for the firm to solve its control problem at the beginning of period t, it must form expectations of a number of variables for periods t through $t+T$. Firm i is assumed to form the following expectations:[b]

$$\frac{PF_{jt}^e}{PF_{jt-1}} = \left(\frac{PF_{it-1}}{PF_{jt-1}}\right)^{\beta_6} \left(\frac{V_{jt-1}}{\beta_1 XF_{jt-1}}\right)^{\beta_7}, \; \beta_6 > 0, \beta_7 < 0, \; \text{[expected price of firm } j \text{ for period } t] \tag{3.23}$$

$$\frac{PF_{jt+k}^e}{PF_{jt+k-1}^e} = \left(\frac{PF_{it+k-1}}{PF_{jt+k-1}^e}\right)^{\beta_6}, \; \text{[expected price of firm } j \text{ for period } t+k \; (k=1,2,\ldots,T)] \tag{3.24}$$

$$\overline{PF}_{t+k}^e = (PF_{it+k} \cdot PF_{jt+k}^e)^{\frac{1}{2}}, \text{ [expected average price for period}$$
$$t+k \ (k=0,1,\ldots,T)] \tag{3.25}$$

$$X_t^e = X_{t-1} \left(\frac{\overline{PF}_t^e}{\overline{PF}_{t-1}} \right)^{\beta_8}, \ \beta_8 < 0, \text{ [expected aggregate demand for goods for}$$
$$\text{period } t] \tag{3.26}$$

$$X_{t+k}^e = X_{t+k-1}^e \left(\frac{\overline{PF}_{t+k}^e}{\overline{PF}_{t+k-1}^e} \right)^{\beta_8}, \text{ [expected aggregate demand for goods for}$$
$$\text{period } t+k \ (k=1,2,\ldots,T)] \tag{3.27}$$

$$\frac{XF_{it}^e}{X_t^e} = \frac{XF_{it-1}}{X_{t-1}} \left(\frac{PF_{it}}{PF_{jt}^e} \right)^{\beta_9}, \ \beta_9 < 0, \text{ [expected market share of goods for period}$$
$$t] \tag{3.28}$$

$$\frac{XF_{it+k}^e}{X_{t+k}^e} = \frac{XF_{it+k-1}^e}{X_{t+k-1}^e} \left(\frac{PF_{it+k}}{PF_{jt+k}^e} \right)^{\beta_9}, \text{ [expected market share of goods for}$$
$$\text{period } t+k \ (k=1,2,\ldots,T)] \tag{3.29}$$

$$\frac{WF_{jt}^e}{WF_{jt-1}} = \left(\frac{WF_{it-1}}{WF_{jt-1}} \right)^{\beta_{10}}, \ \beta_{10} > 0, \text{ [expected wage rate of firm } j \text{ for period } t]$$
$$\tag{3.30}$$

$$\frac{WF_{jt+k}^e}{WF_{jt+k-1}^e} = \left(\frac{WF_{it+k-1}}{WF_{jt+k-1}^e} \right)^{\beta_{10}}, \text{ [expected wage rate of firm } j \text{ for period}$$
$$t+k \ (k=1,2,\ldots,T)] \tag{3.31}$$

$$\overline{WF}_{t+k}^e = (WF_{it+k} \cdot WF_{jt+k}^e)^{\frac{1}{2}}, \text{ [expected average wage rate for period}$$
$$t+k \ (k=0,1,\ldots,T)] \tag{3.32}$$

$$HPUN_t^e = HPUN_{t-1} \left(\frac{\overline{WF}_t^e}{\overline{WF}_{t-1}} \right)^{\beta_{11}} \left(\frac{\overline{PF}_t^e}{\overline{PF}_{t-1}} \right)^{\beta_{12}}, \ \beta_{11} > 0, \beta_{12} < 0,$$
$$\text{[expected aggregate unconstrained supply of}$$
$$\text{labor for period } t] \tag{3.33}$$

$$HPUN_{t+k}^e = HPUN_{t+k-1}^e \left(\frac{\overline{WF}_{t+k}^e}{\overline{WF}_{t+k-1}^e} \right)^{\beta_{11}} \left(\frac{\overline{PF}_{t+k}^e}{\overline{PF}_{t+k-1}^e} \right)^{\beta_{12}}, \text{ [expected aggregate}$$
$$\text{unconstrained}$$
$$\text{supply of labor for}$$
$$\text{period } t+k$$
$$(k=1,2,\ldots,T)]$$
$$\tag{3.34}$$

$$HP_{t+k}^e = HPUN_{t+k}^e, \text{ [expected aggregate constrained supply of labor for period}$$
$$t+k \ (k=0,1,\ldots,T)] \tag{3.35}$$

$$\frac{HPF_{it}^e}{HP_t^e} = \frac{HPF_{it-1}}{HP_{t-1}} \left(\frac{WF_{it}}{WF_{jt}^e}\right)^{\beta_{13}}, \beta_{13} > 0, \text{[expected market share of labor for period } t]$$

(3.36)

$$\frac{HPF_{it+k}^e}{HP_{t+k}^e} = \frac{HPF_{it+k-1}^e}{HP_{t+k-1}^e} \left(\frac{WF_{it+k}}{WF_{jt+k}^e}\right)^{\beta_{13}}, \text{[expected market share of labor for period } t+k \; (k=1,2,\ldots,T)]$$

(3.37)

$$PFF_{it+k}^e = \overline{PF}_{t+k}^e, \text{[expected price of investment goods for period } t+k \; (k=0,1,\ldots,T)]$$

(3.38)

$$RF_{it+k}^e = RF_{it}. \text{[expected loan rate for period } t+k \; (k=1,2,\ldots,T)]$$

(3.39)

The first term on the right-hand side of Equation (3.23) reflects the fact that firm i expects its price setting behavior in period $t-1$ to have an effect on firm j's price setting behavior in period t. The second term is designed to represent the effect of market conditions on firm i's expectation of firm j's price. If, for example, firm j's stock of inventories at the end of period $t-1$ is greater than a certain proportion of sales, then firm i is assumed to expect that firm j will respond to this situation by lowering its price in period t in an effort to increase sales and draw down inventories.

Firm i must also form expectations of firm j's price for periods $t+1$ and beyond. These expectations are specified in Equation (3.24), which is the same as Equation (3.23) without the final term. Equation (3.24) means that firm i expects that firm j is always adjusting its price toward firm i's price. If firm i's price is constant over time, then firm i expects that firm j's price will gradually approach this value.

In Equation (3.25) firm i's expectation of the average price level is taken to be the geometric average of its price and its expectation of firm j's price. Without loss of generality, there is assumed to be only one other firm, firm j, in existence. (As was the case for banks, it should be obvious how the number of other firms in existence can be generalized to be more than one.) The geometric average is used in (3.25) rather than the arithmetic average to make the solution of the model easier. Firm i expects that the aggregate demand for goods is a function of the average price level, as specified in Equations (3.26) and (3.27).[c]

An important difference between Equations (3.26) and (3.27) for firms and Equations (2.11)-(2.13) for banks is that firms are assumed not to observe the unconstrained demand for goods, whereas banks are assumed to observe the unconstrained demand for loans. Equation (3.26), for example, is in terms of the actual (constrained) demand for goods, whereas Equation (2.11) is in terms of the unconstrained demand for loans. The rationale for this difference in assumptions has to do with the fact that the loan constraints on firms and households are likely to be binding more often than are the goods constraints on households.

The maximum number of goods that a firm will sell in a period is equal to the sum of the amount it knows it can produce in the period and the amount it has in inventories at the beginning of the period. Since firms usually hold a nonnegligible stock of inventories, the maximum number of goods that a firm will sell in a period is in most cases likely to be much larger than what it expects to sell and what it actually sells. Therefore, firms will not in general be turning customers away from buying their goods even if they set their prices of goods too low (in the sense that their actual sales exceed their expected sales), whereas banks will be turning customers away from taking out loans if they set their loan rates too low. It thus seems reasonable to assume that banks observe the unconstrained demand for loans because they turn customers away, and that firms do not observe the unconstrained demand for goods because they seldom turn customers away. On this same line of reasoning, it also seems reasonable to assume, as is done below, that firms observe the unconstrained supply of labor because they turn workers away when they set their wage rates too high.

Equations (3.28) and (3.29) determine firm i's expectations of its market share of goods for periods t and beyond and are similar to Equations (2.14) and (2.15) for banks. The equations reflect the assumption that a firm expects that its market share of goods is a function of its price relative to the prices of other firms.

Firm i's expectation of firm j's wage rate is specified in Equations (3.30) and (3.31). Equation (3.30) for the wage rate is similar to Equation (3.23) for the price level, without the final term. Firm i is assumed to have no other basis upon which to base its expectation of firm j's wage rate for period t than its and firm j's wage rates for period $t-1$. Equation (3.32), defining firm i's expectation of the average wage rate, is similar to Equation (3.24).

Firm i expects that the aggregate unconstrained supply of labor is a positive function of the average wage rate and a negative function of the average price level, as specified in Equations (3.33) and (3.34). Equations (3.33) and (3.34) for firms are similar to Equations (2.11) and (2.12) for banks. As mentioned above, firms are assumed to observe the unconstrained supply of labor.[d] Equation (3.35) states that firm i expects that households will not be constrained in their work behavior in periods t and beyond. The same justification for this equation can be made as was made for Equation (2.13) for banks. As will be seen below, firm i does not itself expect to turn any workers away, and so Equation (3.35) merely states that firm i also does not expect any workers in the aggregate to be turned away.

Equations (3.36) and (3.37) determine firm *i*'s expectations of its market share of labor for periods *t* and beyond. The equations are similar to Equations (2.14)–(2.15) and (3.28)–(3.29) and require no further discussion here.

Aside from a few details, the symmetry of specifications among Equations (2.8)–(2.15) for banks and loans, Equations (3.23)–(3.29) for firms and goods, and Equations (3.30)–(3.37) for firms and labor should be obvious. Each set of equations is based on the assumption that a bank or firm expects that its behavior has an effect on the behavior of its competitors and that its market share is a function of the relationship of its price to the prices of its competitors.

Equation (3.38) states that firm *i* expects that the price that it must pay for investment goods each period is the expected average price level for that period. The firm is assumed not to be able to produce its own investment goods. Equation (3.39) states that firm *i* expects that the loan rate for all future periods is going to be the same as the loan rate for period *t*. Regarding this latter assumption, it would be possible, since banks determine optimal loan rate *paths,* to make the alternative assumption that banks inform firms of the planned future values of the loan rate in addition to the current value. It seemed more straightforward in this case, however, just to assume that firms make the expectations themselves.

3.3 BEHAVIORAL ASSUMPTIONS

The objective of the firm is to maximize the present discounted value of expected future after-tax cash flow. The discount rate is assumed to be the loan rate. The objective function of firm *i* at the beginning of period *t* is:

$$OBJF_{it} = \frac{CF_{it}^e - TAXF_{it}^e}{(1+RF_{it})} + \frac{CF_{it+1}^e - TAXF_{it+1}^e}{(1+RF_{it})(1+RF_{it+1}^e)}$$

$$+ \ldots + \frac{CF_{it+T}^e - TAXF_{it+T}^e}{(1+RF_{it})(1+RF_{it+1}^e) \ldots (1+RF_{it+T}^e)} , \tag{3.40}$$

where $CF_{it+k}^e - TAXE_{it+k}^e$ is the expected value of after-tax cash flow for period $t+k$ ($k = 0,1, \ldots ,T$). The decision variables of the firm are its price, PF_{it+k}, its wage rate, WF_{it+k}, the number of each type of machine to buy, I_{1it+k} and I_{2it+k}, the planned number of goods to produce on each type of machine, Y_{1it+k}^p and Y_{2it+k}^p, the amount of money to borrow, LF_{it+k} ($k = 0,1, \ldots ,T$), the maximum number of hours to pay for, $HPFMAX_{it}$, and the maximum number of goods to sell, $XFMAX_{it}$.

Given a set of paths of the decision variables, the corresponding value of the objective function can be computed as follows.

1. Given firm i's price path, firm i's expectation of firm j's price path can be computed from (3.23) and (3.24). The path of the expected average price level can then be computed from (3.25), followed by the path of expected aggregate demand from (3.26) and (3.27). Firm i's expectation of its own sales path can then be computed from (3.28) and (3.29). Given firm i's expected sales path, its expected path of inventories can be computed from (3.7).e

2. Given firm i's wage path, firm i's expectation of firm j's wage path can be computed from (3.30) and (3.31). The path of the expected average wage rate can then be computed from (3.32), followed by the path of the expected aggregate unconstrained supply of labor from (3.33) and (3.34), and then by the path of the expected aggregate constrained supply of labor from (3.35). Firm i's expectation of the supply of labor available to it can then be computed from (3.36) and (3.37).

3. Given paths of the number of each type of machine to buy, the path of investment denominated in goods can be computed from (3.5). The path of depreciation can then be computed from (3.15), given the path of the expected price of investment goods from (3.38).

4. Given the above paths and the path of the expected loan rate from (3.39), the paths of profits, taxes, and cash flow can be computed from (3.16), (3.17), and (3.19), which then means that the value of the objective function can be computed.

The firm is restricted in each period by (3.13) and (3.14) and by various nonegativity properties, such as the fact that the stock of inventories must be nonnegative. For any set of paths of the decision variables, these restrictions can be checked by solving Equations (3.1) through (3.12) and then making the appropriate checks. The firm is also constrained in the current period by the loan constraint (3.22). Regarding the possibility of the loan constraint existing for future periods as well, firm i is assumed to expect that the loan constraint will *not* be binding in periods beyond t. Banks, in other words, are assumed to communicate the maximum loan values to firms only for period t, and firms are assumed to expect that the maximum values in the future will be large enough so as not to be binding. This was the simplest assumption to make, and having the constraint hold only for period t appeared to have an important enough influence on the firm's decision values for period t so as to make further restrictions unnecessary.

The following two end-point constraints were also imposed on the firm.

$$V^e_{it+T} = \beta_1 X F^e_{it+T}, \tag{3.41}$$

$$K^a_{1it-k} + K^a_{2iT-k} \geq \bar{K}, \; k = 0,1,\ldots,m\text{-}1. \tag{3.42}$$

The level of inventories at the end of the decision horizon was forced to be equal to β_1 times sales of the last period, and the number of machines held in each of the last m periods was required to be greater than or equal to a given number. These conditions were imposed to avoid quirks that would otherwise be likely to show up in the optimal paths near the end of the horizon.

A few general remarks can now be made regarding the control problem of the firm. The firm expects that it will gain customers by lowering its price relative to the expected prices of other firms. The main expected costs to the firm from lowering its price, in addition to the lower price it is charging per good, are the adjustment costs (3.9), (3.10), and (3.11) involved in increasing sales, employment, and investment. The firm also expects that other firms will follow it if it lowers its price, so that it does not expect to be able to capture an ever increasing share of the market without further and future price reductions.

The firm expects that it will lose customers by raising its price relative to the expected prices of other firms. The main costs from doing this, aside from the lost customers, are the adjustment costs. On the plus side, the firm expects that other firms will follow it if it raises its price, so that it does not expect to lose an ever increasing share of the market without further and further price increases.

The firm expects that it will gain workers if it raises its wage rate relative to the expected wage rates of other firms and lose workers if it lowers its wage rate relative to the expected wage rates of other firms. The firm also expects that other firms will follow it if it raises (lowers) its wage rate, so that it does not expect to capture (lose) an ever increasing share of the market without further and further wage rate increases (decreases).

Because of the various adjustment costs, the firm, if it chooses to lower its production, may choose in the current period not to lower its employment and capital stock to the minimum levels required. The firm may thus plan to hold either excess labor or excess capital or both during certain periods.

Before concluding this section, the determination of the three decision variables $HPFMAX_{it}$, $XFMAX_{it}$, and LF_{it+k} $(k = 0,1, \ldots, T)$, must be described. Consider $HPFMAX_{it}$ first. As was the case for banks, a firm must prepare for the possibility that its expectations are incorrect. In the case of worker hours paid for, a firm must prepare for the possibility that it underestimates the supply of labor available to it at the wage rate that it has set.

A firm is assumed to prepare for this possibility by announcing to households not only the wage rate that it will pay in the period t, but also the maximum number of hours that it will pay for in the period, $HPFMAX_{it}$. This maximum is assumed to be set equal to the number of hours the firm expects to pay for from Equation (3.36), given its wage rate, its expectation of firm j's wage rate from Equation (3.30), and its expectations of the aggregate supply of labor from Equation (3.35).f Thus

$$HPFMAX_{it} = HPF^e_{it} \, . \tag{3.43}$$

By setting this maximum, a firm will never have to hire more labor than it expects to hire.

Regarding $XFMAX_{it}$, a firm must prepare for the possibility that the demand for its goods at the price it has set is greater than the amount that it can supply. A firm is assumed to prepare for this possibility by announcing to households not only the price that it will charge in period t, but also the maximum number of goods that it will sell in the period, $XFMAX_{it}$. This maximum is assumed to be

$$XFMAX_{it} = min \ \left\{ Y^p_{it}, \ [Y^p_{it} - \lambda_2 \ (EMAXHP_i + EMAXMH_i) + \lambda_2(HPF^e_{it} - MH^e_{it})] \right\}$$
$$+ \ V_{it-1}, \tag{3.44}$$

where

$\qquad Y^p_{it}$ = planned output for period t,

$\quad EMAXHP_i$ = largest error the firm expects to make in overestimating the supply of labor available to it for any period,

$\quad EMAXMH_i$ = largest error the firm expects to make in underestimating its worker hour requirements for any period,

$HPF^e_{it} - MH^e_{it}$ = expected amount of excess labor for period t.

What Equation (3.44) states is the following. If the firm were assured of being able to produce in period t all it had planned at the beginning of the period to produce, then it could sell in period t $Y^p_{it} + V_{it-1}$. It may, however, either overestimate the supply of labor available to it or underestimate its worker hour requirements,g or both, which will force it to produce less than it had planned unless it had planned to hold enough excess labor to make up the slack. Since machines of type 2 are less efficient absolutely than machines of type 1, if a firm has to cut back on its planned production, it will cut production on machines of type 2 first. Therefore, $\lambda_2(EMAXHP_i + EMAXMH_i)$ is the maximum amount of output the firm expects to have to cut back because of its expectation errors. (If the firm is not using any machines of type 2, then λ_1 replaces λ_2 in (3.44)).

If the firm had planned to hold excess labor, then amount $\lambda_2(HPF_t^e - MH_t^e)$ can be produced from taking up the excess labor slack. Therefore, the amount in square brackets in Equation (3.44) is the amount the firm knows it can produce in period t even if it overestimates its labor supply and underestimates its worker hour requirements by the maximum amounts. It is possible, if the firm plans to hold a lot of excess labor in period t, for $HPF_{it}^e - MH_{it}^e$ to be greater than $EMAXHP_i + EMAXMH_i$, in which case the term in square brackets in Equation (3.44) is greater than Y_{it}^p. It is assumed that a firm never produces more in period t than it originally planned, and since the term in square brackets can be greater than Y_{it}^p, the minimum expression is used in (3.44). $XFMAX_{it}$ as defined in (3.44) is thus the maximum number of goods the firm knows with certainty it can supply in period t.

As mentioned above, it is unlikely that goods constraints are very important in practice because of the fact that goods can be held in inventories. In the present case the goods constraints have been included in the model only for the sake of completeness, and the constraints do not play an important role in future discussion of the model and its properties.

Regarding the determination of the firm's demand for loans, consider first the demand deposit needs of the firm. The demand deposit needs are assumed to be of two kinds: the need for transactions purposes and the need to meet unexpected decreases in cash flow net of taxes and dividends. The need for transactions purposes is assumed to be proportional to the firm's wage bill. Let DDF_{1it} denote the value of demand deposits set aside by firm i for transactions purposes in period t. Then DDF_{1it} is assumed to be

$$DDF_{1it} = \beta_{14} WF_{it}\, HPFMAX_{it},\ \beta_{14} > 0. \tag{3.45}$$

Since it is assumed that the firm never hires more than $HPFMAX_{it}$ amount of labor, the firm's wage bill cannot exceed $WF_{it}\, HPFMAX_{it}$, and so the firm is assured by setting aside the value of demand deposits in (3.45) that it will always have enough demand deposits for transactions purposes.

With respect to the second need for demand deposits, firm i only has from Equation (3.20) an expectation of its cash flow net of taxes and dividends for period t because it only has an expectation of the price of investment goods, PFF_{it}^e, and of its level of inventories for the end of period t, V_{it}^e. The firm must prepare for the possibility that it underestimates the price of investment goods or its level of inventories and ends up with less cash flow net of taxes and dividends than it originally expected. The firm is assumed to prepare for this possibility by planning to hold more demand deposits than are needed for transactions purposes. The firm is assumed from past experience to have a good idea of the largest error it is likely to make in underestimating its cash flow, and this is the amount that the firm is assumed to plan to hold in demand deposits over and above its requirements for transactions purposes. Denote this amount as DDF_{2i}. For simplicity DDF_{2i} is assumed not to be a function of time.

Given its expectations, the firm is assumed to borrow money with the aim of holding amount $DDF_{1it} + DDF_{2i}$ in demand deposits in period t. The aimed-for change in demand deposits is $DDF_{1it} + DDF_{2i} - DDF_{it-1}$, where DDF_{it-1} is the actual value of demand deposits held by firm i in period t-1. The firm will need to increase its loans over and above any increase in aimed-for demand deposits if its expected cash flow after taxes and dividends, $\overline{CF}^e_{it}$, is negative, and conversely if $\overline{CF}^e_{it}$ is positive. The change in the value of loans for the firm is thus

$$LF_{it} - LF_{it-1} = (DDF_{1it} + DDF_{2i} - DDF_{it-1}) - \overline{CF}^e_{it}. \tag{3.46}$$

At the end of the period, after all transactions have taken place, actual demand deposits, DDF_{it}, will be equal to $DDF_{1it} + DDF_{2i}$ only in the case in which the firm's expectation of $\overline{CF}_{it}$ is completely accurate. DDF_{it} will be less than $DDF_{1it} + DDF_{2i}$ if the firm underestimates $\overline{CF}_{it}$ and has to use some of DDF_{2i} to meet the unexpected decrease. From the definition of DDF_{2i}, the firm is assured that DDF_{it} will never be less than DDF_{1it}. DDF_{it} will be greater than $DDF_{1it} + DDF_{2i}$ if the firm overestimates $\overline{CF}_{it}$ and takes out more loans than it really needed. The actual change in demand deposits of the firm for period t is a residual and is defined by Equation (3.21). The determination of the value of loans for periods t+1 and beyond is a straightforward extension of the above analysis for period t.

3.4   THE SOLUTION OF THE CONTROL PROBLEM

It was seen in the last section that given the paths of the decision variables, the corresponding value of the objective function can be computed. In order to solve the control problem of the firm, algorithms were written to search over various sets of paths for the optimum. The main algorithm searched over different price paths. The base price path, from which other paths were tried, was taken to be the path in which the price in each period was the same and equal to PF^e_{jt} in (3.23). PF^e_{jt} is the price that firm i expects firm j to set for period t. From (3.24) it can be seen that this price path corresponds to firm i expecting that firm j's price path will be the same as firm i's price path, which from (3.28) and (3.29) corresponds to firm i expecting that its market share will remain the same in periods t and beyond as it was in period t-1.

For each price path chosen by the algorithm, a submaximization problem was solved to determine the optimal production, investment, and employment paths corresponding to the given price path. This submaximization problem was solved by scanning over the various possible paths. First, given the expected sales path corresponding to the price path, various production paths were tried. The production paths are constrained, given the sales path, by the fact that inventories cannot be negative and by the terminal condition on inventories. For each production path, various investment paths were tried. The investment paths are constrained by the fact that there must be enough machines on hand to produce the amount of output required from the production path and by the terminal conditions. For each production and investment path, various employment paths were tried. The employment paths are constrained by the fact worker hours paid for each period must be at least as great as worker hour requirements.

Two extreme production paths that were tried were a path in which production changed as little as possible from period to period, and a path in which inventories changed as little as possible from period to period. Other paths were then tried as weighted averages of these two paths. There is a tradeoff between costs of production fluctuations (due to costs of investment and employment fluctuations) and costs of inventory fluctuations, and so trying various weighted averages of the two extreme paths should lead to a computed optimum path that is close to the true optimum path.

Given the level of production for a particular period and given the past history of investment, one can compute the number of machines of type 1 or of type 2 that need to be purchased in the period to produce the output of the period, assuming that all machines are utilized to full capacity ($\overline{H}$ hours per period). Two investment paths that were tried were a path in which only machines of type 1 were purchased, and a path in which only machines of type 2 were purchased. Both of these paths were taken to be characterized by full capacity utilization all the time, unless full capacity utilization required negative gross investment, which was not allowed. Other paths were tried in which investment fluctuations were lessened by not having the firm be at full capacity utilization all the time. Paths in which some of type 1 machines and some of type 2 machines were purchased were not tried since it was costly to do so and it did not seem likely that the computed optimum values for period t would be sensitive to this omission.

Given the level of production and the number of the two types of machines on hand for a particular period, given the expected deviation of inventories from β_1 times sales for the period, given the expected change in sales for the period, given the change in worker hours paid for of the previous period, and given the value of net investment for the period, worker hour requirements can be computed from Equations (3.1) and (3.8) – (3.11). Two extreme employment paths that were tried were a path in which worker hours paid for were always kept equal to worker hour requirements, and a path in which fluctuations in worker hours paid for were kept small. Other paths were then tried as weighted averages of these two paths. As was the case for the production paths, trying various weighted averages of the two extreme paths should lead to a computed optimum path that is close to the true optimum path. All paths except the path in which worker hours paid for were equal to worker hour requirements were characterized by the firm paying for more hours than required during some periods.

Given a price path for firm i and its path of worker hours paid for, and given firm i's expectation of the price path of firm j and the path of the average price level in the economy, one can compute from Equations (3.30) – (3.37) the wage path that firm i expects is necessary to yield the path of worker hours paid for that it has set. In other words, once the firm has chosen its price path and its path of worker hours paid for, the wage path is automatically determined.

The loan constraint was handled by throwing out as infeasible those paths that implied a loan value greater than the constraint.

3.5   SOME EXAMPLES OF SOLVING
THE CONTROL PROBLEM OF FIRM i
PARAMETER VALUES AND INITIAL CONDITIONS

The parameter values and initial conditions that were used for the first example are presented in Table 3-2. The most important parameters are β_6, the measure of the extent to which firm i expects firm j to respond to firm i's price setting behavior; β_9, the measure of the extent to which firm i loses or gains market share as its price deviates from firm j's price; β_{10}, the measure of the extent to which firm i expects firm j to respond to firm i's wage setting behavior; β_{13}, the measure of the extent to which firm i loses or gains its market share of labor as its wage deviates from firm j's wage; β_7, the measure of the extent to which firm i expects firm j to change its price in period t as a result of firm j's inventory situation in period $t-1$; and the four parameters reflecting inventory, sales adjustment, hours adjustment, and capital adjustment costs, $\beta_2, \beta_3, \beta_4$, and β_5.

The parameter values and initial conditions were chosen, after some experimentation, so that the optimum values of each control variable for periods t through $t+T$ would be essentially the same as the initial value for period $t-1$. This was done to make it easier to analyze the effects on the behavior of the firm of changing various initial conditions. As can be seen from Table 3-2, the initial conditions correspond to firm i's having half the sales in period $t-1$ and half the labor employed. The firm holds no excess labor and excess capital in period $t-1$. The two firms' prices and wage rates in period $t-1$ are the same. All the machines held by firm i are type 1 machines. The length of the decision

Table 3-2   Parameter Values and Initial Conditions for the Control Problem of Firm i

Parameter	Value	Variable	Value
$T+1$	30	K^a_{1it-1}	250.0
d_1	0.5	K^a_{2it-1}	0.0
m	10	$I_{1it-1}, \ldots, I_{1it-m}$	$25.0, \ldots, 25.0$
λ_1	1.3212	$I_{2it-1}, \ldots, I_{2it-m}$	$0.0, \ldots, 0.0$
λ_2	1.3000	V_{it-1}	52.625
μ_1	1.684	HPF_{it-1}	318.65
μ_2	1.684	HPF_{it-2}	318.65
$\overline{H}$	1.0	$PFF_{it-1}, \ldots, PFF_{it-m+1}$	$1.0, \ldots, 1.0$
δ_1	1.0	LF_{it-1}	164.05
δ_2	0.9	DDF_{it-1}	25.15
β_1	0.125	XF_{it-1}	421.0
β_2	0.075	X_{t-1}	842.0
β_3	0.125		
β_4	0.050	PF_{it-1}	1.0
β_5	0.250	PF_{jt-1}	1.0
β_6	0.5	HP_{t-1}	637.3
β_7	−0.03	$HPUN_{t-1}$	637.3
β_8	−0.30	WF_{it-1}	1.0
β_9	−8.0	WF_{jt-1}	1.0
β_{10}	0.5	XF_{jt-1}	421.0
β_{11}	1.0	V_{jt-1}	52.625
β_{12}	−1.0	DDF_{2i}	2.5
β_{13}	2.0	RF_{it}	0.0750
β_{14}	0.07108	Y_{it-1}	$421.0[=\lambda_1 HPF_{it-1}$
			$=\mu_1 K^a_{1it-1}]$
$\overline{K}$	250.0		
$EMAXHP_i$			
$+ EMAXMH_i$	12.7		

horizon is 30 periods, and the length of life, m, of a machine is 10 periods. The values in Table 3-2 correspond to the firm having profitable investment opportunities in the sense that, ignoring adjustment costs, the present discounted value of the revenue stream generated by an extra unit of investment is greater than the initial cost.

THE RESULTS

The results of solving the control problem of the firm for the parameter values and initial conditions in Table 3-2 are presented in the first row of Table 3-3. Only a small subset of the results are presented in Table 3-3, as it is not feasible to present all 30 values for each variable. Values of the price variable are given for periods t, $t+1$, and $t+2$, and then values for period t are given for the

Table 3-3.   Results of Solving the Control Problem of Firm i

Initial Conditions from Table 3-2 except:	PF_{it}	PF_{it+1}	PF_{it+2}	PF^e_{jt}	XF^e_{it}	Y^p_{it}	INV_{it}	HPF^e_{it} ($HPFMAX_{it}$)	WF_{it}	LF_{it}	Planned excess labor for period t	Planned excess capital for period t
1. No exceptions	1.0000	1.0000	1.0000	1.0000	421.0	421.0	25.0	318.65	1.0000	164.05	0.0	0.0
2. (demand increase, firms i and j)[a]	1.0090	1.0095	1.0080	1.0075	425.4	427.0	28.6	337.78	1.0269	171.46	0.0	0.0
3. (demand decrease, firms i and j)[b]	0.9923	0.9933	0.9938	0.9938	416.3	408.3	24.4	314.08	0.9915	154.36	0.0	7.0
4. (demand increase, firm i only)[c]	1.0020	1.0025	1.0010	1.0000	424.6	424.5	24.4*	338.12	1.0244	165.56	0.0	0.0
5. (demand decrease, firm i only)[d]	0.9985	0.9995	1.0000	1.0000	415.5	409.0	24.4	314.46	0.9944	156.41	0.0	6.5
6. $HPUN_{t-1} = 653.2$ (+2.5%)	1.0000	1.0000	1.0000	1.0000	421.0	421.0	25.0	318.65	0.9902	163.83	0.0	0.0
7. (excess labor)[e]	0.9995	1.0000	1.0000	1.0000	422.7	422.5	25.9	320.35	0.9922	163.94	0.0	0.0
8. (excess capital)[f]	1.0000	0.9995	1.0000	1.0000	421.0	421.1	25.0	319.08	1.0005	163.03	0.0	11.2
9. $PF_{jt-1} = 1.0050$ (+0.5%)	1.0025	1.0025	1.0025	1.0025	421.0	421.0	25.0	318.65	1.0000	164.22	0.0	0.0
10. $PF_{jt-1} = 0.9950$ (-0.5%)	0.9975	0.9975	0.9975	0.9975	421.0	421.0	25.0	318.65	1.0000	163.84	0.0	0.0
11. $WF_{jt-1} = 1.0100$ (+1.0%)	1.0000	1.0005	1.0005	1.0000	421.0	421.0	25.0	318.15	1.0034	162.86	0.0	0.0
12. $WF_{jt-1} = 0.9900$ (-1.0%)	1.0000	1.0000	1.0000	1.0000	421.0	421.0	25.0	318.65	0.9960	163.96	0.0	0.0
13. $RF_{it} = 0.0788$ (+5.0%)	1.0000	1.0005	1.0005	1.0000	421.0	420.2	24.5	318.15	0.9994	162.77	0.0	0.0

Table 3-3. (continued)

Initial Conditions from Table 3-2 except:	PF_{it}	PF_{it+1}	PF_{it+2}	PF_{jt}^e	XF_{it}^e	Y_{it}^P	INV_{it}	HPF_{it}^e $(HPFMAX_{it})$	WF_{it}	LF_{it}	Planned excess labor for period t	Planned excess capital for period t
14. $RF_{it} = 0.0825$ (+10.0%)	1.0000	1.0005	1.0005	1.0000	421.0	419.5	22.1*	318.66	1.0000	161.61	0.0	0.0
15. $RF_{it} = 0.0338$ (−55.0%)	0.9995	0.9995	0.9995	1.0000	422.7	422.9	26.1	320.81	1.0026	165.48	0.0	0.0
16. $LFMAX_{it} = 159.13$ (−3.0%)	1.0005	1.0000	1.0005	1.0000	419.3	418.0	20.9*	318.11	0.9994	159.10	0.0	0.0

[a] $X_{t-1} = 863.0, XF_{it-1} = 431.5, V_{it-1} = 42.1, XF_{jt-1} = 431.5, V_{jt-1} = 42.1$

[b] $X_{t-1} = 821.0, XF_{it-1} = 410.5, V_{it-1} = 63.1, XF_{jt-1} = 410.5, V_{jt-1} = 63.1$

[c] $X_{t-1} = 852.5, XF_{it-1} = 431.5, V_{it-1} = 42.1$

[d] $X_{t-1} = 831.5, XF_{it-1} = 410.5, V_{it-1} = 63.1$

[e] $HPF_{t-1} = 326.62, HPF_{it-2} = 326.62, HPUN_{t-1} = 653.2, HP_{t-1} = 653.2, DDF_{it-1} = 25.71$

[f] $K_{Iit-1}^a = 262.5; I_{Iit-1}, \ldots, I_{Iit-m} = 26.25$

*Firm switched to machines of type 2.

expected price of firm j, the expected level of sales, the planned level of production, the expected supply of labor, the wage rate, the value of loans, planned excess labor $(HPF_{it}^e - MH_{it}^e)$, and planned excess capital in units of machines $(K_{1it}^a - KMIN_{1it} + K_{2it}^a - KMIN_{2it})$. The value in the first row of Table 3-3 for each variable for period t is the same as the corresponding initial value in Table 3-2, which reflects the way the parameter values and initial conditions were chosen.

One of the most important reactions of a firm is how the firm responds to an increase or decrease in sales. For the results in row 2 of Table 3-3, sales in period $t-1$ were increased by 2.5 percent. Production for period $t-1$ was not changed, and so inventories for period $t-1$ were assumed to fall. Both firm i and firm j were assumed to have the same rise in sales and thus the same drop in inventories. The drop in inventories of firm j led firm i to expect firm j's price for period t to rise to 1.0075. Firm i raised its price a little above this level, which caused its market share to decrease somewhat. Firm i ended up with expected sales of 425.4 for period t, compared to the level of 431.5 that it would have expected had it kept its price equal to the expected price of firm j.

Planned production, investment, employment,[h] and loans were all higher as a result of the sales increase. The wage rate was also higher since firm i needed to attract more workers to meet the increased employment requirements. Also, since firm i expected the average price in the economy to be higher in period t, this had a negative effect on firm i's expectation of the aggregate supply of labor, which caused the firm to have to raise its wage rate more than it otherwise would have to attract the same amount of labor. Although not shown in the table, the higher expected average price also had a negative effect on firm i's expectation of the aggregate demand for goods.

For the results in row 3 of Table 3-3, sales in period $t-1$ were decreased by 2.5 percent. The results are essentially the opposite to those in row 2. Firm i lowered its price slightly from what it expected firm j's price to be, which had the effect of increasing expected sales somewhat from what would have been the case had firm i kept its price the same as the expected price of firm j. Planned production, investment, employment, loans, and the wage rate were all lower as a result of the sales decrease. The firm also planned to hold excess capital in period t, which means that the firm did not plan to lower investment as much as it could have and still produce the planned output.

For the results in row 4, only the level of sales of firm i in period $t-1$ was increased. This change had essentially the same effects as did the demand increase in row 2, except that the rise in price of firm i was less. The price rise was less in row 4 because in this case firm i did not expect firm j to increase its price in period t. The firm switched to the cheaper type 2 machines in row 4. Although employment was slightly greater in row 4 than in row 2, the wage rate in row 4 was less. The wage rate was less because the expected average price level was less. For the results in row 5, the level of firm i's sales in period $t-1$ was decreased. The results are essentially the opposite to those in row 4. In this case, as was the case in row 3, the firm planned to hold some excess capital in period *t*.

For the results in row 6, $HPUN_{t-1}$, the aggregate unconstrained supply of labor in period *t-1*, was increased. The only major effect this had on firm *i* was for firm *i* to lower its wage rate. Because of the larger expected aggregate supply, firm *i* needed a lower wage rate to attract the same amount of labor.

For the results in row 7, the employment of firm *i* for period *t-1* was increased, with no corresponding increase in production. This meant that firm *i* held excess labor in period *t-1*. This change caused firm *i* to decrease its employment in period *t* from the level existing in period *t-1*, to lower its price slightly in period *t*, and to increase its expected sales, planned production, and investment. Excess labor in period *t-1* thus caused the firm to lower its price and expand slightly in period *t*. Employment was decreased in period *t*, but not all the way back to the level in row 1. The wage rate was lower in this case, which was caused by the fact that the aggregate supply of labor in period *t-1* was also increased for this run.

For the results in row 8, the number of machines held by firm *i* in period *t-1* was increased, with no corresponding increase in production. This meant that firm *i* held excess capital in period *t-1*. This change caused the firm to lower its price slightly for period *t+1*. Investment dropped by 1.25 machines—from past gross investments of 26.25 to a gross investment of 25.0 in period t. The firm chose to hold excess capital in period *t* of 11.2 machines. Employment rose because of the investment adjustment costs.

For the results in row 9, the price of firm *j* in period *t-1* was increased by 0.5 percent to 1.0050. This caused firm *i* to expect firm *j*'s price to be 1.0025 in period *t*. Firm *i* raised its price to this amount, keeping its expected market share the same. Planned production, investment, and employment were unchanged. For the results in row 10, the price of firm *j* in period *t-1* was decreased by 0.5 percent, which had the opposite effect from the price increase in row 9.

For the results in row 11, the wage rate of firm *j* in period *t-1* was increased by 1.0 percent to 1.0100. This caused firm *i* to expect firm *j*'s wage rate for period *t* to be higher than firm *i* expected it to be in row 1. (Although not shown in the table, firm *i* expected firm *j*'s wage rate in period *t* to be 1.0000 for the results in row 1 and 1.0050 for the results in row 11.) The higher expected wage rate of firm *j* for period *t* caused firm *i* to raise its wage rate for period *t*. Firm *i* also raised its price slightly for periods *t+1* and beyond and cut back its production, investment, and employment slightly. For the results in row 12, the wage rate of firm *j* in period *t-1* was decreased by 1.0 percent, which caused firm *i* to lower its wage rate in period *t*. In this case firm *i* was not led to lower its price as a result of the lower expected wage rate of firm *j*.

For the results in row 13, the loan rate was increased by 5.0 percent. This caused the firm to raise its price for periods $t+1$ and beyond and to produce, invest, and borrow less in period t. For the results in row 14, the loan rate was increased by 10.0 percent, which caused the firm to switch to type 2 machines. Investment in terms of the number of goods purchased was thus lower in row 14 than in row 13 because of the switch to the cheaper machines. Employment was higher in row 14 than in row 13 because of the greater employment requirements on type 2 machines. For the results in row 15, the loan rate was decreased by 55.0 percent. This caused the firm to lower its price for periods t and beyond, which caused expected sales to increase and the firm to produce, invest, and borrow more. In this case it is, of course, not possible for the firm to switch to more expensive machines, since only two types of machines were postulated and the firm was already using the more expensive type. It was necessary to decrease the loan rate by slightly over 50.0 percent to get the firm to react in any significant way to the change.

For the results in row 16, the loan constraint was assumed to be binding on the firm. $LFMAX_{it}$ was set to 159.13 compared with the unconstrained choice of the firm of 164.05. This constraint caused the firm to raise its price and to produce and invest less in period t. The firm switched to type 2 machines, which allowed the firm to spend less for investment than it otherwise would have had to, given the level of production, and thus to lower the amount of money it needed to borrow.

For none of the runs in Table 3-3, given the parameter values used, did the firm plan to hold excess labor in period t. The adjustment-cost parameter for employment, β_4, was too low relative to the other cost parameters for it to be profitable for the firm to hold excess labor. In general, however, one would expect firms to adjust to falling demand situations by holding some excess labor in the current period.

Some of the main properties of the model that can be gleaned from the results in Table 3-3 are the following.

1. When demand increases and inventories decrease, the firm raises its price and increases its production, investment, employment, wage rate, and loans. The firm raises its price for two reasons. One is because it expects other firms to raise their prices, and the other is a desire to lower its market share somewhat to avoid having as large an increase in investment and employment as would be required if it kept its market share the same. If only the demand for firm i's goods increases, then firm i raises its price less than otherwise because it does not expect other firms to raise their prices in the current period.

2. The opposite effects from 1 take place when demand decreases and inventories increase.

3. The existence of excess labor in a period causes the firm to decrease employment in the next period and to lower its price and expand production slightly.
4. The existence of excess capital in a period causes the firm to decrease investment in the next period and perhaps to lower its price path slightly.
5. The main effect of an increase in the aggregate unconstrained supply of labor is for the firm to decrease its wage rate.
6. The main effect of a change in other firms' prices or wage rates is for firm *i* to change its price or wage rate in the same direction.
7. The firm responds to an interest rate increase by raising its price, at least for periods *t+1* and beyond, and by lowering its production, investment, and loans. Employment may respond in either direction depending on whether or not the firm moves into cheaper types of machines with higher employment requirements.
8. Essentially the opposite effects from 5 take place for an interest rate decrease.
9. The firm responds to a constraint on its borrowing behavior in a similar way that it responds to an interest rate increase, by raising its price and lowering its production and investment. Lower investment in this case may also take the form of purchasing cheaper machines.

It is also evident from the results in Table 3-3 that the behavior of the firm is not necessarily symmetrical for increases and decreases in a particular variable. For the results in rows 2 and 3 of Table 3-3, for example, the firm chose to increase production by only 6.0 units corresponding to a 10.5 increase in sales of the previous period, whereas it chose to decrease its production by 12.7 units corresponding to a 10.5 decrease in sales.

A second example of an asymmetrical reaction is reflected in rows 11 and 12. An increase in the wage rate of firm *j* led firm *i* to increase its price for period *t+1* and beyond, whereas a decrease in the wage rate of firm *j* did not induce firm *i* to lower its price. A third example of an asymmetrical reaction is reflected in rows 13 and 15. An interest rate increase of only 5.0 percent led to a price increase in periods *t+1* and beyond, but it took an interest rate decrease of about 55.0 percent to lead to a price decrease. The firm's reaction to the loan constraint is, of course, another asymmetrical reaction in the sense that the firm is forced to respond to the constraint, but is not forced in the opposite direction when there is no constraint.

One important reason for the firm's asymmetrical behavior regarding increases and decreases in demand is the ability of the firm to hold excess labor and capital during contractions, but having no corresponding ability during expansions when already at full capacity. A decrease in demand means that the firm has the opportunity to hold excess labor and capital to help smooth out adjustment costs, whereas an increase in demand from a situation in which no excess labor and capital is being held means that the firm must either increase investment and employment immediately or must decrease its inventories. It was quite evident from examining various runs for the firm, using in many cases different sets of parameter values, that the firm was more inclined to choose to raise its price and lower its expected sales and production paths than to lower its price and raise its expected sales and production paths.

Another important factor influencing the firm's proclivity to raise or lower its price is the size of the parameters β_6 and β_9 in Equations (3.23)-(3.24) and (3.28)-(3.29). The larger is β_6, the more does firm i expect firm j to follow its price setting behavior, and the larger is β_9 in absolute value, the more does firm i expect its market share to change as its price deviates from firm j's price. Large values of β_6, other things being equal, increase the proclivity of firm i to raise its price, because in this case firm j is expected to follow quickly along. If firm j follows quickly along, firm i will not lose much of its market share as a result of its higher price. Large absolute values of β_9, other things being equal, decrease the proclivity of firm i to raise its price, because in this case it expects to lose a lot of its market share as a result of the higher price. For the particular values of β_6 and β_9 tried in this study, the proclivity of firm i was definitely toward raising its price.

Regarding the effect of the loan rate on the behavior of the firm, it should be noted that the loan rate can affect the investment of the firm in ways that have nothing to do with capital-labor substitution in the sense of the firm purchasing different types of machines. In row 13 in Table 3-3, for example, an increase in the loan rate caused the firm to produce and invest less, and yet it was still optimal for the firm to purchase the more expensive type 1 machines. The higher loan rate caused the firm to raise its price for periods $t+1$ and beyond, which caused expected sales to be less for periods $t+1$ and beyond, which in turn caused production to be less for periods t and beyond. Production was less in period t, even though the expected level of sales was not changed for period t, because of production smoothing considerations. Because of adjustment costs, it was optimal for the firm to begin lowering production in period t. Because of the lower level of production in period t, investment was also less in period t. The loan rate has in this case affected the level of investment without causing any capital-labor substitution to take place in the sense of the firm switching to the cheaper type of machines.

3.6 THE CONDENSED MODEL FOR FIRMS

The firm behavioral equations for the condensed model are presented in Table 3-4. The superscripts p and pp refer to planned values, which may get modified during the course of the decision process. As was the case for banks, all i subscripts have been dropped, since for the condensed model there is only a firm

Table 3-4. Firm Equations for the Condensed Model

(1) $P_t^p = 0.661(P_{t-1})^{0.50} \left(\dfrac{V_{t-1}}{\beta_1 X_{t-1}}\right)^{-0.03} (X_{t-1})^{0.10}(RL_t)^{0.10} \left(\dfrac{HPF_{t-1}}{MH_{t-1}}\right)^{-0.02}$

$\left(\dfrac{K_{t-1}^a}{KMIN_{t-1}}\right)^{-0.01}$,

(2) $X_t^{ep} = X_{t-1}\left(\dfrac{P_t^p}{P_{t-1}}\right)^{-0.30}$

The values of P_t, Y_t^p, INV_t, $HPFMAX_t$, W_t, LF_t, $XFMAX_t$, $INVUN_t$, and $LFUN_t$ are determined by the following algorithm:

[1] $Y_t^{pp} = X_t^{ep} + \beta_1 X_t^{ep} - V_{t-1}$,

[2] $K_t^{pp} = \dfrac{Y_t^{pp}}{\mu_1 \bar{\bar{H}}}$,

[3] If $K_t^{pp} \geqslant K_{t-1}^a$, then $K_t^p = K_{t-1}^a + 0.5(K_t^{pp} - K_{t-1}^a)$ and $Y_t^p = \mu_1 K_t^p \bar{\bar{H}}$,

[4] If $K_t^{pp} < K_{t-1}^a$, then $K_t^p = K_{t-1}^a + 0.2(K_t^{pp} - K_{t-1}^a)$ and

$Y_t^p = \mu_1(K_{t-1}^a + 0.5(K_t^{pp} - K_{t-1}^a))\bar{\bar{H}}$,

[5] $V_t^p = V_{t-1} + Y_t^p - X_t^{ep}$,

[6] $MH_{1t}^p = \dfrac{Y_t^p}{\lambda_1}$,

[7] $MH_{3t}^p = \beta_2(V_t^p - \beta_1 X_t^{ep})^2$,

[8] $MH_{4t}^p = \beta_3(X_t^{ep} - X_{t-1})^2$,

[9] $MH_{5t}^p = \beta_4(HPF_{t-1} - HPF_{t-2})^2$,

[10] $MH_{6t}^p = \beta_5(K_t^p - K_{t-1}^a)^2$,

[11] $MH_t^p = MH_{1t}^p + MH_{3t}^p + MH_{4t}^p + MH_{5t}^p + MH_{6t}^p$,

[12] If $MH_t^p = HPF_{t-1}$, then $HPF_t^p = MH_t^p$,

[13] If $MH_t^p < HPF_{t-1}$, then $HPF_t^p = HPF_{t-1} + 0.2(MH_t^p - HPF_{t-1})$,

[14] If $MH_t^p > HPF_{t-1}$, then $HPF_t^p = HPF_{t-1} + 0.5(MH_t^p - HPF_{t-1})$;
Y_t^p = maximum amount that can be produced given K_t^p, X_t^{ep}, and $MH_t^p = HPF_t^p$

$K_t^p = \dfrac{Y_t^p}{\mu_1 \bar{\bar{H}}}$;

$MH_t^p = HPF_t^p + \beta_5(K_t^p - K_{t-1}^a)^2 - MH_{6t}^p$;

Table 3-4.   (continued)

$$HPF_t^p = MH_t^p \, ;$$

$$V_t^p = V_{t-1} + Y_t^p - X_t^{ep} \, ,$$

[15] $W_t^p = (W_{t-1})^{0.50} \, (P_t^p)^{0.40} \left(\dfrac{HPF_t^p}{HPF_{t-1}} \right)^{0.40} \left(\dfrac{HPUN_{t-1}}{HP_{t-1}} \right)^{-0.40} ,$

[16] $INV_t^p = K_t^p - K_{t-1}^a + INV_{t-m} \, ,$

[17] $DDF_{1t}^p = \beta_{14} W_t^p \, HPF_t^p ,$

[18] $DEP_t^p = \dfrac{1}{m} \, [P_t^p INV_t^p + P_{t-1} INV_{t-1} + \ldots + P_{t-m+1} INV_{t-m+1}] \, ,$

[19] $\overline{CF}_t^p = DEP_t^p - P_t^p INV_t^p + P_{t-1} V_{t-1} - P_t^p V_t^p ,$

[20] $LF_t^p = LF_{t-1} + DDF_{1t}^p + DDF_2 - DDF_{t-1} - \overline{CF}_t^p ,$

[21] $INVUN_t = INV_t^p, \; LFUN_t = LF_t^p, \; PUN_t = P_t^p, \; Y^p UN_t = Y_t^p, \; WUN_t = W_t^p,$

$$HPFMAXUN_t = HPF_t^p,$$

[22] If $LF_t^p \leqslant LFMAX_t$, go to statement [42],

[23] $P_t = P_t^p + 0.05 \, P_t^p \left(\dfrac{LFUN_t - LFMAX_t}{LFUN_t} \right) ,$

[24] $X_t^e = X_{t-1} \left(\dfrac{P_t}{P_{t-1}} \right)^{-0.30} ,$

[25] $DEP_t^p = \dfrac{1}{m} \, [P_t INV_t^p + P_{t-1} INV_{t-1} + \ldots + P_{t-m+1} INV_{t-m+1}] \, ,$

[26] $V_t^p = V_{t-1} + Y_t^p - X_t^e ,$

[27] $\overline{CF}_t^p = DEP_t^p - P_t INV_t^p + P_{t-1} V_{t-1} - P_t V_t^p ,$

[28] $LF_t^p = LF_{t-1} + DDF_{1t}^p + DDF_2 - DDF_{t-1} - \overline{CF}_t^p ,$

[29] $Y_t^p = old \; Y_t^p - \dfrac{LF_t^p - LFMAX_t}{(\frac{1}{\mu_1 \overline{H}}) \, (\frac{m-1}{m}) \, P_t + P_t} \, ,$

[30] $INV_t = INV_t^p - \left(\dfrac{old \; Y_t^p - new \; Y_t^p}{\mu_1 \overline{H}} \right) ,$

[31] $K_t^a = K_t^p - (INV_t^p - INV_t),$

[32] $HPF_t^p = old \; HPF_t^p - \left(\dfrac{old \; Y_t^p - new \; Y_t^p}{\lambda_1} \right) ,$

Table 3-4. (continued)

[33] $V_t^p = V_{t-1} + Y_t^p - X_t^e$,

[34] MH_t^p = computed as in statements [6] − [11] with X_t^e replacing X_t^{ep}, K_t^a replacing K_t^p, and new Y_t^p and V_t^p being used,

[35] If $MH_t^p > HPF_t^p$, then $HPF_t^p = MH_t^p$,

[36] $W_t = (W_{t-1})^{0.50} (P_t)^{0.40} \left(\dfrac{HPF_t^p}{HPF_{t-1}} \right)^{0.40} \left(\dfrac{HPUN_{t-1}}{HP_{t-1}} \right)^{-0.40}$,

[37] $DEP_t = \dfrac{1}{m} [P_t INV_t + P_{t-1} INV_{t-1} + \ldots + P_{t-m+1} INV_{t-m+1}]$,

[38] $\overline{CF}_t^p = DEP_t - P_t INV_t + P_{t-1} V_{t-1} - P_t V_t^p$,

[39] $DDF_{1t}^p = \beta_{14} W_t HPF_t^p$,

[40] $LF_t = LF_{t-1} + DDF_{1t}^p + DDF_2 - DDF_{t-1} - \overline{CF}_t^p$,

[41] Go to statement [48] ,

[42] $P_t = P_t^p$,

[43] $X_t^e = X_t^{ep}$,

[44] $INV_t = INV_t^p$,

[45] $W_t = W_t^p$,

[46] $LF_t = LF_t^p$,

[47] $K_t^a = K_t^p$,

[48] $HPFMAX_t = HPF_t^p$,

[49] $XFMAX_t = V_{t-1} + min \left\{ Y_t^p, \ [Y_t^p - \lambda_1 (EMAXHP + EMAXMH) + \lambda_1 (HPF_t^p - MH_t^p)] \right\}$,

[50] $KMIN_t^p = \dfrac{Y_t^p}{\mu_1 \overline{H}}$,

[51] $MH_{4t}^p = \beta_3 (X_t^e - X_{t-1})^2$.

sector rather than individual firms. There is also assumed for the condensed model to be only one type of machine in existence, and so the subscripts referring to the types of machines have been dropped. The existence of only one type of machine rules out the possibility of capital-labor substitution, but, as just discussed, the loan rate can still have an effect on the investment decision of the firm. Because of this, it did not seem necessary in specifying the condensed model to consider more than one type of machine. The price for period t is now denoted P_t rather than PF_{it}, the wage rate is denoted W_t rather than WF_{it}, and the loan rate is denoted RL_t rather than RF_{it}.

Equation (1) in Table 3-4 determines the first planned price of the firm sector. The planned price is a positive function of last period's price, of last period's sales, and of the current loan rate, and is a negative function of last period's ratio of the level of inventories to β_1 times sales, of last period's ratio of worker hours paid for to worker hour requirements (excess labor), and of last period's ratio of the number of machines on hand to the minimum number required (excess capital).

Equation (1) is based on the results in Table 3-3. The size of the various coefficients are for the most part consistent with the size of the responses in Table 3-3, although the coefficient for the loan rate was made somewhat larger than the responses in Table 3-3 would indicate it should be. The equation is, of course, also symmetric and does not capture any of the asymmetries in Table 3-3. The choice of the constant term in Equation (1) is explained in Chapter Six. Equation (2), determining the expected demand for goods, is the same as equation (3.26) for the non-condensed model.

The algorithm described in Table 3-4 determines all the values of the decision variables of the firm. The algorithm is written like a FORTRAN program would be written, and so the logic of the algorithm should be fairly clear to readers with a knowledge of the FORTRAN language. The following is a brief verbal description of the algorithms.

Y_t^{pp} in statement [1] is the output that is necessary for the firm sector to produce in period t, given the expected level of sales for period t, in order for it to end up with the level of inventories at the end of period t being equal to β_1 times sales. K_t^{pp} in statement [2] is the minimum number of machines needed to produce this amount. If the number of machines needed is greater than the actual number on hand in period $t-1$, so that positive net investment is necessary to produce Y_t^{pp}, then, as in statement [3], planned net investment $(K_t^p - K_{t-1}^a)$ is taken to be 50.0 percent of that originally planned $(K_t^{pp} - K_{t-1}^a)$. Planned production is then decreased in statement [3] accordingly. If the originally planned net investment is negative, then, as in statement [4], planned net investment is taken to be 20.0 percent of that originally planned. Planned production is then increased in statement [4]. In statement [3] planned production is decreased by the amount necessary for the firm to be able to produce the output, given the fewer number of machines on hand than originally planned. The firm sector plans to hold no excess capital in this case. In statement [4], however, the firm sector plans to hold some excess capital. Planned production is increased, but not enough to correspond to full utilization of the number of machines on hand. Planned production is rather increased to correspond to what would have been full utilization had the new planned investment been 50.0 percent (rather than 20.0 percent) of that originally planned. Statements [3] and [4] are meant to capture the effects of investment-adjustment costs on the behavior of the firm sector.

Statement [5] defines the planned level of inventories, and statements [6]-[11] determine worker hour requirements. If the computed level of worker hour requirements is equal to last period's level of worker hours paid for, then, as in statement [12], the firm sector plans not to change the number of worker hours paid for in the current period. If the computed level of worker hour requirements is less than last period's level of worker hours paid for, then, as in statement [13], the firm sector plans to decrease the level of worker hours paid for in the current period by 20.0 percent of the difference between the computed level of worker hour requirements and last period's level of worker hours paid for. In this case the firm sector plans to hold excess labor in the current period. If the computed level of worker hour requirements is greater than last period's level of worker hours paid for, then, as in statement [14], the firm sector plans to increase the level of worker hours paid for in the current period by 50.0 percent of the difference between the computed level of worker hour requirements and last period's level of worker hours paid for.

Planned production is then decreased in statement [14] by the amount necessary for the firm sector to be able to produce the output. Planned production must be decreased in this case because the new planned level of worker hours paid for is now less than is necessary for the firm sector to be able to produce the originally planned output. Because worker hour requirements are a function of the current level of inventories (statement [7]), computing the level of production in this case requires solving a quadratic equation in output.i The planned number of machines on hand is then decreased in statement [14] to the number necessary to produce the new planned output. This change has an effect on worker-hour requirements (MH^p_{6t} in statement [10]), and so worker hour requirements are recomputed. The planned level of worker hours paid for is then set equal in statement [14] to this recomputed amount. The planned level of inventories is also recomputed using the new planned output. The effect of the new planned level of inventories on worker hour requirements has already been taken into account in the solving of the quadratic equation to compute the new planned level of output. Statements [13] and [14] are meant to capture the effects of employment adjustment costs on the behavior of the firm sector.

Statement [15] determines the first planned wage rate, which is a positive function of last period's wage rate, of the current period's planned price, and of the ratio of the current period's planned level of worker hours paid for to last period's actual level of worker hours paid for, and a negative function of last period's ratio of the unconstrained to the constrained aggregate supply of labor. This equation is again based on the results in Table 3-3.

Statements [16]-[19] determine the variables necessary to compute the planned level of loans of the firm sector. The planned level of loans is then computed in statement [20]. The equations in these statements are all comparable to the equations for the non-condensed model. In statement [21] various unconstrained quantities are defined. These are the values that the firm sector would choose if it were not subject to a loan constraint. The reason that separate notation is established for the unconstrained quantities in statement [21] is because of the presentation of these values in Table 6-6 in Chapter Six. By comparing the values in statement [21] with the final values chosen by the firm sector, one can see directly how the loan constraint has affected the decisions of the firm sector.

If the planned level of loans in statement [20] is less than the maximum value allowed, then the loan constraint is not binding on the firm sector. In this case the actual values are set equal to the planned values, as in statements [42]-[48]. If the planned level of loans is greater than the maximum value allowed, then the firm must modify its original plans. Statement [23]-[40] describe the modifications. In statement [23] the price level is raised from the originally planned level. The size of the increase is a positive function of the percentage difference between the unconstrained and maximum value of loans. The expected demand for goods is then recomputed in statement [24], being based now on a higher price level. The new planned level of loans, based on the higher price, is determined by statements [25]-[28]. A higher price, with the same level of production and investment, has an overall positive effect on the demand for loans, and so LF_t^p in statement [28] is greater than the originally planned level of loans. The new planned level of loans is, of course, not feasible, and it is recomputed in statements [25]-[28] only so it can be used in statement [29]. In statement [29] planned production is decreased. The size of the decrease is a positive function of the difference between the new planned level of loans and the maximum value. The statement is based on the following analysis. Using statements [25]-[27], statement [28] can be written

$$LF_t^p = LF_{t-1} + DDF_{1t}^p + DDF_2 - DDF_{t-1}$$
$$- \frac{1}{m}[P_{t-1}INV_{t-1} + \ldots + P_{t-m+1}INV_{t-m+1}] + \frac{m-1}{m}P_tINV_t^p - P_{t-1}V_{t-1}$$
$$+ P_tV_{t-1} + P_tY_t^p - P_tX_t^e. \tag{3.47}$$

Now, for each unit decrease in Y_t^p, LF_t^p decreases by P_t units, and for each unit decrease in INV_t^p, LF_t^p decreases by $\frac{m-1}{m} P_t$ units. Also, for each unit decrease in Y_t^p, INV_t^p can decrease by $\frac{1}{\mu_1 \bar{H}}$ units. Therefore, a unit decrease in Y_t^p, with the appropriate decrease in INV_t^p, corresponds to a decrease in LF_t^p of $P_t + \left|\frac{1}{\mu_1 \bar{H}}\right| \left|\frac{m-1}{m}\right| P_t$ units. Since the firm must cut back its loans by $LF_t^p - LFMAX_t$ units, the planned level of output must be cut back by $(LF_t^p - LFMAX_t) / (P_t + \left|\frac{1}{\mu_1 \bar{H}}\right| \left|\frac{m-1}{m}\right| P_t)$ units, which is the expression in statement [29]. In statement [30] investment is cut back by the appropriate amount. Statement [31] then defines the resulting new value for the number of machines on hand.

In statement [32] the planned number of hours paid for per worker is decreased corresponding to the decrease in planned production. The new planned level of inventories is computed in statement [33], and the new level of worker hour requirements is computed as described in statement [34]. If the new level of worker hour requirements is greater than the planned level of worker hours paid for, then, as in statement [35], the latter is set equal to the former. In statement [36] the wage rate is changed as a result of the change in the price level and the planned number of worker hours paid for. Statements [37]–[40] determine the new level of loans corresponding to the various changes.

It should be noted that the new level of loans will not be exactly equal to $LFMAX_t$ because the wage rate and the planned number of worker hours paid for, both of which have an effect on DDF_{ft}^p in statement [39], are decreased from their original values. This decrease was not taken into account when planned production was changed in statement [29], and so LF_t as computed in statement [40] will be slightly less than $LFMAX_t$. This is a very small effect, however, which is the reason it was ignored in computing the change in planned production in statement [29].

Statements [48] and [49], determining the maximum number of worker hours that the firm will pay for and the maximum number of goods that the firm will sell, are the same as in the non-condensed models. Statement [50] defines the minimum number of machines needed to produce the planned output ($KMIN_t^p$), and statement [51] defines the number of worker hours required to meet the expected change in sales (MH_{4t}^p). The value of $KMIN_t^p$ is needed for the results in Table 6-6, where the ratio of K_t^a to $KMIN_t^p$ is presented. The ratio is a measure of the planned excess capital of the firm sector. The value of MH_{4t}^p is also presented in Table 6-6. Since the actual level of sales will generally not be equal to the expected level, MH_{4t}^p will generally not be equal to the number of worker hours required to meet the actual change in sales. The value of MH_{4t}^p is presented in Table 6-6 because it is of some interest to compare this number to the number of worker hours actually required to meet the change in sales.

In summary, while the details of the algorithm in Table 3-4 are somewhat tedious, the overall design is fairly clear. The price level and expected sales are determined first in equations (1) and (2). Statements [1]-[14] are then concerned with computing the levels of production, investment, and employment. The decisions involved in statements [3], [4], [13], and [14] reflect the fact that there are costs involved in changing net investment and employment. These statements are designed to approximate the actual production smoothing decisions of the firms in the non-condensed model. Given the planned level of employment and the price level, the wage rate is computed in statement [15]. Statements [16]-[20] then determine the planned value of loans. If the planned value is less than the maximum value, then the algorithm is essentially finished. Otherwise, the firm sector modifies its decisions in a fairly straightforward way in statements [23]-[40].

The optimal control problem of the firm is clearly the most complicated of the control problems in the model, and the algorithm in Table 3-4 can certainly only be considered to be an approximation to it. One of the main differences between the actual control problem and the approximation in Table 3-4 is that the latter is recursive while the former is not. In the actual control problem the decisions on price, production, investment, employment, the wage rate, and loans are made simultaneously (all coming out of the solution of the maximization problem), whereas in Table 3-4 the decisions are made more or less recursively.

NOTES

[a]It should be obvious in what follows that the number of different types of machines can be generalized to any number.

[b]Since all expectations are made by firm i, no i subscript or superscript has been added to the relevant symbols to denote the fact that it is firm i making the expectation.

[c]In the programming for the non-condensed model, firm i was assumed to estimate the parameter β_8 in Equations (3.26) and (3.27) on the basis of its past observations of the correlation between changes in the aggregate demand for goods and changes in the average price level. Similarly, the parameters β_{11} and β_{12} in Equations (3.33) and (3.34) were assumed to be estimated by firm i. The exact procedure by which these parameters were assumed to be estimated is described in the Appendix.

[d]There is an asymmetry in the specification of Equations (3.26)-(3.27) and (3.33)-(3.34), aside from the fact that the former are in terms of the *constrained* demand for goods and the latter are in terms of the *unconstrained* supply of labor. In (3.26)-(3.27) firm i's expectation of the aggregate demand for goods is only a function of prices and not wages, whereas in (3.33)-(3.34) its expectation of the aggregate supply of labor is a function of both prices and wages. In general, a firm's expectation of the aggregate demand for goods may also be a function of wages, but for reasons of computational convenience this possibility was not allowed for here.

[e]As was the case for banks, although Equations (3.1)-(3.21) are written only for period t, they are also meant to hold for periods $t+1, \ldots, t+T$ as well. In addition, an e or a p superscript should be added to a variable when firm i only has an expectation or a planned value of that variable. For example, Equation (3.7) should be written

$$V_{it}^e = V_{it-1} + Y_{it}^p - XF_{it}^e ,$$
 (3.7)'

$$V_{it+k}^e = V_{it+k-1}^e + Y_{it+k}^p - XF_{it+k}^e , \quad k=1,2,\ldots,T.$$
 (3.7)''

To conserve space, Equations (3.1)–(3.21) will not be written out in this expanded way, but the expansion in each case is straightforward.

[f]A firm's expectation of the aggregate (constrained) supply of labor depends, of course, on its expectation of the aggregate unconstrained supply of labor from Equation (3.33), which in turn depends on its price and wage expectations from Equations (3.23), (3.25), and (3.32).

[g]Since actual worker hour requirements for period t are dependent on the actual level of sales in period t and since a firm only has at the beginning of period t an expectation of sales for the period, it likewise only has at the beginning of period t an expectation of worker hour requirements for the period.

[h]By employment in this case and in what follows is meant the expected supply of labor, HPF_{it}^e.

[i]The quadratic equation is $Y_t^p/\lambda_1 + \beta_2(V_{t-1} + Y_t^p - X_t^{ep} - \beta_1 X_t^{ep})^2 + MHP_{4t}^p + MHP_{5t}^p + MHP_{6t}^p = HPF_t^p$. This equation is obtained by substituting [5] in [7], adding [6] through [10], and setting this sum equal to HPF_t^p, the planned number of worker hours.

Chapter Four

Households

4.1 THE BASIC EQUATIONS

In Table 4-1 the important symbols used in this chapter are listed in alphabetic order. Each household receives wage income from firms and the government $(WH_{it}HPH_{it})$, purchases goods from firms (XH_{it}), and pays taxes to the government $(TAXH_{it})$. All goods that are purchased in a period are consumed in that period. A household either has a positive amount of savings or is in debt. If it has savings, the savings can take the form of demand deposits (DDH_{it}), savings deposits (SDH_{it}), or stocks (S_{it}). If it is in debt, the debt takes the form of loans from banks (LH_{it}). It is assumed that a household does not both borrow from banks and have savings deposits or stocks at the same time.

At the beginning of period t, each household receives information on the rate that it will be paid on its savings deposits in the period (the bill rate, r_t), on the aggregate stock price for the period (PS_t), on the loan rate that it will be charged (RH_{it}), on the maximum amount of money that it will be able to borrow $(LHMAX_{it})$, on the price that it will be charged for goods (PH_{it}), on the wage rate that it will be paid (WH_{it}), on the maximum number of goods that it will be able to purchase $(XHMAX_{it})$, and on the maximum number of hours that it will be able to be paid for $(HPHMAX_{it})$. The two main decision variables of a household are the number of hours to work (HPH_{it}), and the number of goods to purchase (XH_{it}).

Table 4-1.   Notation for Households in Alphabetic Order

Non-Condensed Model

Subscript i denotes variable for household i. Subscript t denotes variable for period t. An e superscript in the text denotes an expected value of the variable.

A_{it}	= value of non-demand-deposit assets or liabilities
CG_{it}	= capital gains or losses on stocks
d_3	= personal tax rate
DDH_{it}	= demand deposits
DIV_t	= total dividends paid and received in the economy
$DIVH_{it}$	= dividends received by the household
HPH_{it}	= number of hours that the household is paid for
$HPHMAX_{it}$	= maximum number of hours that the household can be paid for
$HPHUN_{it}$	= unconstrained supply of hours of the household
LH_{it}	= value of loans taken out
$LHMAX_{it}$	= maximum value of loans that the household can take out
$LHUN_{it}$	= unconstrained demand for loans of the household
PH_{it}	= price paid for goods
PS_t	= price of the aggregate share of stock
r_t	= bill rate
RH_{it}	= loan rate paid
S_{it}	= fraction of the aggregate share of stock held
SAV_{it}	= savings net of capital gains or losses
SDH_{it}	= savings deposits
$TAXH_{it}$	= taxes paid
WH_{it}	= wage rate received
XH_{it}	= number of goods purchased
$XHMAX_{it}$	= maximum number of goods that the household can purchase
$XHUN_{it}$	= unconstrained demand for goods of the household
YG	= minimum guaranteed level of income (also can be thought of as the level of transfer payments to each household)
YH_{it}	= before-tax income excluding capital gains or losses

Condensed Model (For equations in Table 4–6 only.)

Subscript t denotes variable for period t. Superscript p in Table 4–6 denotes a planned value of the variable, and superscript e denotes an expected value of the variable. Asset variables pertain to household 1; liability variables pertain to household 2. Only the notation that differs from the notation for the non-condensed model is presented here.

CG_t	= capital gains or losses on stocks (household 1)
LH_t	= value of loans taken out (household 2)
$LHMAX_t$	= maximum value of loans that the household can take out (household 2)
$LHUN_t$	= unconstrained demand for loans of the household (household 2)
P_t	= price paid for goods.
RL_t	= loan rate paid
SD_t	= savings deposits (household 1)

$SDUN_t$ = unconstrained savings deposits of household 1 (corresponding to $HPHUN_{1t}$ and $XHUN_{1t}$)

W_t = wage rate received

The basic equations for household i for period t are the following:

$$CG_{it} = (PS_{t+1} - PS_t)S_{it}, \quad \text{[capital gains or losses on stocks]} \tag{4.1}$$

$$YH_{it} = WH_{it}HPH_{it} + r_t SDH_{it} + DIVH_{it}, \quad \text{[before-tax income net of capital gains or losses]} \tag{4.2}$$

$$TAXH_{it} = d_3(YH_{it} + CG_{it} - RH_{it}LH_{it}) - YG, \quad \text{[taxes paid]} \tag{4.3}$$

$$DDH_{it} = \gamma_1 PH_{it}XH_{it}, \quad \text{[demand deposits]} \tag{4.4}$$

$$SAV_{it} = YH_{it} - TAXH_{it} - RH_{it}LH_{it} - PH_{it}XH_{it}, \quad \text{[savings net of capital gains or losses]} \tag{4.5}$$

$$SDH_{it} - LH_{it} = SDH_{it-1} - LH_{it-1} - (DDH_{it} - DDH_{it-1})$$
$$+ SAV_{it} - PS_t(S_{it} - S_{it-1}), \quad \text{[equation determining savings deposits or loans]} \tag{4.6}$$

$$A_{it} = SDH_{it} + PS_{t+1}S_{it} - LH_{it}, \quad \text{[total value of non-demand-deposit assets or liabilities at the end of period } t\text{]} \tag{4.7}$$

$$LH_{it} \leqslant LHMAX_{it}, \quad \text{[loan constraint]} \tag{4.8}$$

$$XH_{it} \leqslant XHMAX_{it}, \quad \text{[goods constraint]} \tag{4.9}$$

$$HPH_{it} \leqslant HPHMAX_{it}. \quad \text{[hours constraint]} \tag{4.10}$$

Equation (4.1) defines the capital gains or losses that are recorded for period t on the fraction of the aggregate share of stock held by household i in period t. PS_{t+1} is the value of the aggregate share of stock at the end of period t or the beginning of period $t+1$. S_{it} is the fraction of the aggregate share of stock held by household i in period t. Equation (4.2) defines before-tax income net of capital gains or losses. If the household is a debtor, then the last two terms are zero. Equation (4.3) defines taxes paid. d_3 is the (proportional) personal income tax rate, and YG is the minimum guaranteed level of income. Capital gains or losses are assumed to be taxed as regular income, and interest payments are assumed to be tax deductible. The tax parameter YG, which will be called the "minimum guaranteed level of income" in this study, can also be thought of as the level of transfer payments from the government to each household.

Equation (4.4) defines demand deposits. The demand deposit need of a household is assumed to be proportional to the value of goods purchased. Households are assumed to hold no demand deposits except those necessary for transactions purposes. Equation (4.5) defines savings net of capital gains or losses, and Equation (4.6) determines savings deposits or loans. The last term in Equation (4.6) is the amount of money that household i spends (receives) on stock purchases (sales) in period t. Equation (4.7) defines total non-demand-deposit assets or liabilities as of the end of period t or the beginning of period $t+1$. Household i is subject to the three constraints (4.8)–(4.10).

4.2   THE FORMATION OF EXPECTATIONS

Let $N+1$ denote the expected remaining length of household i's life. Household i is assumed to form the following expectations.

$$r^e_{t+k} = r_t, \quad \text{[expected bill rate for period } t+k \ (k=1,2,\ldots)] \tag{4.11}$$

$$RH^e_{it+k} = RH_{it}, \quad \text{[expected loan-rate for period } t+k \ (k=1,2,\ldots,N)] \tag{4.12}$$

$$PH^e_{it+k} = PH_{it}, \quad \text{[expected price for period } t+k \ (k=1,2,\ldots,N)] \tag{4.13}$$

$$WH^e_{it+k} = WH_{it}, \text{[expected wage rate for period } t+k \ (k=1,2,\ldots,N)] \tag{4.14}$$

$$DIV^e_{t+k} = \tfrac{1}{5}(DIV_{t-1} + DIV_{t-2} + DIV_{t-3} + DIV_{t-4} + DIV_{t-5}),$$
$$\text{[expected aggregate level of dividends for period } t+k$$
$$(k=0,1,\ldots)] \tag{4.15}$$

$$PS^e_{t+k} = \frac{DIV^e_{t+k}}{(1+r^e_{t+k})} + \frac{DIV^e_{t+k+1}}{(1+r^e_{t+k})\,(1+r^e_{t+k+1})}$$

$$+ \frac{DIV^e_{t+k+2}}{(1+r^e_{t+k})\,(1+r^e_{t+k+1})\,(1+r^e_{t+k+2})} + \ldots \text{ [expected stock price for}$$
$$\text{period } t+k \ (k=1,2,\ldots,N)]$$

$$= \frac{DIV^e_t}{r_t}. \qquad \text{[from (4.11) and (4.15)]} \tag{4.16}$$

Equations (4.11)–(4.14) state that household i expects that the future values of the bill rate, the loan rate that it will be charged, the price that it will be charged, and the wage rate that it will be paid will be equal to the last observed values of the variables. These assumptions of no change expected from the last observed value are consistent with the aim of keeping the expectational assumptions as simple as possible in the model. Since banks determine optimal loan rate paths and since firms determine optimal price and wage paths, it would have been possible to assume that banks and firms inform households of the planned future values in addition to the current values. As was the case for firms and the loan rates, it seemed more straightforward in this case just to assume that the households make the expectations themselves.

In Equation (4.15), household i is assumed to average the past five dividend levels and to expect that the future dividend levels will be equal to this average. The level of dividends is a fairly erratic variable (being a residual of sorts), and this is the reason for the averaging. In Equation (4.16) the expected stock price is assumed to be equal to the present discounted value of the expected future dividend levels, the discount rates being the expected future bill rates. As will be seen in the next chapter, this is the same formula that is used by the bond dealer to set the actual stock price. Because of (4.11) and (4.15), Equation (4.16) means that household i expects that all the future values of the stock price will be the same and will be equal to the expected dividend level for period t divided by the bill rate for period t.

One minor point regarding the expectations of future stock prices in (4.16) should be noted. Since firms are assumed in Chapter Three to maximize the present discounted value of expected future after-tax *cash flow* and since households are assumed in (4.16) to base their expectations of stock prices on expected future *dividends,* firms do not behave so as to maximize the value of their stocks outstanding. This is also true because firms are assumed to use the loan rate as their discount rate, whereas households are assumed in (4.16) to use the bill rate. These differences are, however, fairly minor, and it is easier to specify the model in this way than it is to have the objective function of firms be the value of their stocks outstanding.

4.3 BEHAVIORAL ASSUMPTIONS

The objective of a household is to maximize the present discounted value of its expected remaining lifetime utility. Utility in any period is assumed to be a negative function of hours worked in the period and a positive function of consumption. The form of the utility function is taken to be the log of the CES function:

$$U_{it+k} = \log \left[\eta_i \, (\overline{HPH} - HPH_{it+k})^{-\rho_i} + (1-\eta_i) \, XH_{it+k}^{-\rho_i} \right]^{-\frac{1}{\rho_i}}, \qquad (4.17)$$

where U_{it+k} denotes the utility of household i for period $t+k$ and $\overline{HPH}$ is the total number of hours in a period. $\overline{HPH} - HPH_{it+k}$ is the amount of leisure time that household i has in period $t+k$. The objective function of household i at the beginning of period t is assumed to be

$$OBJH_{it} = \frac{U_{it}}{1+RDH_i} + \frac{U_{it+1}}{(1+RDH_i)^2} + \ldots + \frac{U_{it+N}}{(1+RDH_i)^{N+1}}, \qquad (4.18)$$

where RDH_i is the discount rate of household i. All problems associated with the fact that the lengths of the remaining lives of households are uncertain have been ignored here. Each household is assumed to expect that the length is $N+1$ and to behave as if the actual length were exactly this.

The household chooses HPH_{it+k} and XH_{it+k} ($k=0,1,\ldots,N$) so as to maximize $OBJH_{it}$. One of the constraints facing a household is a lifetime budget constraint. This constraint is handled by assuming that household i plans to end its life with a particular level of non-demand-deposit assets or liabilities:

$$A^e_{it+N} = \overline{A}_i , \tag{4.19}$$

where A^e_{it+N} is the expected level of non-demand-deposit assets or liabilities for the end of period $t+N$ and $\overline{A}_i$ is the target level.

A household with positive non-demand-deposit assets can either hold its assets in the form of stocks or savings deposits. Because of Equation (4.16), a household expects the before-tax, one-period rate of return on stocks (including capital gains and losses) for a given period to be the same as the expected bill rate for that period. Since the bill rate is the rate paid on savings deposits and since capital gains and losses are taxed at the same rate as other income, a household then expects that the after-tax rates of return on stocks and savings deposits are the same. A household can therefore be assumed to be indifferent between holding its assets in the form of stocks or savings deposits, and one need not distinguish between stocks and savings deposits for purposes of analyzing a household's decision. The expected one-period rate of return on the non-demand-deposit assets held during period $t+k$, A_{it+k}, is r^e_{t+k} for a creditor household. Using this fact, Equations (4.1)–(4.7) can be rewritten for purposes of analyzing a creditor household's decision as follows:

$$YYH^e_{it+k} = WH^e_{it+k} \, HPH_{it+k} + r^e_{t+k} \, A^e_{it+k} ,$$
[expected before-tax income including capital gains or losses for period $t+k$ ($k=0,1,\ldots,N$)]   (4.20)

$$DDH^e_{it+k} = \gamma_1 PH^e_{it+k} \, XH_{it+k} ,$$
[expected level of demand deposits for period $t+k$ ($k=0,1,\ldots,N$)]   (4.21)

$$A^e_{it+k} = A^e_{it+k-1} - (DDH^e_{it+k} - DDH^e_{it+k-1})$$
$$+ (1-d_3) \, YYH^e_{it+k} + YG - PH^e_{it+k} \, XH_{it+k}$$
[expected value of non-demand-deposit assets for the end of period $t+k$ ($k=0,1,\ldots,N$)]   (4.22)

Equations (4.20)–(4.22) have been written to hold for all periods of the decision horizon, and e superscripts have been added to the relevant variables to denote the fact that household i only has expectations of the variables for periods beyond $t-1$ or t. For purposes of analyzing a debtor household's decision, equations (4.2)–(4.7) can likewise be rewritten

$$YH^e_{it+k} = WH^e_{it+k} HPH_{it+k}, \quad \text{[expected before-tax income for period}$$
$$t+k \ (k=0,1,\ldots,N)] \quad (4.23)$$

$$DDH^e_{it+k} = \gamma_1 PH^e_{it+k} XH_{it+k}, \text{ [expected level of demand deposits}$$
$$\text{for period } t+k \ (k=0,1,\ldots,N)] \quad (4.24)$$

$$LH^e_{it+k} = LH^e_{it+k-1} + (DDH^e_{it+k} - DDH^e_{it+k-1})$$

$$- (1-d_3)(YH^e_{it+k} - RH^e_{it+k} LH^e_{it+k}) \quad \text{[expected value of loans}$$
$$\text{for the end of period}$$
$$- YG + PH^e_{it+k} XH_{it+k}. \qquad\qquad t+k \ (k=0,1,\ldots,N)] \quad (4.25)$$

The terminal condition (4.19) for debtor households is merely $LH^e_{it+N} = -\overline{A}_i$.

The maximization problem of a household is easy to describe. Given a path of hours worked, HPH_{it+k}, and a path of consumption, XH_{it+k}, $(k=0,1,\ldots,N)$, the objective function can be computed directly. The two paths must satisfy the terminal condition (4.19). Given the two paths and given the expectations from (4.11)–(4.14), Equations (4.20)–(4.22) and (4.23)–(4.25) each form a set of three linear equations in three unknowns for each period, which can be solved through time to obtain a terminal value of non-demand-deposit assets or liabilities. The hours and consumption paths must be chosen so that the resulting terminal value of non-demand-deposit assets or liabilities is equal to $\overline{A}_i$. The hours and consumption paths must also, of course, be chosen to satisfy the inequality constraints (4.8)–(4.10). Regarding the possibility of the loan, goods, and hours constraints existing for periods beyond t, households were assumed to expect that the constraints would *not* be binding for periods beyond t. As was the case for firms, having the constraints hold only for period t appeared to have an important enough influence on the households' decision values for period t so as to make further restrictions unnecessary.

4.4 THE SOLUTION OF THE CONTROL PROBLEM

Two algorithms were written to solve the control problem of a household; one to search over different hours paths and one to search over different consumption paths, given an hours path. For each hours path chosen by the first algorithm, a submaximization problem was solved using the second algorithm. Particular importance was attached to searching over values for the first two periods. The three constraints were handled by throwing out as infeasible those paths that failed to meet one or more of the constraints. Whenever a particular constraint was not met, an alternative path was always tried in which the value of the variable in question was set equal to the constraint. Given an hours path, the consumption paths tried by the second algorithm were always chosen so as to satisfy the terminal condition.

4.5   SOME EXAMPLES OF SOLVING THE CONTROL PROBLEMS OF THE HOUSEHOLDS

PARAMETER VALUES AND INITIAL CONDITIONS

For purposes of the simulation work, two different households were considered; a creditor household (household 1) and a debtor household (household 2). The parameter values and initial conditions used for the first example for each household are presented in Table 4-2. The values of prices and wages were set equal to 1.0, the bill rate was set equal to 0.0650, and the loan rate was set equal to 0.0750. The only values for period $t-1$ needed for household 1 were A_{1t-1} and DDH_{1t-1}, and the only values for period $t-1$ needed for household 2 were LH_{2t-1} and DDH_{2t-1}. The discount rates for the two households were chosen, after some experimentation, to yield fairly constant paths of hours and consumption over the life of the households. The terminal condition for household 1 was taken to be the level of wealth in period $t-1$, and the terminal condition for household 2 was taken to be the negative of the value of loans held in period $t-1$. Neither household, in other words, was taken to be a net saver or dissaver over its remaining life. Household 2, for example, was assumed to plan to end its life in debt to the same extent that it was in period $t-1$. As with banks and firms, this was done to make it easier to analyze the effects on the behavior of the households of changing various initial conditions. The values of ρ_1 and ρ_2 were chosen to make the supply of labor on the part of the two households a positive function of the wage rate.

THE RESULTS

The results of solving the control problems of households 1 and 2 are presented in Tables 4-3 and 4-4, respectively. Values of hours, consumption, and expected assets or liabilities are presented for the first two periods of the 30-period decision horizon.

Consider the behavior of household 1 in Table 4-3 first. The first set of results in the table is based on the assumption that no constraints were binding on the household. The results in the first row are based on the parameter values and initial conditions in Table 4-2. For this run the household essentially

Table 4-2. Parameter Values and Initial Conditions for the Control Problems of Households 1 and 2

Parameter	Value
$N+1$	30
$\overline{HPH}$	1143.45
η_1	0.5808
η_2	0.5811
ρ_1	−0.3
ρ_2	−0.3
γ_1	0.1609
d_3	0.1934
YG	0.0
RDH_1	0.0603
RDH_2	0.0695

Variable	Value
Household 1	
A_{1t-1}	2159.8
DDH_{1t-1}	60.1
r_t	0.0650
PH_{1t}	1.0
WH_{1t}	1.0
$\overline{A}_1$	2159.8
Household 2	
LH_{2t-1}	482.1
DDH_{2t-1}	51.8
RH_{2t}	0.0750
PH_{2t}	1.0
WH_{2t}	1.0
$\overline{A}_2$	−482.1

chose a flat path of the variables throughout its remaining life, a result that reflects the way the parameter values and initial conditions were chosen in the first place.

An important set of reactions of a household is how it responds to changes in wages and prices. For the results in row 2 in Table 4-3, the wage rate of household 1 for period t was increased by 5.0 percent. This meant that the household expected its wage rates for periods $t+1$ and beyond to be higher by 5.0 percent as well. This change caused the household to work more (+3.4 percent) and consume more (+5.7 percent) in period t and likewise in future periods as well. The planned or expected level of wealth for period t decreased slightly.

The rest of the results in Table 4-3 are fairly self-explanatory. Decreasing the wage rate (row 3) caused the household to work less and consume less, as did increasing the price level (row 4). Decreasing the price level (row 5) caused the household to work more and consume more. It is interesting to note that with respect to its hours worked the household responded slightly more to changes in the wage rate than to changes in the price level, and with respect to its consumption slightly more to changes in the price level than to

Table 4-3.   Results of Solving the Control Problem of Household 1

A. No Constraints Binding

Initial Conditions from Table 4-2 except:	HPH_{1t}	HPH_{1t+1}	XH_{1t}	XH_{1t+1}	A^e_{1t}	A^e_{1t+1}
1. No exceptions	323.0	323.8	373.8	374.3	2160	2160
2. $WH_{1t} = 1.05$ (+5.0%)	334.0 (+3.4%)	333.8	395.0 (+5.7%)	395.5	2157	2158
3. $WH_{1t} = 0.95$ (−5.0%)	311.0 (−3.7%)	311.8	352.6 (−5.7%)	352.5	2162	2162
4. $PH_{1t} = 1.05$ (+5.0%)	317.0 (−1.9%)	316.8	352.0 (−5.8%)	351.3	2160	2160
5. $PH_{1t} = 0.95$ (−5.0%)	330.0 (+2.2%)	329.8	399.6 (+6.9%)	399.1	2159	2159
6. $r_t = 0.0683$ (+5.0%)	334.8 (+3.7%)	333.3	365.8 (−2.1%)	365.6	2186	2211
7. $r_t = 0.0618$ (−5.0%)	310.0 (−4.0%)	311.8	380.9 (+1.9%)	381.1	2134	2110
8. $d_3 = 0.2031$ (+5.0%)	317.0 (−1.9%)	317.8	370.8 (−0.8%)	370.2	2154	2148
9. $d_3 = 0.1837$ (−5.0%)	329.0 (+1.9%)	327.8	377.9 (+1.1%)	377.1	2165	2170
10. $YG = 10.0$ (+10.0)	316.0 (−2.2%)	315.8	377.5 (+1.0%)	377.9	2160	2160
11. $YG = -10.0$ (−10.0)	332.0 (+2.8%)	330.8	370.4 (−0.9%)	370.2	2161	2161
12. $A_{1t-1} = 2268$ (+5.0%)	317.0 (−1.9%)	316.8	376.4 (+0.7%)	376.6	2265	2263
13. $A_{1t-1} = 2052$ (−5.0%)	329.0 (+1.9%)	328.8	371.1 (−0.7%)	371.6	2054	2055

B. $HPHMAX_{1t} = 306.8$

	HPH_{1t}	HPH_{1t+1}	XH_{1t}	XH_{1t+1}	A^e_{1t}	A^e_{1t+1}
1. No exceptions	306.8	322.8	368.6	374.0	2152	2151
2. $WH_{1t} = 1.05$ (+5.0%)	306.8 (+0.0%)	333.8	384.2 (+4.2%)	395.8	2146	2144
3. $WH_{1t} = 0.95$ (−5.0%)	306.8 (+0.0%)	311.8	351.9 (−4.5%)	352.9	2160	2160
4. $PH_{1t} = 1.05$ (+5.0%)	306.8 (+0.0%)	315.8	349.3 (−5.2%)	351.7	2155	2153
5. $PH_{1t} = 0.95$ (−5.0%)	306.8 (+0.0%)	329.8	390.6 (+6.0%)	399.7	2149	2147

C. $XHMAX_{1t} = 350.0$

	HPH_{1t}	HPH_{1t+1}	XH_{1t}	XH_{1t+1}	A^e_{1t}	A^e_{1t+1}
1. No exceptions	319.0	321.8	350.0	374.5	2186	2181
2. $WH_{1t} = 1.05$ (+5.0%)	327.0 (+2.5%)	332.8	350.0 (+0.0%)	396.1	2206	2200
3. WH_{1t} 0.95 (−5.0%)	311.0 (−2.5%)	311.8	350.0 (+0.0%)	352.5	2166	2165
4. $PH_{1t} = 1.05$ (+5.0%)	317.0 (−0.6%)	316.8	350.0 (+0.0%)	351.3	2162	2162
5. $PH_{1t} = 0.95$ (−5.0%)	322.0 (+0.9%)	327.8	350.0 (+0.0%)	399.8	2210	2202

D. $HPHMAX_{1t} = 306.8$, $XHMAX_{1t} = 350.0$

	HPH_{1t}	HPH_{1t+1}	XH_{1t}	XH_{1t+1}	A^e_{1t}	A^e_{1t+1}
1. No exceptions	306.8	321.8	350.0	374.3	2175	2170
2. $WH_{1t} = 1.05$ (+5.0%)	306.8 (+0.0%)	332.8	350.0 (+0.0%)	397.0	2188	2180
3. $WH_{1t} = 0.95$ (−5.0%)	306.8 (+0.0%)	311.8	350.0 (+0.0%)	352.1	2162	2162
4. $PH_{1t} = 1.05$ (+5.0%)	306.8 (+0.0%)	315.8	349.3 (−0.2%)	351.7	2155	2153
5. $PH_{1t} = 0.95$ (−5.0%)	306.8 (+0.0%)	328.8	350.0 (+0.0%)	400.0	2197	2189

changes in the wage rate. Because of wealth holdings and income taxes, one would not necessarily expect the response of a household to be symmetric with respect to wage and price changes. It is also important to note that the value of ρ_1 was chosen to make the supply of labor a positive function of the wage rate. Different results would be obtained for different values of ρ_1, as will be seen in the Cobb-Douglas case of ρ_1 equal to zero below.

Two other important sets of reactions of a household are how the household responds to changes in interest rates and tax rates. Increasing the bill rate for household 1 (row 6) had a positive effect on hours worked and caused the household to save more and consume less. Decreasing the bill rate (row 7) caused the household to work less, save less, and consume more. Because the

Table 4-4. Results of Solving the Control Problem of Household 2

A. No Constraints Binding
Initial Conditions from Table 4-2 except:

	HPH_{2t}	HPH_{2t+1}	XH_{2t}	XH_{2t+1}	LH_{2t}	LH^e_{2t+1}
1. No exceptions	435.0	434.8	321.7	321.5	482.1	482.1
2. $WH_{2t} = 1.05\ (+5.0\%)$	440.0 (+1.1%)	438.8	342.5 (+6.5%)	343.2	484.6	485.6
3. $WH_{2t} = 0.95\ (-5.0\%)$	430.0 (−1.1%)	430.8	301.3 (−6.3%)	301.2	479.6	479.8
4. $PH_{2t} = 1.05\ (+5.0\%)$	429.0 (−1.4%)	429.8	302.4 (−6.0%)	302.4	482.1	482.1
5. $PH_{2t} = 0.95\ (-5.0\%)$	440.0 (+1.1%)	440.8	343.3 (+6.7%)	343.4	483.3	483.2
6. $RH_{2t} = 0.0788$ (+5.0%)	452.0 (+3.9%)	449.8	313.3 (−2.6%)	313.2	458.5	436.7
7. $RH_{2t} = 0.0713$ (−5.0%)	418.3 (−3.8%)	420.3	332.3 (+3.3%)	333.3	508.0	533.1
8. $d_3 = 0.2031\ (+5.0\%)$	430.0 (−1.1%)	429.8	319.0 (−0.8%)	318.8	487.0	492.8
9. $d_3 = 0.1837\ (-5.0\%)$	440.0 (+1.1%)	439.8	324.5 (+0.9%)	324.3	477.2	471.3
10. $YG = 10.0\ (+10.0)$	428.0 (−1.6%)	426.8	325.5 (+1.2%)	325.1	482.1	482.1
11. $YG = -10.0\ (-10.0)$	443.0 (+1.8%)	442.8	318.6 (−1.0%)	318.1	482.1	482.1
12. $LH_{2t-1} = 506.2$ (+5.0%)	437.0 (+0.5%)	436.8	321.2 (−0.2%)	321.0	505.4	504.6
13. $LH_{2t-1} = 458.0$ (−5.0%)	434.0 (−0.2%)	433.8	322.9 (+0.4%)	322.9	458.8	459.6

B. $HPHMAX_{2t} = 413.2$

1. No exceptions	413.2	434.8	313.6	321.4	490.7	492.6
2. $WH_{2t} = 1.05\ (+5.0\%)$	413.2 (+0.0%)	440.8	330.9 (+5.5%)	342.9	494.5	496.0
3. $WH_{2t} = 0.95\ (-5.0\%)$	413.2 (+0.0%)	428.8	297.2 (−5.2%)	300.4	488.3	490.3
4. $PH_{2t} = 1.05\ (+5.0\%)$	413.2 (+0.0%)	429.8	297.0 (−5.3%)	301.9	488.6	489.4
5. $PH_{2t} = 0.95\ (-5.0\%)$	413.2 (+0.0%)	441.8	332.7 (+6.1%)	343.4	493.8	495.3

C. $XHMAX_{2t} = 300.0$

1. No exceptions	431.0	433.8	300.0	322.5	458.7	462.9
2. $WH_{2t} = 1.05\ (+5.0\%)$	432.0 (+0.2%)	437.8	300.0 (+0.0%)	343.6	439.3	446.2
3. $WH_{2t} = 0.95\ (-5.0\%)$	431.0 (+0.0%)	430.8	300.0 (+0.0%)	300.3	477.2	476.3
4. $PH_{2t} = 1.05\ (+5.0\%)$	429.0 (−0.5%)	429.8	300.0 (+0.0%)	302.4	479.0	479.2
5. $PH_{2t} = 0.95\ (-5.0\%)$	434.0 (+0.7%)	438.8	300.0 (+0.0%)	344.3	437.6	444.4

D. $LHMAX_{2t} = 458.0$

1. No exceptions	445.0	432.8	309.1	323.1	458.0	462.3
2. $WH_{2t} = 1.05\ (+5.0\%)$	450.0 (+1.1%)	436.8	328.3 (+6.2%)	343.7	458.0	462.3
3. $WH_{2t} = 0.95\ (-5.0\%)$	439.0 (−1.3%)	428.8	289.7 (−6.3%)	301.7	458.0	461.0
4. $PH_{2t} = 1.05\ (+5.0\%)$	439.0 (−1.3%)	426.8	290.5 (−6.0%)	303.3	458.0	462.4
5. $PH_{2t} = 0.95\ (-5.0\%)$	450.0 (+1.1%)	437.8	329.1 (+6.5%)	345.2	458.0	463.3

E. $HPHMAX_{2t} = 413.2$, $XHMAX_{2t} = 300.0$, $LHMAX_{2t} = 458.0$

1. No exceptions	413.2	434.8	287.1	322.4	458.0	463.5
2. $WH_{2t} = 1.05\ (+5.0\%)$	413.2 (+0.0%)	438.8	300.0 (+4.5%)	343.4	456.2	463.1
3. $WH_{2t} = 0.95\ (-5.0\%)$	413.2 (+0.0%)	428.8	272.7 (−5.0%)	301.4	458.0	463.5
4. $PH_{2t} = 1.05\ (+5.0\%)$	413.2 (+0.0%)	438.8	273.4 (−4.8%)	303.3	458.0	463.7
5. $PH_{2t} = 0.95\ (-5.0\%)$	413.2 (+0.0%)	438.8	300.0 (+4.5%)	344.2	455.4	463.3

terminal condition states that household 1 must end its life with the same level of assets that it started with, changes in savings in the current period corresponding to changes in the bill rate eventually reversed themselves during the expected life of the household. Increasing the proportional tax rate (row 8) caused the household to work less and consume less, and decreasing the tax rate (row 9) had the opposite effect. Increasing the minimum guaranteed level of income (row 10) caused the household to work less and consume more, and decreasing the level (row 11) had the opposite effect. (When the tax parameters d_3 and YG were changed for these experiments, the changes were assumed to be permanent. In other words, the household was assumed to expect that the new value of the tax parameter would persist throughout its remaining lifetime.)

Tax decreases in the form of a decrease in the tax rate thus have a positive effect on work effort, while tax decreases in the form of an increase in the minimum guaranteed level of income have a negative effect. This is, of course, as expected because the parameter ρ_1 was chosen so that the (negative) income effect of a change in the wage rate on work effort was smaller in absolute value than the (positive) substitution effect. Capital gains and losses affect the wealth of creditor households, and so it is of interest to examine the effect of wealth changes on household 1. Increasing wealth of the previous period (row 12) caused household 1 to work less and consume more, and decreasing wealth (row 13) had the opposite effect.

For the second set of results in Table 4-3, household 1 was constrained in the number of hours it could work in period t. This constraint led it to work as much as it was allowed in period t—which was always less than the unconstrained amount—and to consume less. The values for period $t+1$ were much less affected. The household's responses in period t to changes in wages and prices were zero in terms of hours worked, but the household still responded in terms of the number of goods consumed. An increase in the wage rate of 5.0 percent, for example, led it to increase its consumption by 4.2 percent. This figure compares to 5.7 percent for the unconstrained case.

For the third set of results in Table 4-3, household 1 was constrained in the number of goods it could purchase in period t. For all five runs, this constraint led it to purchase the maximum number of goods it was allowed in period t. In two of the cases (rows 3 and 4) it worked the same as in the unconstrained case, but in the other three cases it worked less. Again, the values for period $t+1$ were much less affected.

For the fourth set of results in Table 4-3, both constraints were imposed on household 1. For all five runs this caused it to work the maximum number of hours allowed and to consume, with one exception, the maximum number of goods allowed. In this case, changing wages and prices merely changed how much the household saved in period t.

The results in Table 4-4 for household 2 are similar to the results in Table 4-3 for household 1 and require little further discussion. For household 2, an increase in savings means, of course, a decrease in loans. For the fourth set of results in Table 4-4, household 2 was constrained in the value of loans that it could take out for period t. For all five runs this caused it to work more and consume less in period t than in the corresponding unconstrained case. In all five cases the household chose to borrow the maximum amount of money that it was allowed for period t. For the fifth set of results in Table 4-4, all three constraints were imposed on household 2 for period t. When this happens, only two of the three constraints are really binding on the household, since given values for two of the three decision variables for period t the value of the other variable is automatically determined.

As mentioned above, the choice of the values of p_i in the CES utility function is important in determining how household i responds to wage and price changes and to changes in the other relevant variables. The case of $\rho_i = 0$ corresponds to the Cobb-Douglas function, and some results using this function are presented in Table 4-5. In this case the work effort of households is less responsive to changes in wages and prices. In the simple case of one time period and no nonlabor income, it can be easily shown that for a Cobb-Douglas utility function in consumption and leisure, work effort is not a function of the wage rate.[b] Although the present situation is more complicated, it is still true that for the Cobb-Douglas function work effort does not respond very much to the wage rate or the price level.

Table 4-5. Results of Solving the Control Problems of Households 1 and 2 Based on a Cobb-Douglas Utility Function

Household 1

Initial Conditions from Table 4-2 except	HPH_{1t}	HPH_{1t+1}	XH_{1t}	XH_{1t+1}	A^e_{1t}	A^e_{1t+1}
1. No exceptions	322.0	321.8	374.1	373.8	2159	2157
2. WH_{1t} 1.05 (+5.0%)	327.0 (+1.5%)	326.8	388.9 (+4.0%)	389.7	2159	2159
3. WH_{1t} 0.95 (−5.0%)	318.0 (−1.2%)	317.8	357.3 (−4.5%)	357.1	2162	2162
4. PH_{1t} 1.05 (+5.0%)	322.0 (+0.0%)	321.8	355.3 (−5.0%)	356.1	2160	2159
5. PH_{1t} 0.95 (−5.0%)	322.0 (+0.0%)	321.8	393.7 (+5.2%)	393.4	2159	2158

Household 2

	HPH_{2t}	HPH_{2t+1}	XH_{2t}	XH_{2t+1}	LH_{2t}	LH^e_{2t+1}
1. No exceptions	434.0	433.8	321.0	321.7	482.1	483.3
2. WH_{2t} 1.05 (+5.0%)	433.0 (−0.2%)	432.8	337.4 (+5.1%)	338.1	484.6	485.6
3. WH_{2t} 0.95 (−5.0%)	436.0 (+0.5%)	435.8	305.3 (−4.9%)	305.1	479.6	479.8
4. PH_{2t} 1.05 (+5.0%)	434.0 (+0.0%	433.8	305.7 (−4.8%)	306.5	482.1	483.4
5. PH_{2t} 0.95 (−5.0%)	434.0 (+0.0%)	433.8	338.9 (+5.6%)	338.6	483.3	484.4

For the results in this table $\eta_1 = 0.6375$, $RDH_1 = 0.0558$, $\eta_2 = 0.6380$, $RDH_2 = 0.0644$.

From the results in Tables 4-3 and 4-4, the behavior of the households can be summarized as follows. The main characteristic of households is that they maximize subject to constraints imposed on them by firms, banks, and the government. Unconstrained, their work effort (for $\rho_i = -0.3$) and consumption respond positively to the wage rate and negatively to the price level. Constrained, there may be no response at all or a much smaller response. Unconstrained, an increase in the bill rate or the loan rate causes households to work more, consume less, and save more, and conversely for a decrease in the rates. Increasing (decreasing) taxes has a negative (positive) effect on consumption, but may increase or decrease work effort depending on whether the proportional tax rate is changed or the minimum guaranteed level of income is changed. For a creditor household, an increase in initial wealth has a negative effect on work effort and a positive effect on consumption, and a decrease in initial wealth has the opposite effect.

4.6   THE CONDENSED MODEL
FOR HOUSEHOLDS

The household behavioral equations for the condensed model are presented in Table 4-6. Subscript 1 refers to household 1 and subscript 2 to household 2. The subscript 1 was dropped from the asset variables, since only household 1 has assets, and the subscript 2 was dropped from the liability variables, since only household 2 has liabilities. Also, the loan rate for period t is denoted as RL_t rather than RH_{it}, the price is denoted as P_t rather than PH_{it}, the wage rate is denoted as W_t rather than WH_{it}, and the level of savings deposits is denoted as SD_t rather than SDH_{it}. Since household 1 owns all the stock, the variable S_{it} can be dropped completely. The value of stocks held by household 1 is merely the price of the aggregate share of stock, PS_t.

Table 4-6.   Household Equations for the Condensed Model

Household 1

$$DIV_t^e = \frac{1}{5}\,(DIV_{t-1} + DIV_{t-2} + DIV_{t-3} + DIV_{t-4} + DIV_{t-5})\,, \tag{1}$$

$$HPHUN_{1t} = e^{10.18}(P_t)^{-0.41}\,(W_t)^{0.71}\,(r_t)^{0.77}\,(d_3)^{-0.38}\,(SD_{t-1} + PS_t)^{-0.38}$$
$$- 0.80YG\,, \tag{2}$$

$$XHUN_{1t} = e^{3.44}\,(P_t)^{-1.27}\,(W_t)^{1.14}\,(r_t)^{-0.40}\,(d_3)^{-0.19}\,(SD_{t-1}+PS_t)^{0.14}$$
$$+ 0.36YG\,, \tag{3}$$

$$SDUN_t^p = \frac{1}{1-(1-d_3)r_t}\,[SD_{t-1} - (\gamma_1 P_t\,XHUN_{1t} - DDH_{1t-1})$$
$$+ (1-d_3)\,(W_t HPHUN_{1t} + DIV_t^e) + YG - P_t XHUN_{1t}]\,, \tag{4}$$

$$HPH_{1t} = HPHUN_{1t} \text{ if } HPHUN_{1t} \leqslant HPHMAX_{1t}$$
$$= HPHMAX_{1t} \text{ if } HPHUN_{1t} > HPHMAX_{1t}, \tag{5}$$

If $HPHUN_{1t} > HPHMAX_{1t}$, then $\tag{6}$

Table 4-6. (continued)

Household 1

$$SD_t^p = SDUN_t^p - 0.074 \ SDUN_t^p \left| \frac{HPHUN_{1t} - HPHMAX_{1t}}{HPHUN_{1t}} \right| ,$$

If $HPHUN_{1t} \leqslant HPHMAX_{1t}$, then $SD_t^p = SDUN_t^p$,

$XH_{1t} = XHUN_{1t}$ if $HPHUN_{1t} \leqslant HPHMAX_{1t}$ and $XHUN_{1t} \leqslant XHMAX_{1t}$ $\qquad$ (7)

$$= \frac{1}{\gamma_1 P_t + P_t} \ [-(1-(1-d_3)r_t)SD_t^p + SD_{t-1} + DDH_{1t-1} + (1-d_3)(W_t HPH_{1t} + DIV_t^e) + YG]$$

$\qquad$ if $HPHUN_{1t} > HPHMAX_{1t}$ and the computed value of XH_{1t}

$\qquad$ does not exceed $XHMAX_{1t}$

$\qquad = XHMAX_{1t}$ if $HPHUN_{1t} \leqslant HPHMAX_{1t}$ and $XHUN_{1t} > XHMAX_{1t}$

$\qquad$ or if $HPHUN_{1t} > HPHMAX_{1t}$ and the computed value of XH_{1t}

$\qquad$ above exceeds $XHMAX_{1t}$; SD_t^p is then recomputed in these two cases.

Household 2

$HPHUN_{2t} = e^{7.28} (P_t)^{-0.25} (W_t)^{0.22} (RL_t)^{0.77} (d_3)^{-0.22} (LH_{t-1})^{0.07} - 0.75 \ YG,$ $\quad$ (1)'

$XHUN_{2t} = e^{4.34} (P_t)^{-1.27} (W_t)^{1.28} (RL_t)^{-0.59} (d_3)^{-0.17} (LH_{t-1})^{-0.06} + 0.35 \ YG,$ $\quad$ (2)'

$$LHUN_t = \frac{1}{1-(1-d_3)RL_t} \ [LH_{t-1} + (\gamma_1 P_t \ XHUN_{2t} - DDH_{2t-1}) - (1-d_3)W_t HPHUN_{2t}$$
$$- YG + P_t \ XHUN_{2t}] , \qquad (3)'$$

If $HPHUN_{2t} \leqslant HPHMAX_{2t}$, $XHUN_{2t} \leqslant XHMAX_{2t}$, and $LHUN_{2t} \leqslant LHMAX_t$, then

$HPH_{2t} = HPHUN_{2t} ,$ $\qquad\qquad$ (4)'

$XH_{2t} = XHUN_{2t} ,$ $\qquad\qquad$ (5)'

$LH_t = LHUN_t .$ $\qquad\qquad$ (6)'

Otherwise, the actual values are determined by the following algorithm:

[1] If $HPHUN_{2t} \leqslant HPHMAX_{2t}$, then $HPH_{2t}^p = HPHUN_{2t}$ and go to statement [8] ,

[2] $HPH_{2t}^p = HPHMAX_{2t}$,

[3] $LH_t^p = LHUN_t + 0.36 \ LHUN_t \left| \frac{HPHUN_{2t} - HPHMAX_{2t}}{HPHUN_{2t}} \right|$

[4] If $LH_t^p > LHMAX_t$, then $LH_t^p = LHMAX_t$,

[5] $XH_{2t}^p = \frac{1}{-\gamma_1 P_t - P_t} \ [-(1-(1-d_3)RL_t)LH_t^p + LH_{t-1} - DDH_{2t-1} - (1-d_3)W_t HPH_{2t}^p - YG] ,$

[6] If $XH_{2t}^p > XHMAX_{2t}$, then $XH_{2t}^p = XHMAX_{2t}$ and

Table 4-6.   (continued)

Household 2

$$LH_t^p = \frac{1}{1-(1-d_3)RL_t} \; [LH_{t-1} + \gamma_1 P_t XH_{2t}^p - DDH_{2t-1} - (1-d_3)W_t HPH_{2t}^p$$
$$- YG + P_t XH_{2t}^p \,] \,,$$

[7] Go to statement [18],

[8] If $LHUN_t \leqslant LHMAX_t$, then $LH_t^p = LHUN_t$ and go to statement [15],

[9] $LH_t^p = LHMAX_t$,

[10] $HPH_{2t}^p = HPHUN_{2t} + 0.46 \, HPHUN_{2t} \left(\dfrac{LHUN_t - LHMAX_t}{LHUN_t} \right)$,

[11] If $HPH_{2t}^p > HPHMAX_{2t}$, then $HPH_{2t}^p = HPHMAX_{2t}$,

[12] $XH_{2t}^p = \dfrac{1}{-\gamma_1 P_t - P_t} \; [-(1-(1-d_3)RL_t) \, LH_t^p + LH_{t-1} - DDH_{2t-1} - (1-d_3) \, W_t HPH_{2t}^p - YG]$,

[13] If $XH_{2t}^p > XHMAX_{2t}$, then $XH_{2t}^p = XHMAX_{2t}$ and

$$LH_t^p = \frac{1}{1-(1-d_3)RL_t} \; [LH_{t-1} + \gamma_1 P_t XH_{2t}^p - DDH_{2t-1} - (1-d_3)W_t HPH_t^p - YG + P_t XH_{2t}^p],$$

[14] Go to statement [18],

[15] If $XHUN_{2t} \leqslant XHMAX_{2t}$, then $XH_{2t}^p = XHUN_{2t}$ and go to statement [18],

[16] $XH_{2t}^p = XHMAX_{2t}$,

[17] $LH_t^p = \dfrac{1}{1-(1-d_3)RL_t} \; [LH_{t-1} + \gamma_1 P_t XH_{2t}^p - DDH_{2t-1} - (1-d_3)W_t HPH_{2t}^p - YG + P_t XH_{2t}^p]$,

[18] $HPH_{2t} = HPH_{2t}^p$,

[19] $XH_{2t} = XH_{2t}^p$,

[20] $LH_t = LH_t^p$.

Consider household 1 in Table 4-6 first. Equation (1) merely defines the expected level of dividends. It is the same as the equation in the non-condensed model. Equations (2) and (3) are based on the results in Table 4-3. The unconstrained number of hours worked is a positive function of the wage rate and the bill rate, and a negative function of the price level, the tax rate, the level of wealth of the previous period, and the minimum guaranteed level of income. The unconstrained number of goods purchased is a positive function of the wage rate, the level of wealth of the previous period, and the minimum guaranteed level of income, and a negative function of the price level, the bill rate, and the tax rate. The coefficients in Equations (2) and (3) were chosen to be consistent with the size of the reactions in Table 4-3.

Equation (4) defines the expected level of savings deposits, given the two unconstrained values and the expected level of dividends. The equation is derived as follows. Because of assumptions (4.11), (4.15), and (4.16), household 1 always expects the stock price to remain unchanged over time. Household 1 does not, therefore, expect to receive any capital gains or losses on its stocks, which means that CG_{it} in Equation (4.1) is expected to be zero. Now, Equations (4.2), (4.3), and (4.5) can be combined for household 1 to yield, using the notation for the condensed model:

$$SAV_{1t}^e = (1-d_3)(W_t HPH_{1t} + r_t SD_t^e + DIV_t^e) + YG - P_t XH_{1t}. \qquad (4.26)$$

The e superscripts have been added to the appropriate variables to denote the fact that household 1 only has at the beginning of period t an expectation of these variables. Equations (4.4) and (4.6) can be similarly combined for household 1 to yield, again using the notation for the condensed model:

$$SD_t^e = SD_{t-1} - (\gamma_1 P_t XH_{1t} - DDH_{1t-1}) + SAV_{1t}^e. \qquad (4.27)$$

The final term in Equation (4.6) is zero because household 1 always owns all the stock. Finally, Equations (4.26) and (4.27) can be solved to yield:

$$SD_t^e = \frac{1}{1-(1-d_3)r_t} [SD_{t-1} - (\gamma_1 P_t XH_{1t} - DDH_{1t-1})$$

$$+ (1-d_3)(W_t HPH_{1t} + DIV_t^e) + YG - P_t XH_{1t}], \qquad (4.28)$$

which is the same as Equation (4) in Table 4-6 with the appropriate change of notation.

Equation (5) in Table 4-6 determines the actual number of hours worked. If the unconstrained number is less than the maximum number allowed, then the actual number is the unconstrained number. Otherwise, the actual number is set equal to the maximum number. In Equation (6), the planned level of savings is lowered if the unconstrained number of hours worked is greater than the maximum number allowed. In row B.1 in Table 4-3 it can be seen that planned savings decreased slightly when household 1 was constrained in the number of hours that it could work, and this is the assumption reflected in Equation (6). The −0.074 coefficient is estimated from Table 4-3, where

$$-0.074 = (\frac{2152 - 2160}{2160}) / (\frac{323.0 - 306.8}{323.0}) .$$

Equation (7) determines the actual number of goods purchased. If the unconstrained number of hours worked is less than the maximum number allowed and if the unconstrained number of goods purchased is less than the maximum number allowed, then the actual number of goods purchased is the unconstrained number. If the unconstrained number of hours worked is greater than the maximum number allowed, so that the actual number is set equal to the maximum, then the actual number of goods purchased is set equal to the number necessary to have the planned level of savings deposits be what it is in Equation (6), given the new lower level of hours worked. This is the expression following the second equal sign in (7). This expression is obtained by solving Equations (4.26) and (4.27) for XH_{1t}.

If the computed number of goods purchased from this exercise is greater than the maximum number allowed or if (in the unconstrained hours case) the unconstrained number of goods purchased is greater than the maximum number allowed, then the actual number of goods purchased is set equal to the maximum number. This is the expression following the third equal sign in (7). It should be noted that this procedure reflects the assumption that a binding goods constraint has no effect on hours worked. In row C.1 in Table 4-3 it can be seen that the goods constraint had a negative effect on the number of hours worked by household 1, but for simplicity this behavioral response was not incorporated into the condensed model.

The condensed model for household 1 is thus fairly simple. If the household is not constrained, then the number of hours worked and the number of goods purchased are determined from Equation (2) and (3). Otherwise, the household modifies its decisions according to Equations (4)–(7). Because of Equations (4.26) and (4.27), given two of the three values of HPH_{1t}, XH_{1t}, and SD_t^e, the other value is automatically determined, and this property was used in Equations (4) and (7) in determining how the household's decisions were modified.

The equations for household 2 in the condensed model are based on the results in Table 4-4. The problem is more complicated for household 2 because of the possibly binding loan constraint in addition to the hours and goods constraints. In Equation (1)′ the unconstrained number of hours worked is a positive function of the wage rate, the loan rate, and the value of loans of the previous period, and a negative function of the price level, the tax rate, and the minimum guaranteed level of income. In Equation (2)′ the unconstrained number of goods purchased is a positive function of the wage rate and the minimum guaranteed level of income, and a negative function of the price level, the loan rate, the tax rate, and the value of loans of the previous period.

Equation (3)′ defines the unconstrained value of loans, given the unconstrained number of hours worked and the unconstrained number of goods purchased. The equation is derived in a similar way that Equation (4.28) was derived above for household 1. Equations (4.2), (4.3), and (4.5) can be combined for household 2 to yield, using the notation for the condensed model:

$$SAV_{2t} = (1-d_3) (W_t HPH_{2t} - RL_t LH_t) + YG - P_t XH_{2t}. \tag{4.29}$$

Equations (4.4) and (4.6) can be combined to yield, again using the notation for the condensed model:

$$LH_t = LH_{t-1} + (\gamma_1 P_t XH_{2t} - DDH_{2t}) - SAV_{2t}. \tag{4.30}$$

Equations (4.29) and (4.30) can then be solved to yield:

$$LH_t = \frac{1}{1-(1-d_3)RL_t} [LH_{t-1} + (\gamma_1 P_t XH_{2t} - DDH_{2t-1})$$

$$- (1-d_3) W_t HPH_{2t} - YG + P_t XH_{2t}], \tag{4.31}$$

which is the same as equation $(3)'$ in Table 4-6 with the appropriate change of notation.

If none of the unconstrained values in Equations $(1)'-(3)'$ is greater than the maximum values, then, as in Equations $(4)'-(6)'$, the actual values are the unconstrained values. Otherwise, the actual values are determined by the algorithm in Table 4-6. As was the case for the algorithm in Table 3-4 for the condensed model for the firm sector, the algorithm in Table 4-6 is written like a FORTRAN program. The following is a brief verbal description of the algorithm.

If the hours constraint is binding, then statements [2]-[6] hold. The actual number of hours worked is set equal to the maximum number in statement [2]. In statement [3] the planned value of loans is then increased. In row B.1 in Table 4-4 it can be seen that the planned value of loans increased when household 2 was constrained in the number of hours that it could work, and this is the assumption reflected in statement [3]. The 0.36 coefficient is estimated from Table 4-4, where

$$0.36 = (\frac{490.7 - 482.1}{482.1}) / (\frac{435.0 - 413.2}{435.0})$$

If the new planned value of loans is greater than the maximum value, then in statement [4] the actual value is set equal to the maximum value.

Statement [5] determines the number of goods purchased, given the number of hours worked and the value of loans. The equation in statement [5] is derived by solving Equations (4.29) and (4.30) for XH_{2t}. If the new number of goods purchased is greater than the maximum value, then in statement [6] the actual number is set equal to the maximum value and a new value of loans is computed. The new value of loans is guaranteed to be less than the previous value because the new number of goods purchased is in this case less than the previous number. The equation for loans in statement [6] is, of course, the same as Equation (3)' with the appropriate change of notation.

As was the case for household 1, the procedure in statement [6] reflects the assumption that a binding goods constraint has no effect on hours worked. In row C.1 in Table 4-4 it can be seen that the goods constraint had a negative effect on the number of hours worked by household 2, but for simplicity this behavioral response was not incorporated into the condensed model. Statement [6] ends the computations for household 2 in the case of an originally binding hours constraint, and the algorithm finishes off with statements [18]–[20], where the actual values are set equal to the planned values.

If the hours constraint is not binding but the loan constraint is, then statements [9]–[13] hold. The actual value of loans is set equal to the maximum value in statement [9]. In statement [10] the planned number of hours worked is then increased. In row D.1 in Table 4-4 it can be seen that the planned number of hours worked increased when household 2 was constrained in the value of loans that it could take out, and this is the assumption reflected in statement [10]. The 0.46 coefficient is estimated from Table 4–4, where

$$0.46 = (\frac{445.0 - 435.0}{435.0}) / (\frac{482.1 - 458.0}{482.1}) \ .$$

If the new planned number of hours worked is greater than the maximum number, then in statement [11] the actual number is set equal to the maximum number. Statements [12] and [13] are then exactly like statements [5] and [6]. Statement [13] then ends the computations for household 2 in this case.

If the hours and loan constraints are not binding but the goods constraint is, then statements [16] and [17] hold. The actual number of goods purchased is set equal to the maximum number in statement [16]. In statement [19] the value of loans is recomputed. Again, the new value of loans is guaranteed to be less than the previous value because the new number of goods purchased is less than the previous number. Statement [17] then ends the computation for household 2 in this case.

To summarize the condensed model for household 2, the number of hours worked, the number of goods purchased, and the value of loans taken out are determined by Equations $(1)'-(3)'$ if the household is not constrained. If the hours constraint is binding, then statements $[2]-[6]$ hold. If the loan constraint is binding but the hours constraint is not, then statements $[9]-[13]$ hold. If the goods constraint is binding but the hours and loan constraints are not, then statements $[16]-[17]$ hold. As was the case for household 1, the algorithm for household 2 uses the fact that given two of the three values of HPH_{2t}, XH_{2t}, and LH_t, the other value is automatically determined (because of Equations (4.29) and (4.30)).

NOTES

[a]Since all expectations are made by household i, no i subscript or superscript has been added to the relevant symbols to denote the fact that it is household i making the expectation.
[b]See, for example, Henderson and Quandt [28], p. 24.

Chapter Five

The Government and the Bond Dealer

5.1 THE GOVERNMENT

In Table 5-1 the important symbols used in this chapter are listed in alphabetic order. With a few exceptions, the notation used for the government and the bond dealer is the same for both the non-condensed and condensed models. The government collects taxes from banks ($TAXB_{it}$), from firms ($TAXF_{it}$), from households ($TAXH_{it}$), and from the bond dealer ($TAXD_t$). It hires labor from households (HPG_t), buys goods from firms (XG_t), issues bills and bonds ($VBILLG_t$ and $BONDG_t$), and pays interest on its bills and bonds ($r_t VBILLG_t + BONDG_t$). The government also sets the various tax parameters in the system and the reserve requirement ratio. It is subject to the following budget constraints:[a]

$$
PG_t XG_t + WG_t HPG_t + r_t VBILLG_t + BONDG_t - \sum_{i=1}^{NB} TAXB_{it} - \sum_{i=1}^{NF} TAXF_{it}
$$

$$
- \sum_{i=1}^{NH} TAXH_{it} - TAXD_t = VBILLG_t - VBILLG_{t-1}
$$

$$
+ \frac{BONDG_t - BONDG_{t-1}}{R_t} + \sum_{i=1}^{NB} BR_{it} - \sum_{i=1}^{NB} BR_{it-1} \quad . \tag{5.1}
$$

The first four terms in Equation (5.1) are government expenditures, and the next four terms are government tax collections. The left-hand side of Equation (5.1) is thus expenditures minus taxes, and this value must equal the change in the value of bills plus bonds plus bank reserves.

Table 5-1.   Notation for the Government and the Bond Dealer in Alphabetic Order

---

Non-Condensed and Condensed Models

The Government

$BONDG_t$ = number of bonds issued
HPG_t = hours paid for
PG_t = price paid [= P_t in the condensed model]
$TAXB_{it}$ = taxes paid by bank i [=$TAXB_t$ in the condensed model]
$TAXD_t$ = taxes paid by the bond dealer
$TAXF_{it}$ = taxes paid by firm i [=$TAXF_t$ in the condensed model]
$TAXH_{it}$ = taxes paid by household i
$VBILLG_t$ = value of bills issued
WG_t = wage rate paid [= W_t in the condensed model]
XG_t = number of goods purchased

The Bond Dealer

$BONDD_t$ = number of bonds held
DDD_t = demand deposits
DIV_t = total dividends paid and received in the economy
$DIVD_t$ = dividends paid
PS_t = price of the aggregate share of stock
r_t = bill rate
R_t = bond rate
$TAXD_t$ = taxes paid
$VBD*$ = value of bills and bonds that the bond dealer desires to hold
$VBILLD_t$ = value of bills held
ΠD_t = before-tax profits

5.2   THE BOND DEALER

The bond dealer is taken in the model to represent the government bill and bond market and the stock market. The three decision variables of the bond dealer are the bill rate (r_t), the bond rate (R_t), and the stock price (PS_t). The assets of the bond dealer consist of bills $(VBILLD_t)$, bonds $(BONDD_t)$, and demand deposits (DDD_t). Households own the stock of the bond dealership. The profits of the bond dealer consist of the interest received on its bill and bond holdings $(r_t VBILLD_t + BONDD_t)$, and capital gains or losses on its bond holdings $(BONDD_t/R_{t+1} - BONDD_t/R_t)$. The bond dealer pays taxes to the government on its profits $(TAXD_t)$. After-tax profits are paid to households in the form of dividends $(DIVD_t)$. The basic equations for the bond dealer are the following:

$$\Pi D_t = r_t VBILLD_t + BONDD_t + \left(\frac{BONDD_t}{R_{t+1}} - \frac{BONDD_t}{R_t} \right), \text{ [before-tax profits]}$$

(5.2)

$TAXD_t = d_1 \Pi D_t$, [taxes paid] (5.3)

$DIVD_t = \Pi D_t - TAXD_t$, [dividends paid] (5.4)

$$DDD_t = DDD_{t-1} - (VBILLD_t - VBILLD_{t-1}) - \frac{(BONDD_t - BONDD_{t-1})}{R_t}$$
$$- \left(\frac{BONDD_t}{R_{t+1}} - \frac{BONDD_t}{R_t} \right) \text{ [demand deposits]} \quad (5.5)$$
$$= DDD_{t-1} - (VBILLD_t - VBILLD_{t-1}) - \left(\frac{BONDD_t}{R_{t+1}} - \frac{BONDD_t}{R_t} \right) .$$

Equation (5.5) states that the change in demand deposits of the bond dealer is equal to minus the change in the value of its bills and bonds and minus the capital gains or losses on its bond holdings. Since the bond dealer pays out in the form of taxes and dividends any capital gains made in the period (and conversely for capital losses), and yet does not receive any cash flow from the capital gains, capital gains take away from (and conversely capital losses add to) demand deposits.

In any period the bond dealer is assumed to absorb the difference between the supply of bills and bonds from the government and the demand for bills and bonds from the banks:

$$VBILLD_t = VBILLG_t - \sum_{i=1}^{NB} VBILLB_{it} , \quad (5.6)$$

$$BONDD_t = BONDG_t - \sum_{i=1}^{NB} BONDB_{it} . \quad (5.7)$$

The bond dealer is assumed to have a certain desired value of bills and bonds, denoted as VBD^*, that it aims to hold in inventories each period. Now, the total demand for bills and bonds from the banks in, say, period $t-1$ is $\sum_{i=1}^{NB} VBB_{it-1}$. Therefore, the total demand for bills and bonds from both the banks and the bond dealer in period $t-1$ is $\sum_{i=1}^{NB} VBB_{it-1} + VBD^*$. The total supply of bills and bonds from the government in period $t-1$ is, of course, $VBILLG_{t-1} + BONDG_{t-1}/R_{t-1}$. The bond dealer is assumed to have knowledge of $\sum_{i=1}^{NB} VBB_{it-1}, VBILLG_{t-1}$, and $BONDG_{t-1}$ near the end of period $t-1$, and it is assumed to set at this time the bill rate for period t according to the following formula

$$\frac{r_t - r_{t-1}}{r_{t-1}} = \lambda \left[\frac{\left(VBILLG_{t-1} + \dfrac{BONDG_{t-1}}{R_{t-1}} \right) - \left(\sum_{i=1}^{NB} VBB_{it-1} + VBD^* \right)}{\sum_{i=1}^{NB} VBB_{it-1} + VBD^*} \right], \lambda > 0. \tag{5.8}$$

The numerator of the term in brackets is the excess supply of bills and bonds in period t-1. Equation (5.8) thus states that the bond dealer raises the bill rate for period t if there was an excess supply of bills and bonds in period t-1 and lowers the bill rate for period t if there was an excess demand (negative excess supply).[b]

It was mentioned in Section 1.2 that banks are assumed to communicate to the bond dealer near the end of period t-1 their expectations of the future bill rates. All banks are assumed to have the same expectations. Let r_{t+k}^e denote the banks' expectation of the bill rate for period $t+k$ ($k=1, 2, \ldots$). Then given the value of r_t and given these expectations, the bond dealer is assumed to set the bond rate, R_t, according to the formula

$$\frac{1}{R_t} = \frac{1}{(1+r_t)} + \frac{1}{(1+r_t)(1+r_{t+1}^e)} + \frac{1}{(1+r_t)(1+r_{t+1}^e)(1+r_{t+2}^e)} + \ldots \; . \tag{5.9}$$

The price of a bond, in other words, is set equal to the presented discounted value of a perpetual stream of one-dollar payments, the discount rates being the current and expected future bill rates. Equation (5.9) is consistent with Equation (2.19) in Chapter Two, which is the equation describing the way that banks *expect* the bond rate to be set. Since banks are assumed always to expect that the bill rate will remain unchanged from its last observed value, the bond rate that the bond dealer sets is always equal to the bill rate:[c]

$$R_t = r_t \; . \tag{5.10}$$

It was also mentioned in Section 1.2 that households are assumed to communicate to the bond dealer near the end of period t-1 their expectations of the future bill rates and dividend levels. All households are assumed to have the same expectations. Let r_{t+k}^e now denote the households' expectation of the bill rate for period $t+k$ ($k=1, 2, \ldots$), and let DIV_{t+k}^e denote their expectation of the dividend level for period $t+k$ ($k=0, 1, 2, \ldots$). Then given the value of r_t and given these expectations, the bond dealer is assumed to set the stock price, PS_t, according to the formula

$$PS_t = \frac{DIV_t^e}{(1+r_t)} + \frac{DIV_{t+1}^e}{(1+r_t)(1+r_{t+1}^e)} + \frac{DIV_{t+2}^e}{(1+r_t)(1+r_{t+1}^e)(1+r_{t+2}^e)} + \dots \quad .$$

(5.11)

The stock price, in other words, is set equal to the present discounted value of the expected future dividend levels, the discount rates being the current and expected future bill rates. Equation (5.11) is consistent with Equation (4.16) in Chapter Four, which is the equation describing the way that households *expect* the stock price to be set. Since households are assumed always to expect that the bill rate will remain unchanged from its last observed value and are assumed always to expect that the dividend level will remain unchanged from the level expected for period t, the stock price that the bond dealer sets is merely[d]

$$PS_t = \frac{DIV_t^e}{r_t} \quad .$$

(5.12)

DIV_t^e in (5.12) is determined in Equation (4.15) in Chapter Four as the average of the past five dividend levels:[e]

$$DIV_t^e = \frac{1}{5}(DIV_{t-1} + DIV_{t-2} + DIV_{t-3} + DIV_{t-4} + DIV_{t-5}).$$

(5.13)

This completes the discussion for the bond dealer. Although the bond dealer represents the bill and bond market and the stock market, it is important to note that the bond dealer is not an auctioneer. The bond dealer sets the bill rate for period t according to the excess supply or demand situation for bills and bonds that exists in period $t-1$. Any difference between the supply of bills and bonds from the government and the demand from the banks in a period is absorbed by the bond dealer. Although the bond dealer can be thought of as always trying to achieve a zero excess supply and demand for bills and bonds in the next period, it does not continually call out rates in the current period until a zero excess supply and demand for bills and bonds is reached in the current period.

5.3   THE CONDENSED MODEL FOR THE GOVERNMENT AND THE BOND DEALER

The condensed model for the government and the bond dealer is the same as the non-condensed model. The equations for the condensed model are presented in Table 5-2. The only difference between the equations in Table 5-2 and the equations for the non-condensed model is the change in notation for some of the variables.

Table 5-2   The Government and Bond Dealer Equations for the Condensed Model

The Government

(1) $P_t XG_t + W_t HPG_t + r_t VBILLG_t + BONDG_t - TAXB_t - TAXF_t$
$- TAXH_{1t} - TAXH_{2t} - TAXD_t = VBILLG_t - VBILLG_{t-1}$
$+ \dfrac{BONDG_t - BONDG_{t-1}}{R_t} + BR_t - BR_{t-1}$, [government budget constraint]

The Bond Dealer

(2) $\dfrac{r_t - r_{t-1}}{r_{t-1}} = \lambda \left[\dfrac{(VBILLG_{t-1} + \dfrac{BONDG_{t-1}}{R_{t-1}}) - (VBB_{t-1} + VBD^*)}{(VBB_{t-1} + VBD^*)} \right]$, [equation determining the bill rate]

(3) $R_t = r_t$, [equation determining the bond rate]

(4) $PS_t = \dfrac{\frac{1}{5}(DIV_{t-1} + DIV_{t-2} + DIV_{t-3} + DIV_{t-4} + DIV_{t-5})}{r_t}$. [equation determining the stock price]

NOTES

[a]NB in (5.1) is the number of banks in existence, NF is the number of firms, and NH is the number of households.

[b]In the programming for the non-condensed model, the bond dealer was assumed to estimate the parameter λ in Equation (5.8) each period on the basis of its past observations of the correlation between percentage changes in the demand for bills and bonds from the banks and percentage changes in the bill rate. The exact procedure by which λ was assumed to be estimated is described in the Appendix.

[c]In order for the r^e_{t+k} ($k=1, 2, \ldots$) in Equation (5.9) to be equal to r_t, so that (5.10) holds, it must be assumed that the banks know the value of r_t before they form their future expectations. Therefore, the bond dealer must be thought of as communicating the value of r_t (obtained from (5.8)) to the banks, who then in turn communicate their future expectations to the bond dealer. All this communication takes place near the end of period $t-1$.

[d]The same assumption regarding the communication flow to and from the bond dealer has to be made here as was made for banks in footnote c.

[e]In order for the value of DIV^e_t to be communicated to the bond dealer near the end of period $t-1$, the households must be assumed to know at this time the value of DIV_{t-1}. As will be seen in Tables 6-2 and A-2, this assumption introduces a slight degree of simultaneity into the model. This simultaneity could have been eliminated by assuming that DIV^e_t in (5.13) is the average of the past five dividend levels starting with period $t-2$, but because the degree of simultaneity was so slight, the assumption in (5.13) was retained.

Chapter Six

The Dynamic Properties of the Model

6.1 THE COMPLETE SET OF EQUATIONS FOR THE MODEL

The complete set of equations for the condensed model is presented in Table 6-2, and the complete set of equations for the non-condensed model is presented in the Appendix in Table A-2. For ease of reference, the complete notation for the condensed model is presented in alphabetic order in Table 6-1, and the complete notation for the non-condensed model is presented in alphabetic order in Table A-1. Attention will be concentrated in this chapter on the condensed model.

The equations in Table 6-2 are listed in the order in which the model is solved. At the end of period $t-1$ the bond dealer determines the bill rate, the bond rate, and the stock price for period t (Equation (1)). Equations (2) through (12) then refer to the decisions made at the beginning of period t before any transactions take place. In Equation (2) the government sets the values of the tax parameters (d_1, d_2, d_3, YG, g_2) and the value of the reserve reserve requirement ratio (g_1) and decides on the number of goods to purchase (XG_t), the number of worker hours to pay for (HPG_t), the value of bills to issue ($VBILLG_t$), and the number of bonds to have outstanding ($BONDG_t$). The decisions regarding these variables are treated as exogenous in the model.

In Equation (3) the bank sector determines the loan rate (RL_t), the value of bills and bonds to purchase (VBB_t), and the maximum amount of money to lend in the period ($LBMAX_t$). As can be seen from Table 2-4 (Chapter Two), the important determinants of these variables are the expected level of funds for the current period ($FUNDS_t^e$), the loan rate of the previous period

Table 6-1. The Complete Notation for the Condensed Model in Alphabetic Order

Subscript t denotes variable for period t. Superscripts p and pp in the text denote a planned value of the variable, and superscript e denotes an expected value of the variable.

$BONDB_t$	= number of bonds held by the bank sector
$BONDD_t$	= number of bonds held by the bond dealer
$BONDG_t$	= number of bonds issued by the government
BR_t	= actual reserves of the bank sector
BR_t^*	= required reserves of the bank sector $[g_1 DDB_t]$
BR_t^{**}	= desired reserves of the bank sector $[g_1 (DDB_t - EMAXDD) + EMAXDD + EMAXSD]$
CF_t	= cash flow before taxes and dividends of the firm sector
$\overline{CF}_t$	= cash flow net of taxes and dividends of the firm sector
CG_t	= capital gains or losses on stocks of household 1
CGB_t	= capital gains or losses on bonds of the bank sector $[BONDB_t/R_{t+1} - BONDB_t/R_t]$
CGD_t	= capital gains or losses on bonds of the bond dealer $[BONDD_t/R_{t+1} - BONDD_t/R_t]$
d_1	= profit tax rate
d_2	= penalty tax rate on the composition of banks' portfolios
d_3	= personal tax rate
DDB_t	= demand deposits of the bank sector
DDD_t	= demand deposits of the bond dealer
DDF_t	= actual demand deposits of the firm sector
DDF_{1t}	= demand deposits set aside by the firm sector for transactions purposes
DDF_2	= demand deposits set aside by the firm sector to be used as a buffer to meet unexpected decreases in cash flow
DDH_{it}	= demand deposits of household i $(i=1,2)$
DEP_t	= depreciation of the firm sector
DIV_t	= total dividends paid and received in the economy
$DIVB_t$	= dividends paid by the bank sector
$DIVD_t$	= dividends paid by the bond dealer
$DIVF_t$	= dividends paid by the firm sector
$EMAXDD$	= largest error the bank sector expects to make in overestimating its demand deposits for any period
$EMAXHP$	= largest error the firm sector expects to make in overestimating the supply of labor available to it for any period
$EMAXMH$	= largest error the firm sector expects to make in underestimating its worker hour requirements for any period
$EMAXSD$	= largest error the bank sector expects to make in overestimating its savings deposits for any period
$EXBB_t$	= excess supply of bills and bonds $[(VBILLG_t + BONDG_t/R_t) - (VBB_t + VBD^*)]$
$FUNDS_t^e$	= amount that the bank sector knows it will have available to lend to households and firms and to buy bills and bonds even if it overestimates its demand and savings deposits by the maximum amounts

Table 6-1. (continued)

g_1	= reserve requirement ratio
g_2	= no-tax proportion of banks' portfolio held in bills and bonds
$\bar{H}$	= maximum number of hours that each machine can be used each period
HP_t	= total number of worker hours paid for in the economy
HPF_t	= number of worker hours paid for by the firm sector
$HPFMAX_t$	= maximum number of worker hours that the firm sector will pay for
$HPFMAXUN_t$	= maximum number of worker hours that the firm sector would pay for if it were not constrained
HPG_t	= number of worker hours paid for by the government
HPH_{it}	= number of hours that household i is paid for ($i=1,2$)
$HPHMAX_{it}$	= unconstrained supply of hours of household i ($i=1,2$)
$HPUN_t$	= total unconstrained supply of hours in the economy
INV_t	= number of goods purchased by the firm sector for investment purposes (one good = one machine)
$INVUN_t$	= unconstrained investment demand of the firm sector
K_t^a	= actual number of machines held by the firm sector
KH_t	= number of machine hours worked
$KMIN_t$	= minimum number of machines required to produce Y_t
L_t	= total value of loans of the bank sector
$LBMAX_t$	= maximum value of loans that the bank sector will make
LF_t	= value of loans taken out by the firm sector
$LFMAX_t$	= maximum value of loans that the firm sector can take out
$LFUN_t$	= unconstrained demand for loans of the firm sector
LH_t	= value of loans taken out by household 2
$LHMAX_t$	= maximum value of loans that household 2 can take out
$LHUN_t$	= unconstrained demand for loans of household 2
LUN_t	= total unconstrained demand for loans
m	= length of life of one machine
MH_{1t}	= number of worker hours worked on the machines
MH_{3t}	= number of worker hours required to handle deviations of inventories from β_1 times sales
MH_{4t}	= number of worker hours required to handle fluctuations in sales
MH_{5t}	= number of worker hours required to handle fluctuations in worker hours paid for
MH_{6t}	= number of worker hours required to handle fluctuations in net investment
MH_t	= total number of worker hours required
P_t	= price level
PS_t	= price of the aggregate share of stock
PUN_t	= price level that the firm sector would set if it were not constrained
r_t	= bill rate
R_t	= bond rate
RL_t	= loan rate of the bank sector
SAV_{it}	= savings net of capital gains or losses of household i ($i=1,2$)
SD_t	= savings deposits of household 1 (and of the bank sector)
$SDUN_t$	= unconstrained savings deposits of household 1 (corresponding to $HPHUN_{1t}$ and $XHUN_{1t}$)

Table 6-1. (continued)

TAX_t	= total taxes paid
$TAXB_t$	= taxes paid by the bank sector
$TAXD_t$	= taxes paid by the bond dealer
$TAXF_t$	= taxes paid by the firm sector
$TAXH_{it}$	= taxes paid by household i ($i=1,2$)
V_t	= stock of inventories of the firm sector
VBB_t	= value of bills and bonds that the bank sector chooses to purchase $[VBILLB_t + BONDB_t/R_t]$
VBD^*	= value of bills and bonds that the bond dealer desires to hold
$VBILLB_t$	= value of bills held by the bank sector
$VBILLD_t$	= value of bills held by the bond dealer
$VBILLG_t$	= value of bills issued by the government
W_t	= wage rate
WUN_t	= wage rate that the firm sector would set if it were not constrained
X_t	= total number of goods sold in the economy
$XFMAX_t$	= maximum number of goods that the firm sector will sell
XG_t	= number of goods purchased by the government
XH_{it}	= number of goods purchased by household i ($i=1,2$)
$XHMAX_{it}$	= maximum number of goods that household i can purchase ($i=1,2$)
$XHUN_{it}$	= unconstrained demand for goods of household i ($i=1,2$)
XUN_t	= total unconstrained demand for goods
Y_t	= total number of goods produced
YG	= minimum guaranteed level of income (also can be thought of as the level of transfer payments to each household)
YH_{it}	= before-tax income excluding capital gains or losses of household i ($i=1,2$)
Y^PUN_t	= number of goods that the firm sector would plan to produce it it were not constrained
λ_1	= amount of output produced per worker hour
μ_1	= amount of output produced per machine hour
ΠB_t	= before-tax profits of the bank sector
ΠD_t	= before-tax profits of the bond dealer
ΠF_t	= before-tax profits of the firm sector

Table 6-2. The Complete Set of Equations for the Condensed Model

(1) r_t, R_t, and PS_t are determined by the bond dealer at the end of period $t-1$. See (42) and (62) below for the determination of the values for period $t+1$.

(2) The government sets d_1, d_2, d_3, YG, g_1, g_2, XG_t, HPG_t, $VBILLG_t$, and $BONDG_t$.

(3) The bank variables RL_t, VBB_t, and $LBMAX_t$ are determined as in Table 2-4.

(4) $LHMAX_t = (\dfrac{LHUN_{t-1}}{LHUN_{t-1}+LFUN_{t-1}}) LBMAX_t$. [allocation of the aggregate loan constraint to household 2 and the firm sector]

Table 6-2. (continued)

(5) $LFMAX_t = LBMAX_t - LHMAX_t.$

(6) The firm variables P_t, INV_t, Y_t^p, W_t, LF_t, $HPFMAX_t$, $XFMAX_t$, $INVUN_t$, and $LFUN_t$ are determined as in Table 3–4.

(7) The variables $HPHUN_{1t}$ and $XHUN_{1t}$ for household 1 and the variables $HPHUN_{2t}$, $XHUN_{2t}$, and $LHUN_t$ for household 2 are determined as in Table 4–6.

(8) $HPHMAX_{1t} = (\dfrac{HPHUN_{1t}}{HPHUN_{1t}+HPHUN_{2t}})\,(HPFMAX_t + HPG_t).$ [allocation of the aggregate hours constraint to households 1 and 2]

(9) $HPHMAX_{2t} = (HPFMAX_t+HPG_t) - HPHMAX_{1t}.$

(10) $XHMAX_{1t} = (\dfrac{XHUN_{1t}}{XHUN_{1t}+XHUN_{2t}})(XFMAX_t - INV_t - XG_t).$
[allocation of the aggregate goods constraint to households 1 and 2]

(11) $XHMAX_{2t} = (XFMAX_t - INV_t - XG_t) - XHMAX_{1t}.$

(12) The variables HPH_{1t} are XH_{1t} for household 1 and the variables HPH_{2t}, XH_{2t}, LH_t for household 2 are determined as in Table 4–6.

(13) $XUN_t = XHUN_{1t} + XHUN_{2t} + INVUN_t + XG_t.$ [aggregate unconstrained demand for goods]

(14) $LUN_t = LFUN_t + LHUN_t.$ [aggregate unconstrained demand for loans]

(15) $HPUN_t = HPHUN_{1t} + HPHUN_{2t}.$ [aggregate unconstrained supply of labor]

(16) $X_t = XH_{1t} + XH_{2t} + INV_t + XG_t.$ [aggregate number of goods sold]

(17) $L_t = LF_t + LH_t.$ [aggregate value of loans]

(18) $HP_t = HPH_{1t} + HPH_{2t}.$ [total number of worker hours paid for]

(19) $HPF_t = HP_t - HPG_t.$ [number of worker hours allocated to the firm sector]

(20) $K_t^a = K_{t-1}^a + INV_t - INV_{t-m}.$ [actual number of machines on hand]

(21) $V_t = V_{t-1} + Y_t^p - X_t.$ [Equations (21) – (29) are concerned with the determination of output and inventories.]

(22) $MH_{1t}^p = \dfrac{Y_t^p}{\lambda_1}.$

(23) $MH_{3t}^p = \beta_2(V_t - \beta_1 X_t)^2.$

(24) $MH_{4t} = \beta_3(X_t - X_{t-1})^2.$

(25) $MH_{5t} = \beta_4(\overline{HPF_{t-1} - HPF_{t-2}})^2.$

Table 6-2.   (continued)

(26) $MH_{6t} = \beta_5 (K_t^a - K_{t-1}^a)^2.$

(27) $MH_t^p = MH_{1t}^p + MH_{3t}^p + MH_{4t} + MH_{5t} + MH_{6t}.$

(28)   If $MH_t^p \leqslant HPF_t$, then $Y_t = Y_t^p$, $V_t = V_t$, and $MH_t = MH_t^p.$

(29)   If $MH_t^p > HPF_t$, then $MH_t = HPF_t$; $Y_t =$ maximum amount that can be
        produced given K_t^a, X_t and MH_t; and $V_t = V_{t-1} + Y_t - X_t.$

(30) $KMIN_t = \dfrac{Y_t}{\mu_1 \bar{H}}.$ [minimum number of machines needed to produce Y_t]

(31) $DEP_t = \dfrac{1}{m}(P_t INV_t + \ldots + P_{t-m+1} INV_{t-m+1}).$ [depreciation]

(32) $\Pi F_t = P_t Y_t - W_t HPF_t - DEP_t - RL_t LF_t + (P_t - P_{t-1})V_{t-1}.$
        [before-tax profits of the firm sector]

(33) $TAXF_t = d_1 \Pi F_t.$ [taxes of the firm sector]

(34) $DIVF_t = \Pi F_t - TAXF_t.$ [dividends of the firm sector]

(35) $CF_t = P_t X_t - W_t HPF_t - P_t INV_t - RL_t LF_t.$ [gross cash flow of the firm sector]

(36) $\overline{CF}_t = CF_t - TAXF_t - DIVF_t$

        $= DEP_t - P_t INV_t + P_{t-1}V_{t-1} - P_t V_t.$ [cash flow net of taxes and
        dividends of the firm sector]

(37) $DDF_t = DDF_{t-1} + LF_t - LF_{t-1} + \overline{CF}_t.$ [demand deposits of the firm sector]

(38) $VBILLD_t = 0.$ [value of bills held by the bond dealer]

(39) $VBILLB_t = VBILLG_t.$ [value of bills held by the bank sector]

(40) $BONDB_t = R_t (VBB_t - VBILLB_t).$ [number of bonds held by the bank sector]

(41) $BONDD_t = BONDG_t - BONDB_t.$ [number of bonds held by the bond dealer]

(42)   The bond dealer determines r_{t+1} and R_{t+1} as in equations (2) and (3) (led one
        period) in Table 5-2.

(43) $\Pi D_t = BONDD_t + (\dfrac{BONDD_t}{R_{t+1}} - \dfrac{BONDD_t}{R_t}).$ [before-tax profits of the bond
        dealer]

(44) $TAXD_t = d_1 \Pi D_t.$ [taxes of the bond dealer]

(45) $DIVD_t = \Pi D_t - TAXD_t.$ [dividends of the bond dealer]

(46) $DDD_t = DDD_{t-1} - (\dfrac{BONDD_t}{R_{t+1}} - \dfrac{BONDD_t}{R_t}).$ [demand deposits of the bond
        dealer]

(47) $DDH_{1t} = \gamma_1 P_t XH_{1t}.$ [demand deposits of household 1]

Table 6-2. (continued)

(48) $DDH_{2t} = \gamma_1 P_t XH_{2t}$. [demand deposits of household 2]

(49) $DDB_t = DDF_t + DDD_t + DDH_{1t} + DDH_{2t}$. [total value of demand deposits]

(50) $YH_{2t} = W_t HPH_{2t}$. [before-tax income of household 2]

(51) $TAXH_{2t} = d_3 (YH_{2t} - RL_t LH_t) - YG$. [taxes of household 2]

(52) $SAV_{2t} = YH_{2t} - TAXH_{2t} - P_t XH_{2t} - RL_t LH_t$. [savings of household 2]

[Equations (53) – (62) are solved simultaneously]

(53) $CG_t = PS_{t+1} - PS_t$. [capital gains or losses of household 1]

(54) $YH_{1t} = W_t HPH_{1t} + r_t SD_t + DIV_t$. [income net of capital gains or losses of household 1]

(55) $TAXH_{1t} = d_3(YH_{1t} + CG_t) - YG$. [taxes of household 1]

(56) $SAV_{1t} = YH_{1t} - TAXH_{1t} - P_t XH_{1t}$. [savings net of capital gains or losses of household 1]

(57) $SD_t = SD_{t-1} - (DDH_{1t} - DDH_{1t-1}) + SAV_{1t}$. [savings deposits of household 1]

(58) $\Pi B_t = RL_t L_t + r_t VBILLB_t + BONDB_t - r_t SD_t + (\dfrac{BONDB_t}{R_{t+1}} - \dfrac{BONDB_t}{R_t})$.

[before-tax profits of the bank sector]

(59) $TAXB_t = d_1 \, \Pi B_t + d_2 \, [VBB_t - g_2(VBB_t + L_t)]^2$. [taxes of the bank sector]

(60) $DIVB_t = \Pi B_t - TAXB_t$. [dividends of the bank sector]

(61) $DIV_t = DIVF_t + DIVD_t + DIVB_t$. [total value of dividends].

(62) $PS_{t+1} = \dfrac{\frac{1}{5}(DIV_t + DIV_{t-1} + DIV_{t-2} + DIV_{t-3} + DIV_{t-4})}{r_{t+1}}$.

[stock price for period t]

(63) $TAX_t = TAXH_{1t} + TAXH_{2t} + TAXF_t + TAXD_t + TAXB_t$. [total value of taxes]

(64) $BR_t = DDB_t + SD_t - L_t - VBILLB_t - \dfrac{BONDB_t}{R_{t+1}}$ [bank reserves]

$= BR_{t-1} + P_t XG_t + W_t HPG_t + r_t VBILLG_t + BONDG_t - TAX_t$

$- (VBILLG_t - VBILLG_{t-1}) - \left(\dfrac{BONDG_t - BONDG_{t-1}}{R_t}\right)$.

[government budget constraint]

(RL_{t-1}), the bill rate for the current period (r_t)—the bill rate for the current period having already been set by the bond dealer—the unconstrained demand for loans of the previous period (LUN_{t-1}), and the no-tax proportion (g_2) of bills and bonds. The expected level of funds for the current period is a function of the reserve requirement ratio and of the level of demand deposits and savings deposits of the previous period $[FUNDS_t^e = (1-g_1)(DDB_{t-1} - EMAXDD) + (SD_{t-1} - EMAXSD)]$.

In equations (4) and (5) the loan constraint from the bank sector is allocated to the household $(LHMAX_t)$ and firm $(LFMAX_t)$ sectors. The allocation is based on the ratio of the sector's unconstrained demand for loans of the previous period to the total unconstrained demand for loans of the previous period. These two equations are new and have not been discussed in the previous chapters.

In Equation (6) the firm sector determines the price of goods (P_t), the number of goods to purchase for investment purposes (INV_t), the planned level of production (Y_t^p), the wage rate (W_t), the amount of money to borrow (LF_t), the maximum number of worker hours to pay for in the period $(HPFMAX_t)$, and the maximum number of goods to sell in the period $(XFMAX_t)$. The unconstrained demands for investment goods $(INVUN_t)$ and for loans $(LFUN_t)$ are also by-products of the decisions of the firm sector. Two of the important determinants of the decision variables of the firm sector are the current loan rate (RL_t) and the current loan constraint $(LFMAX_t)$, both of which are available from the bank sector's decisions. As can be seen from Table 3-4 (Chapter Three), other important determinants of the decision variables are the lagged values of the price level (P_{t-1}), the inventory-sales ratio $(V_{t-1}/\beta_1 X_{t-1})$, the sales level (X_{t-1}), the amounts of excess labor (HPF_{t-1}/MH_{t-1}) and excess capital $(K_{t-1}^a/KMIN_{t-1})$ on hand, the wage rate (W_{t-1}), and the aggregate unconstrained $(HPUN_{t-1})$ and constrained (HP_{t-1}) supplies of labor.

In Equation (7) the household sector determines the unconstrained supply of labor $(HPHUN_{1t}$ and $HPHUN_{2t})$, the unconstrained demand for goods $(XHUN_{1t}$ and $XHUN_{2t})$, and the unconstrained demand for loans $(LHUN_t)$. In equations (8) and (9) the hours constraint is allocated to households 1 and 2 $(HPHMAX_{1t}$ and $HPHMAX_{2t})$. The allocation is based on the ratio of the household's unconstrained supply of labor for the current period to the total unconstrained supply of labor for the current period. The total number of hours to be allocated is the sum of the maximum number from the firm sector and the number the government chooses to pay for.

In Equations (10) and (11) the goods constraint is allocated to households 1 and 2 $(XHMAX_{1t}$ and $XHMAX_{2t})$. The allocation is based on the ratio of the household's unconstrained demand for goods for the current period to the total unconstrained demand for goods from the household sector for the current period. The total number of goods to be allocated is the maximum number the firm sector will sell, less the number of goods the firm sector chooses to purchase for investment purposes and the number the government chooses to purchase. As mentioned in Section 1.2 (Chapter One), the firm sector and the government are assumed to get all the goods that they want to purchase, and the household sector is the one that is assumed to be subject to a goods constraint. Equations (8) – (11) are new and have not been discussed in previous chapters.

In Equation (12) the household sector determines the constrained supply of labor (HPH_{1t} and HPH_{2t}), the constrained demand for goods (XH_{1t} and XH_{2t}), and the constrained demand for loans (LH_t). The loan, hours, and goods constraints for the current period are important determinants of the decision variables of the household sector, all the information on the constraints being available from the prior decisions of the bank and firm sectors and the government. As can be seen from Table 4-6 (Chapter Four), other variables that may be important determinants of the decision variables, depending on the degree to which the constraints are binding, are the proportional tax parameter (d_3), the minimum guaranteed level of income (YG), the previous period's savings deposits (SD_{t-1}) and loans (LH_{t-1}), and the current period's price of goods (P_t), wage rate (W_t), bill rate (r_t), loan rate (RL_t), and stock price (PS_t).

After the household sector makes its decisions in Equation (12), transactions take place. Equations (13) through (64) refer to these transactions and complete the determination of all the variables in the model. Equations (13)-(15) define the aggregate unconstrained demand for goods, demand for loans, and supply of labor, respectively, and Equations (16)-(18) do likewise for the total constrained quantities. The constrained quantities are the actual quantities traded in the period. Equation (19) determines the actual number of worker hours that the firm sector receives, which is the difference between the total number of hours supplied and the number purchased by the government. The government receives all the labor that it wants in the period, and the firm sector receives the rest. Equation (20) defines the actual number of machines on hand in the current period.

Equations (21)-(29) determine the output and inventory levels of the firm sector. Equation (21) defines the level of inventories that would exist if the firm sector produced the amount planned. Equations (22)-(27) determine the level of worker hour requirements for the planned output. If this level is less than the number of worker hours on hand, then the actual values of production and inventories are the planned values (Equation (28)). If the level is greater than the number of worker hours on hand, then the firm sector must produce less than originally planned. In this case the firm sector produces the maximum amount it can with the number of worker hours that it has on hand (Equation (29)). The computation of output (Y_t) in Equation (29) requires the solution of a quadratic equation in output.[a] Equation (30) then defines the minimum number of machines required to produce the output of the period.

Equations (31)-(37) determine the financial variables of the firm sector: depreciation, before-tax profits, taxes, dividends, total cash flow, cash flow net of taxes and dividends, and demand deposits. These equations have all been discussed in Chapter Three, and the only difference between the equations in Table 6-2 and the equations in Chapter Three is the change of notation for the condensed model.

Equations (38)-(41) determine the allocation of bills and bonds to the bank sector and the bond dealer. The bond dealer is assumed to hold no bills

(Equation (38)), so that all the government bills are allocated to the bank sector (Equation (39)). The bank sector holds the rest of its demand for bills and bonds in bonds (Equation (40)), and the bond dealer absorbs the difference between the supply of bonds from the government and the demand from the bank sector (Equation (41)). Since the bank sector is indifferent between holding bills or bonds, the allocation of VBB_t between bills and bonds can be done in any arbitrary way. The choice here was merely to assume that the bond dealer never held any bills, so that the bank sector always held all of the bills issued by the government. The rest of VBB_t was then allocated to bonds. This procedure assumes, of course, that VBB_t is always greater than $VBILLG_t$, which it was for the simulation results below.

  Enough information on bills and bonds is now available for the bond dealer to be able to determine the value of the bill rate and the value of the bond rate for the next period (Equation (42)). Equations (43)–(46) determine the other variables of the bond dealer: before-tax profits, taxes, dividends, and demand deposits. These equations are the same as the equations in Chapter Five.

  Equations (47) and (48) determine the demand deposits of the household sector, and Equation (49) determines the total level of demand deposits of the bank sector. Equations (50)–(52) determine the before-tax income, taxes, and savings of household 2. Equations (47)–(48) and (50)–(52) are the same as in Chapter Four, with the appropriate change of notation.

  Equations (53)–(62) form a system of ten linear simultaneous equations. The simultaneity comes about for two reasons. One reason is that the level of savings deposits of household 1 is a function of the level of dividends, while the level of dividends from the bank sector is a function of the level of savings deposits. The other reason is that the bond dealer needs to know the level of dividends for period t in order to set the stock price for period $t+1$, and yet the stock price for period $t+1$ is needed to compute the capital gains or losses of household 1 for period t. The level of capital gains or losses has an effect on the level of the savings deposits of household 1 and thus on the level of dividends of the bank sector. The level of capital gains has an effect on household 1's savings deposits because household 1 pays taxes on its capital gains, and the level of taxes has an effect on household 1's savings in the period. Capital losses, of course, have the opposite effect from capital gains. Since the level of dividends of the bank sector (which is the cause of both simultaneity problems) is small, the degree of simultaneity in the model is not very important, and no attempt was made to eliminate the simultaneity by specifying a more recursive structure.

  Equations (53)–(57) define the variables for household 1: capital gains or losses, before-tax income, taxes, savings net of capital gains or losses, and the level of savings deposits. These equations are the same as in Chapter Four, with the appropriate change of notation. Equations (58)–(60) define the variables for the bank sector: before-tax profits, taxes, and dividends. These equations are likewise the same as in Chapter Two, with the appropriate change of notation. Equation (61) defines the total level of dividends in the economy, and Equation (62) defines the stock price for the next period as set by the bond dealer.

Equation (63) determines the total value of taxes collected by the government. Equation (64) determines the level of bank reserves. Because of the government budget constraint, the level of bank reserves can be determined in two ways: one way using the equation for the government budget constraint, and one way using the definition of bank reserves as the sum of demand and savings deposits less the sum of loans and bills and bonds held. A good test that the model has been programmed correctly is to compute the level of bank reserves both ways in Equation (64) and check to see if both answers are the same.

Once the value of bank reserves for period t has been computed in Equation (64), enough information is available for the model to be solved for period $t+1$, starting with equation (2). The values computed for period t obviously have an important effect on the values for period $t+1$. The aggregate unconstrained demand for loans in Equation (14), for example, has a positive effect on the loan rate for the next period (Equation (2) in Table 2-4), and the aggregate unconstrained supply of labor in Equation (15) has a negative effect on the wage rate for the next period (statements [15] and [36] in Table 3-4). The aggregate unconstrained demand for goods in Equation (13) does not, however, have any effect on next period's values. As discussed in Chapter Three, the firm sector is assumed not to observe this demand. The unconstrained demand is computed in Equation (13) because values for it are presented in Table 6-6 below. The difference between the unconstrained and constrained demands for goods is one measure of the disequilibrium nature of the economy.

There are many links in the model between the financial variables and the real variables. Interest rates, for example, have an important influence on the decisions of the firm and household sectors, as does the loan constraint from the bank sector. The stock price also influences the decisions of household 1. The savings behavior of household 1, on the other hand, influences the decisions of the bank sector with a lag of one period. The borrowing behavior of the firm sector and household 2 also influences the decisions of the bank sector with a lag of one period.

One important property of the model, as stressed before, is that all of the flows of funds between the behavioral units have been accounted for. Accounting for these flows already provides important links between the real and financial sectors even without considering interest rate effects. In order to see the flow of funds constraints in the model more explicitly, the model has been translated in terms of the flow-of-funds accounts in Table 6-3. Except for the value of common stocks, which is an asset of the household sector, but not a liability of the bank, firm, and bond-dealer sectors, the total stock of assets in

Table 6-3.   Flow-of-Funds Accounts for the Condensed Model: Stocks of Assets and Liabilities

	Household Sector		Firm Sector		Bank Sector		Bond Dealer		Government	
	A	L	A	L	A	L	A	L	A	L
1. Demand Deposits	$\sum_{i=1}^{2} DDH_{it}$	—	DDF_t	—	—	DDB_t	DDD_t	—	—	—
2. Bank Reserves	—	—	—	—	BR_t	—	—	—	—	BR_t
3. Savings Deposits	SD_t	—	—	—	—	SD_t	—	—	—	—
4. Bank Loans	—	LH_t	—	LF_t	LB_t	—	—	—	—	—
5. Government Bills	—	—	—	—	$VBILLB_t$	—	$VBILLD_t$	—	—	$VBILLG_t$
6. Government Bonds	—	—	—	—	$VBONDB_t$	—	$VBONDD_t$	—	—	$VBONDG_t$
7. Common Stocks	PS_t	—	—	—	—	—	—	—	—	—

Note: Total Assets − PS_t = Total Liabilities

$$VBONDG_t = \frac{BONDG_t}{R_t}; \quad VBONDB_t = \frac{BONDB_t}{R_t}; \quad VBONDD_t = \frac{BONDD_t}{R_t}$$

Table 6-3 must equal the total stock of liabilities. This is another useful restriction that can be used to test whether the model has been programmed correctly.

The model can also be translated in terms of the national income accounts, and this is done in Table 6-4. On the income side, the capital gains or losses of the bank sector and the bond dealer must be subtracted from profits in the computation of the national income accounts definition of profits. Also, the national income accounts definition of profits must be adjusted for inventory valuation before being added to wages, capital consumption allowances, and net interest to compute gross national product on the income side. Another good test that the model has been programmed correctly is to compute gross national product in the three ways in Table 6-4 and check to see if all three answers are the same.

A natural definition of the unemployment rate in the model, denoted as UR_t, is

$$UR_t = 1 - \frac{HP_t}{HPUN_t},$$

(6.1)

where, as above, HP_t is the aggregate constrained supply of labor (and the actual amount traded) and $HPUN_t$ is the aggregate unconstrained supply of labor. On this definition it is possible for the unemployment rate to be negative. If household 2 is constrained in its borrowing behavior, but not in the number of hours that it can work, then, as described in statement [10] in Table 4-6, the household chooses to work more. This means that the unconstrained supply of labor of household 2 in this case is less than the constrained supply, which, depending on the values for household 1, can cause the aggregate unemployment rate to be negative. There is, of course, no frictional unemployment in the model, so that "full employment" corresponds to a zero unemployment rate. The fact that there is no frictional unemployment in the model is a consequence of not treating search as a decision variable of the households.

The only important exogenous variables in the model are the government values presented in Equation (2) in Table 6-2. One useful way of analyzing the properties of the model is to see how the model responds to various changes in these variables, and the purpose of the next section is to carry out such an analysis. Because of the complexity of even the condensed version of the model, the properties of the model cannot be shown in any convenient graphical way. The condensed model consists of a set of difference equations along with algorithms for determining some of the key variables of the model. The non-condensed model consists of a set of difference equations along with a set of optimal control problems that are solved each period to determine some

Table 6–4.   National Income Accounts for the Condensed Model

Expenditure Side

(1)   Consumption (real) = $XH_{1t} + XH_{2t}$
(2)   Consumption (money) = $P_t(XH_{1t} + XH_{2t})$
(3)   Fixed Investment (real) = INV_t
(4)   Fixed Investment (money) = $P_t INV_t$
(5)   Government Expenditures on Goods (real) = XG_t
(6)   Government Expenditures on Goods (money) = $P_t XG_t$
(7)   Government Expenditures on Labor (real) = HPG_t
(8)   Government Expenditures on Labor (money) = $W_t HPG_t$
(9)   Inventory Investment (real) = $V_t - V_{t-1}$
(10)   Inventory Investment (money) = $P_t(V_t - V_{t-1})$
　　　Gross National Product (real) = (1) + (3) + (5) + (7) + (9)
　　　Gross National Product (money) = (2) + (4) + (6) + (8) + (10)

Income Side

(1)   Wages = $W_t(HPH_{1t} + HPH_{2t})$
(2)   Before-Tax Profits Net of Capital Gains and Losses =

$$\Pi B_t - \left(\frac{BONDB_t}{R_{t+1}} - \frac{BONDB_t}{R_t}\right) + \Pi F_t + \Pi D_t - \left(\frac{BONDD_t}{R_{t+1}} - \frac{BONDD_t}{R_t}\right)$$

(3)   Inventory Valuation Adjustment = $-(P_t - P_{t-1})V_{t-1}$
(4)   Profits and Inventory Valuation Adjustment = (2) + (3)
(5)   Capital Consumption Allowances = DEP_t
(6)   Net Interest = $r_t SD_t - RL_t LH_t - BONDG_t - r_t VBILLG_t$
　　　Gross National Product (money) = (1) + (4) + (5) + (6)

Production Side

(1)   Production of Goods (real) = Y_t
(2)   Production of Goods (money) = $P_t Y_t$
(3)   Government Expenditures on Labor (real) = HPG_t
(4)   Government Expenditures on Labor (money) = $W_t HPG_t$
　　　Gross National Product (real) = (1) + (3)
　　　Gross National Product (money) = (2) + (4)

of the key variables. Since neither of these versions is open to any convenient graphical analysis, one must resort to analyzing the properties of the model by means of computer simulation, as is done in the next section.

6.2   THE RESPONSE OF THE MODEL TO SHOCKS FROM A POSITION OF EQUILIBRIUM

In this section the results of twelve experiments will be described. Each of the experiments corresponds to changing one or two government values for period t. The twelve experiments are:

1.   A decrease in the number of goods purchased by the government in period t (XG_t: -5.0).

2. An increase in the value of bills issued in period t ($VBILLG_t$: +5.0).
3. An increase in the number of goods purchased by the government in period t (XG_t: +5.0).
4. A decrease in the value of bills issued in period t ($VBILLG_t$: -5.0).
5. A combination of experiments 1 and 4 (XG_t: -5.0 and $VBILLG_t$: -5.0).
6. A combination of experiments 2 and 3 (XG_t: +5.0 and $VBILLG_t$: +5.0).
7. An increase in the personal income tax parameter in period t (d_3: +0.00554 in period t).
8. A decrease in the personal income tax parameter in period t (d_3: -0.00554 in period t).
9. A decrease in the minimum guaranteed level of income in period t (YG: -2.5 in period t).
10. An increase in the minimum guaranteed level of income in period t (YG: +2.5 in period t).
11. A decrease in the number of worker hours paid for by the government in period t (HPG_t: -5.0).
12. An increase in the number of worker hours paid for by the government in period t (HPG_t: +5.0).

For all the experiments only the government values for period t were changed. The values for periods $t+1$ and beyond were changed back to the original values. It should be noted, however, that when the tax parameters d_3 and YG were changed in period t, the households were assumed to expect in period t that the change would be permanent. Then in period $t+1$, when the original value was returned to, the households were assumed to expect that the original value would be permanent.

It is also important to note that except for experiments 5 and 6, only one government variable was changed at a time. When, for example, the number of goods purchased by the government was decreased for period t in experiment 1, no change was made in either the value of bills or the number of bonds issued. This meant that any surplus in the government budget resulting from the decrease in spending led to a decrease in bank reserves. No results are presented in Table 6-6 of changing the number of bonds issued by the government ($BONDG_t$) and of changing the reserve requirement ratio (g_1), since the effects of these changes are similar to the effects of changing the value of bills issued.

The base run from which the changes were made was a run in which none of the variables changed from period to period. By an appropriate choice of the constant terms (in the equations in Tables 2-4, 3-4, and 4-6), the various parameter values, the initial conditions, and the government values, it was possible to concoct a run in which the model simply repeated itself each period. When the model repeats itself each period, it will be said to be in equilibrium. The experiments described in this section are thus characterized as experiments in which the model in period t is shocked from a prior position of equilibrium.

The shock is a one-period shock in the sense that the value of the shocked variable for periods t+1 and beyond is returned to the equilibrium value.

The parameter values, initial conditions, and government values that were used for the base run are presented in Table 6-5. Only the values that are needed to solve the model for period t are presented in the table. The run for period t is assumed to start with Equation (3) in Table 6-2, so that the values of r_t, R_t, and PS_t, which are set by the bond dealer near the end of period $t-1$, are presented in Table 6-5. The government values for period t and for all future periods are also presented in Table 6-5. One of the tricks involved in concocting a run that repeated itself was to choose the values of the constant terms in Equations (2) and (3) in Table 2-4, Equation (1) in Table 3-4, and Equations (2), (3), (1)′, and (2)′ in Table 4-6 in appropriate ways. Basically, what was done was to pick a consistent[b] set of values of the endogenous variables for period $t-1$ and then choose the values of the constant terms and a few of the other parameters so that this set would be the set of solution values for period t. Most of the parameter values in Table 6-5 are the same as were used for the simulation results in Chapters Two through Four. The adjustment-cost parameters β_2, β_3, and β_5 are, however, smaller in Table 6-5 than they are in Table 3-2. The firm sector is double the size of firm i in Chapter Three, and because the adjustment costs are deviations *squared,* doubling the size of firm i causes more than a doubling of the cost of any given aggregate deviation. Before, the aggregate deviation would be split between the two firms, but now it occurs all in the firm sector. Consequently, the values of the four parameters were lowered for the condensed model. The values for the endogenous variables were chosen, whenever possible, to be of the same order of magnitude as data that existed for the U.S. economy.

The results for the base run are presented in Table 6-6 for periods t, $t+1$, and $t+2$. The first three variables in the table are real GNP, the unemployment rate, and the government surplus or deficit. Real GNP is defined in Table 6-4, the unemployment rate is defined in Equation (6.1), and the government surplus or deficit is the left-hand side of Equation (1) in Table 5-2. Except for the last five variables, the remaining variables in Table 6-6 are presented in roughly the order in which they are determined in Table 6-2. Some of the less important variables in Table 6-2 have been omitted from Table 6-6 because of space limitations. A number of unconstrained values for the firm and household sectors are presented in Table 6-6, in addition to the maximum values and the constrained values, so that the reader can see how the constraints affect the decisions of the two sectors.

A number of expected or planned values are also presented in Table 6-6, in addition to the actual values, so that the reader can see when expectation errors have been made. *LBMAX*, for example, is the bank sector's expectation of the unconstrained and constrained demands for loans, and *LUN* and *L* are the actual unconstrained and constrained demands for loans, respectively. *L* cannot,

Table 6-5.   Parameter Values, Initial Conditions, and Government
Values for the Base Run in Table 6-6

The Government

$d_1 = 0.5$	$BONDG_{t-1} = 12.025$
$d_2 = 0.0028$	$BONDG_{t+k} = 12.025$ $(k=0,1,\ldots)$
$d_3 = 0.1934$	$HPG_{t+k} = 120.7$ $(k=0,1,\ldots)$
$g_1 = 0.1667$	$VBILLG_{t-1} = 185.0$
$g_2 = 0.2956$	$VBILLG_{t+k} = 185.0$ $(k=0,1,\ldots)$
$YG = 0.0$	$XG_{t+k} = 96.5$ $(k=0,1,\ldots)$

The Bond Dealer

$VBD^* = 30.0$	$r_t = 0.06500$
$\lambda = 0.25$	$R_t = 0.06500$
$BONDD_{t-1} = 1.95$	$VBILLD_{t-1} = 0.0$
$DDD_{t-1} = 30.0$	

The Bank Sector

$EMAXDD = 3.8$	$DDB_{t-1} = 192.2$
$EMAXSD = 20.2$	$LUN_{t-1} = 810.2$
$BR_{t-1} = 55.4$	$RL_{t-1} = 0.07500$

The Firm Sector

$DDF_2 = 5.0$	$HPF_{t-1} = 637.3$
$EMAXHP + EMAXMH = 25.5$	$HPF_{t-2} = 637.3$
$\bar{H} = 1.0$	$HPUN_{t-1} = 758.0$
$m = 10$	$INV_{t-1} = \ldots = INV_{t-m+1} = 50.0$
$\beta_1 = 0.125$	$K^a_{t-1} = 500.0$
$\beta_2 = 0.001$	$KMIN_{t-1} = 500.0$
$\beta_3 = 0.015$	$LF_{t-1} = 328.1$
$\beta_4 = 0.005$	$LFUN_{t-1} = 328.1$
$\beta_5 = 0.025$	$MH_{t-1} = 637.3$
$\beta_{14} = 0.07108$	$P_{t-1} = \ldots = P_{t-m+1} = 1.0000$
$\lambda_1 = 1.3212$	$V_{t-1} = 105.3$
$\mu_1 = 1.684$	$W_{t-1} = 1.0000$
$HP_{t-1} = 758.0$	$X_{t-1} = 842.0$

Household 1

$\gamma_1 = 0.1609$	$PS_t = 1146.4$
$DDH_{1t-1} = 60.1$	$SD_{t-1} = 1013.4$
$DIV_{t-1} = \ldots = DIV_{t-4} = 74.5$	

Household 2

$\gamma_1 = 0.1609$	$LH_{t-1} = 482.1$
$DDH_{2t-1} = 51.8$	$LHUN_{t-1} = 482.1$

Table 6-6.   Results of Solving the Condensed Model

	Base Run t	t+1	t+2		t	t+1	t+2
Real GNP	962.7	962.7	962.7	X	842.0	842.0	842.0
UR	0.0000	0.0000	0.0000	LUN	810.2	810.1	810.1
Surplus (+)	0.0	0.0	0.0	L	810.2	810.1	810.1
or Deficit (−)				$HPUN$	758.0	758.0	758.0
r	0.06500	0.06500	0.06500	HP	758.0	758.0	758.0
PS	1146.4	1146.4	1146.4	HPF	637.3	637.3	637.3
$FUNDS^e$	1150.2	1150.2	1150.2	MH_4	0.0	0.0	0.0
RL	0.07500	0.07500	0.07500	Y	842.0	842.0	842.0
VBB	340.0	340.0	340.0	V	105.2	105.2	105.2
$LBMAX$	810.2	810.2	810.1	ΠF	130.1	130.1	130.1
$LHMAX$	482.1	482.1	482.1	$TAXF$	65.0	65.0	65.0
$LFMAX$	328.1	328.1	328.1	$\overline{CF}$	0.0	0.0	0.0
$LFUN$	328.1	328.1	328.1	DDF	50.3	50.3	50.3
PUN	1.0000	1.0000	1.0000	$VBILLB$	185.0	185.0	185.0
$INVUN$	50.0	50.0	50.0	$BONDB$	10.07	10.07	10.07
Y^PUN	842.0	842.0	842.0	$BONDD$	1.95	1.95	1.95
WUN	1.0000	1.0000	1.0000	ΠD	1.95	1.95	1.95
$HPFMAXUN$	637.3	637.3	637.3	$TAXD$	0.98	0.98	0.98
LF	328.1	328.1	328.1	CGD	0.00	0.00	0.00
P	1.0000	1.0000	1.0000	DDD	30.0	30.0	30.0
INV	50.0	50.0	50.0	DDH_1	60.1	60.1	60.1
Y^P	842.0	842.0	842.0	DDH_2	51.8	51.8	51.8
X^e	842.0	842.0	842.0	DDB	192.2	192.2	192.2
V^P	105.2	105.2	105.2	YH_2	435.0	435.0	435.0
W	1.0000	1.0000	1.0000	$TAXH_2$	77.1	77.1	77.1
$HPFMAX$	637.3	637.3	637.3	SAV_2	0.0	0.0	0.0
$K^a/KMIN^P$	1.000	1.000	1.000	CG	0.0	0.0	0.0
$HPFMAX/MH^P$	1.000	1.000	1.000	YH_1	463.4	463.4	463.4
MH_4^P	0.0	0.0	0.0	$TAXH_1$	89.6	89.6	89.6
$HPHUN_1$	323.0	323.0	323.0	SAV_1	0.0	0.0	0.0
$XHUN_1$	373.8	373.8	373.8	SD	1013.3	1013.3	1013.3
$HPHUN_2$	435.0	435.0	435.0	CGB	0.0	0.0	0.0
$XHUN_2$	321.7	321.7	321.7	ΠB	17.0	17.0	17.0
$LHUN$	482.1	482.1	482.1	$TAXB$	8.5	8.5	8.5
$HPHMAX_1$	323.0	323.0	323.0	$DIVB$	8.5	8.5	8.5
$HPHMAX_2$	435.0	435.0	435.0	DIV	74.5	74.5	74.5
HPH_1	323.0	323.0	323.0	TAX	241.3	241.3	241.3
XH_1	373.8	373.8	373.8	BR	55.4	55.4	55.4
SD^P	1013.3	1013.3	1013.3	$BR**$	55.4	55.4	55.4
HPH_2	435.0	435.0	435.0	$V/(\beta_1 X)$	1.000	1.000	1.000
XH_2	321.7	321.7	321.7	HPF/MH	1.000	1.000	1.000
LH	482.1	482.1	482.1	$K^a/KMIN$	1.000	1.000	1.000
XUN	842.0	842.0	842.0	$EXBB$	0.0	0.0	0.0

Table 6-6. (continued)

	Experiment 1 (XG_t:-5.0)						
	t	$t+1$	$t+2$		t	$t+1$	$t+2$
Real GNP	962.2	955.3	955.7	X	837.0	836.1	836.5
UR	0.0000	0.0035	0.0052	LUN	810.2	812.3	806.0
Surplus (+)	4.5	-4.7	-3.7	L	810.2	807.3	805.1
or Deficit (-)				$HPUN$	758.0	758.0	758.7
r	0.06500	0.06500	0.06505	HP	758.0	755.3	754.8
PS	1146.4	1145.6	1137.7	HPF	637.3	634.6	634.1
$FUNDS^e$	1150.2	1146.4	1146.8	MH_4	0.4	0.0	0.0
RL	0.07500	0.07507	0.07517	Y	841.5	834.6	835.0
VBB	340.0	338.9	339.0	V	109.7	108.3	106.8
$LBMAX$	810.2	807.5	807.8	ΠF	129.6	125.8	127.0
$LHMAX$	482.1	480.5	478.8	$TAXF$	64.8	62.9	63.5
$LFMAX$	328.1	327.0	329.0	$\overline{CF}$	-4.5	4.1	2.0
$LFUN$	328.1	330.8	326.3	DDF	45.8	48.7	50.1
PUN	1.0000	0.9979	0.9974	$VBILLB$	185.0	185.0	185.0
$INVUN$	50.0	48.9	49.4	$BONDB$	10.07	10.00	10.02
Y^pUN	842.0	837.3	835.0	$BONDD$	1.95	2.02	2.01
WUN	1.0000	0.9987	0.9961	ΠD	1.95	2.00	1.99
$HPFMAXUN$	637.3	636.6	634.1	$TAXD$	0.98	1.00	1.00
LF	328.1	326.8	326.3	CGD	0.00	-0.02	-0.02
P	1.0000	0.9985	0.9974	DDD	30.0	28.9	29.1
INV	50.0	47.3	49.4	DDH_1	60.1	59.9	59.7
Y^p	842.0	834.6	835.0	DDH_2	51.8	51.3	51.1
X^e	842.0	837.4	836.3	DDB	187.7	188.8	190.1
V^p	105.2	106.9	107.0	YH_2	435.0	432.7	431.6
W	1.0000	0.9977	0.9961	$TAXH_2$	77.1	76.7	76.5
$HPFMAX$	637.3	634.6	634.1	SAV_2	0.0	1.1	1.5
$K^a/KMIN^p$	1.000	1.003	1.002	CG	-0.8	-7.9	-6.0
$HPFMAX/MH^p$	1.000	1.004	1.003	YH_1	463.1	458.9	458.9
MH^p_4	0.0	0.0	0.0	$TAXH_1$	89.4	87.2	87.6
$HPHUN_1$	323.0	322.7	323.2	SAV_1	-0.1	-0.7	0.1
$XHUN_1$	373.8	373.5	373.0	SD	1013.3	1012.8	1013.1
$HPHUN_2$	435.0	435.3	435.6	CGB	0.0	-0.1	-0.1
$XHUN_2$	321.7	321.2	320.8	ΠB	17.0	16.7	16.6
$LHUN$	482.1	481.5	479.7	$TAXB$	8.5	8.3	8.3
$HPHMAX_1$	323.0	321.6	321.5	$DIVB$	8.5	8.3	8.3
$HPHMAX_2$	435.0	433.7	433.3	DIV	74.3	72.2	72.8
HPH_1	323.0	321.6	321.5	TAX	240.8	236.2	236.9
XH_1	373.8	372.9	372.2	BR	50.9	55.5	59.2
SD^p	1013.3	1013.1	1012.9	$BR**$	54.7	54.8	55.0
HPH_2	435.0	433.7	433.3	$V/(\beta_1 X)$	1.049	1.036	1.021
XH_2	321.7	319.3	318.4	HPF/MH	1.000	1.004	1.003
LH	482.1	480.5	478.8	$K^a/KMIN$	1.001	1.003	1.002
XUN	837.0	840.1	839.7	$EXBB$	0.0	1.1	0.9

Table 6-6.   (continued)

	Experiment 2 ($VBILLG_t$:+5.0)						
	t	$t+1$	$t+2$		t	$t+1$	$t+2$
Real GNP	962.7	961.7	958.7	X	842.0	838.5	837.8
UR	0.0000	0.0028	0.0035	LUN	810.2	809.2	808.9
Surplus (+)	-1.4	-0.4	-2.2	L	810.2	807.8	808.6
or Deficit (−)				$HPUN$	758.0	759.6	759.3
r	0.06500	0.06522	0.06524	HP	758.0	757.5	756.6
PS	1146.4	1142.0	1141.3	HPF	637.3	636.8	635.9
$FUNDS^e$	1150.2	1146.8	1149.2	MH_4	0.0	0.2	0.0
RL	0.07500	0.07516	0.07517	Y	842.0	841.0	838.0
VBB	340.0	339.0	339.7	V	105.2	107.8	107.9
$LBMAX$	810.2	807.8	809.5	ΠF	130.1	130.2	128.1
$LHMAX$	482.1	480.7	481.2	$TAXF$	65.0	65.1	64.1
$LFMAX$	328.1	327.1	328.3	$\overline{CF}$	0.0	-2.2	0.9
$LFUN$	328.1	328.1	329.2	DDF	50.3	47.1	49.1
PUN	1.0000	1.0002	0.9991	$VBILLB$	190.0	185.0	185.0
$INVUN$	50.0	50.0	49.4	$BONDB$	9.75	10.05	10.09
$Y^p UN$	842.0	842.0	838.6	$BONDD$	2.28	1.98	1.93
WUN	1.0000	1.0001	0.9982	ΠD	2.16	1.97	1.94
$HPFMAXUN$	637.3	637.3	636.4	$TAXD$	1.08	0.99	0.97
LF	328.1	327.1	328.2	CGD	-0.12	-0.01	0.01
P	1.0000	1.0004	0.9992	DDD	25.1	29.7	30.4
INV	50.0	49.6	49.0	DDH_1	60.1	60.0	59.8
Y^p	842.0	841.3	838.0	DDH_2	51.8	51.5	51.5
X^e	842.0	841.9	838.8	DDB	187.3	188.2	190.8
V^p	105.2	104.6	106.9	YH_2	435.0	434.3	433.1
W	1.0000	0.9998	0.9979	$TAXH_2$	77.1	77.0	76.8
$HPFMAX$	637.3	636.8	635.9	SAV_2	0.0	1.1	0.3
$K^a/KMIN^p$	1.000	1.000	1.002	CG	-4.4	-0.8	-3.3
$HPFMAX/MH^p$	1.000	1.000	1.003	YH_1	463.3	463.6	461.6
MH_4^p	0.0	0.0	0.0	$TAXH_1$	88.7	89.5	88.6
$HPHUN_1$	323.0	324.0	323.7	SAV_1	0.7	1.4	1.1
$XHUN_1$	373.8	373.0	372.7	SD	1014.1	1015.7	1017.0
$HPHUN_2$	435.0	435.6	435.6	CGB	-0.5	0.0	0.0
$XHUN_2$	321.7	321.1	320.8	ΠB	16.4	16.5	16.6
$LHUN$	482.1	481.0	479.8	$TAXB$	8.2	8.3	8.3
$HPHMAX_1$	323.0	323.1	322.5	$DIVB$	8.2	8.3	8.3
$HPHMAX_2$	435.0	434.4	434.0	DIV	74.3	74.4	73.3
HPH_1	323.0	323.1	322.5	TAX	240.2	240.9	238.8
XH_1	373.8	372.5	372.1	BR	51.8	57.2	59.4
SD^p	1013.3	1015.7	1017.3	$BR**$	54.6	54.7	55.2
HPH_2	435.0	434.4	434.0	$V/(\beta_1 X)$	1.000	1.028	1.031
XH_2	321.7	319.9	320.2	HPF/MH	1.000	1.000	1.002
LH	482.1	480.7	480.4	$K^a/KMIN$	1.000	1.000	1.002
XUN	842.0	840.5	839.3	$EXBB$	5.0	0.4	-0.4

Table 6-6.   (continued)

Experiment 3 (XG_t: +5.0)

	t	$t+1$	$t+2$		t	$t+1$	$t+2$
Real GNP	962.1	962.0	961.6	X	847.0	843.2	842.8
UR	0.0000	0.0000	0.0000	LUN	810.2	805.1	808.3
Surplus (+)	−5.5	0.4	−0.1	L	810.2	805.1	808.3
or Deficit (−)				$HPUN$	758.0	757.8	757.2
r	0.06500	0.06500	0.06494	HP	758.0	757.8	757.2
PS	1146.4	1145.6	1147.4	HPF	637.3	637.1	636.5
$FUNDS^e$	1150.2	1154.7	1151.3	MH_4	0.4	0.2	0.0
RL	0.07500	0.07492	0.07479	Y	841.4	841.3	840.9
VBB	340.0	341.3	340.3	V	99.7	97.7	95.8
$LBMAX$	810.2	813.4	811.0	ΠF	129.5	130.9	130.6
$LHMAX$	482.1	484.0	486.2	$TAXF$	64.8	65.4	65.3
$LFMAX$	328.1	329.4	324.8	$\overline{CF}$	5.6	0.3	1.8
$LFUN$	328.1	322.4	324.3	DDF	55.9	50.5	54.1
PUN	1.0000	1.0025	1.0037	$VBILLB$	185.0	185.0	185.0
$INVUN$	50.0	51.4	50.1	$BONDB$	10.07	10.16	10.09
Y^pUN	842.0	844.4	844.5	$BONDD$	1.95	1.86	1.94
WUN	1.0000	1.0022	1.0039	ΠD	1.95	1.89	1.94
$HPFMAXUN$	637.3	639.2	639.2	$TAXD$	0.98	0.94	0.97
LF	328.1	322.4	324.3	CGD	0.00	0.03	0.00
P	1.0000	1.0025	1.0037	DDD	30.0	31.3	30.2
INV	50.0	51.4	50.1	DDH_1	60.1	60.2	60.4
Y^p	842.0	844.4	844.5	DDH_2	51.8	51.9	52.0
X^e	842.0	846.4	843.0	DDB	197.8	194.0	196.7
V^p	105.2	97.7	99.3	YH_2	435.0	435.5	435.8
W	1.0000	1.0022	1.0039	$TAXH_2$	77.1	77.2	77.3
$HPFMAX$	637.3	639.2	639.2	SAV_2	0.0	−0.5	−1.2
$K^a/KMIN^p$	1.000	1.000	1.000	CG	−0.8	1.8	0.6
$HPFMAX/MH^p$	1.000	1.000	1.000	YH_1	463.1	464.6	464.8
MH^p_4	0.0	0.0	0.0	$TAXH_1$	89.4	90.2	90.0
$HPHUN_1$	323.0	323.2	323.2	SAV_1	−0.1	−0.1	−0.4
$XHUN_1$	373.8	373.5	373.9	SD	1013.3	1013.1	1012.5
$HPHUN_2$	435.0	434.6	434.1	CGB	0.0	0.1	0.0
$XHUN_2$	321.7	321.8	322.3	ΠB	17.0	16.8	16.8
$LHUN$	482.1	482.7	484.0	$TAXB$	8.5	8.4	8.4
$HPHMAX_1$	323.0	324.1	324.3	$DIVB$	8.5	8.4	8.4
$HPHMAX_2$	435.0	435.8	435.6	DIV	74.2	74.8	74.7
HPH_1	323.0	323.2	323.2	TAX	240.8	242.2	242.0
XH_1	373.8	373.5	373.9	BR	60.9	60.4	60.5
SD^p	1013.3	1013.2	1012.5	$BR**$	56.3	55.7	56.1
HPH_2	435.0	434.6	434.1	$V/(\beta_1 X)$	0.942	0.927	0.910
XH_2	321.7	321.8	322.3	HPF/MH	1.000	1.000	1.000
LH	482.1	482.7	484.0	$K^a/KMIN$	1.001	1.004	1.004
XUN	847.0	843.2	842.8	$EXBB$	0.0	−1.3	−0.2

Table 6-6.   (continued)

		Experiment 4 ($VBILLG$:-5.0)						
	t	$t+1$	$t+2$		t	$t+1$	$t+2$
Real GNP	962.7	960.4	961.5	X	842.0	843.1	842.5
UR	0.0000	0.0000	-0.0008	LUN	810.2	811.1	808.0
Surplus (+)	1.4	-0.6	-0.3	L	810.2	811.1	806.6
or Deficit (−)				$HPUN$	758.0	756.3	756.6
r	0.06500	0.06478	0.06477	HP	758.0	756.3	757.1
PS	1146.4	1150.9	1150.6	HPF	637.3	635.6	636.4
$FUNDS^e$	1150.2	1153.5	1150.6	MH_4	0.0	0.0	0.0
RL	0.07500	0.07484	0.07483	Y	842.0	839.7	840.8
VBB	340.0	340.9	340.1	V	105.2	101.8	100.1
$LBMAX$	810.2	812.5	810.5	ΠF	130.1	129.4	130.2
$LHMAX$	482.1	483.5	482.7	$TAXF$	65.0	64.7	65.1
$LFMAX$	328.1	329.1	327.8	$\overline{CF}$	0.0	3.5	1.6
$LFUN$	328.1	328.0	323.8	DDF	50.3	53.7	51.1
PUN	1.0000	0.9998	1.0010	$VBILLB$	180.0	185.0	185.0
$INVUN$	50.0	50.0	49.9	$BONDB$	10.40	10.10	10.05
Y^pUN	842.0	842.0	841.9	$BONDD$	1.63	1.92	1.98
WUN	1.0000	0.9999	1.0014	ΠD	1.71	1.93	1.97
$HPFMAXUN$	637.3	637.3	637.3	$TAXD$	0.85	0.96	0.98
LF	328.1	328.0	323.8	CGD	0.08	0.01	-0.01
P	1.0000	0.9998	1.0010	DDD	34.9	30.3	29.5
INV	50.0	50.0	49.9	DDH_1	60.1	60.2	60.3
Y^p	842.0	842.0	841.9	DDH_2	51.8	51.8	51.8
X^e	842.0	842.1	842.8	DDB	197.1	196.1	192.7
V^p	105.2	105.2	100.9	YH_2	435.0	434.3	435.5
W	1.0000	0.9999	1.0014	$TAXH_2$	77.1	77.0	77.2
$HPFMAX$	637.3	637.3	637.3	SAV_2	0.0	-1.0	0.3
$K^a/KMIN^p$	1.000	1.000	1.000	CG	4.4	-0.3	-0.3
$HPFMAX/MH^p$	1.000	1.000	1.000	YH_1	463.5	461.8	462.6
MH_4^p	0.0	0.0	0.0	$TAXH_1$	90.5	89.2	89.4
$HPHUN_1$	323.0	322.0	322.2	SAV_1	-0.8	-1.9	-1.7
$XHUN_1$	373.8	374.5	374.5	SD	1012.6	1010.6	1008.8
$HPHUN_2$	435.0	434.3	434.3	CGB	0.5	0.0	-0.1
$XHUN_2$	321.7	322.2	322.3	ΠB	17.6	17.4	17.0
$LHUN$	482.1	483.1	484.1	$TAXB$	8.8	8.7	8.5
$HPHMAX_1$	323.0	322.7	322.8	$DIVB$	8.8	8.7	8.5
$HPHMAX_2$	435.0	435.3	435.1	DIV	74.7	74.3	74.6
HPH_1	323.0	322.0	322.2	TAX	242.3	240.6	241.2
XH_1	373.8	374.5	374.5	BR	59.0	54.6	54.9
SD^p	1013.3	1010.7	1008.7	$BR**$	56.2	56.0	55.5
HPH_2	435.0	434.3	434.9	$V/(\beta_1 X)$	1.000	0.966	0.950
XH_2	321.7	322.2	321.5	HPF/MH	1.000	1.000	1.000
LH	482.1	483.1	482.7	$K^a/KMIN$	1.000	1.003	1.001
XUN	842.0	843.1	843.2	$EXBB$	-5.0	-0.3	0.5

Table 6-6. (continued)

Experiment 5 (XG_t:-5.0, $VBILLG_t$:-5.0)

	t	$t+1$	$t+2$		t	$t+1$	$t+2$
Real GNP	962.2	956.1	959.2	X	837.0	839.6	839.3
UR	0.0000	0.0007	0.0021	LUN	810.2	813.3	807.3
Surplus (+)	5.9	-4.4	-1.3	L	810.2	809.7	805.0
or Deficit (−)				$HPUN$	758.0	756.4	757.4
r	0.06500	0.06478	0.06482	HP	758.0	755.8	755.7
PS	1146.4	1150.1	1142.5	HPF	637.3	635.1	635.0
$FUNDS^e$	1150.2	1149.7	1147.9	MH_4	0.4	0.1	0.0
RL	0.07500	0.07491	0.07499	Y	841.5	835.4	838.5
VBB	340.0	339.8	339.3	V	109.7	105.5	104.7
$LBMAX$	810.2	809.9	808.6	ΠF	129.6	125.4	129.4
$LHMAX$	482.1	481.9	479.7	$TAXF$	64.8	62.7	64.7
$LFMAX$	328.1	328.0	328.8	$\overline{CF}$	-4.5	6.5	0.3
$LFUN$	328.1	330.8	325.2	DDF	45.8	52.1	49.9
PUN	1.0000	0.9977	0.9985	$VBILLB$	180.0	185.0	185.0
$INVUN$	50.0	48.9	50.2	$BONDB$	10.40	10.03	10.00
Y^pUN	842.0	837.3	838.5	$BONDD$	1.63	2.00	2.02
WUN	1.0000	0.9986	0.9980	ΠD	1.71	1.98	2.00
$HPFMAXUN$	637.3	636.6	635.0	$TAXD$	0.85	0.99	1.00
LF	328.1	327.8	325.2	CGD	0.08	-0.02	-0.03
P	1.0000	0.9981	0.9985	DDD	34.9	29.2	28.8
INV	50.0	47.7	50.2	DDH_1	60.1	60.1	60.0
Y^p	842.0	835.4	838.5	DDH_2	51.8	51.6	51.2
X^e	842.0	837.5	839.5	DDB	192.7	193.0	189.9
V^p	105.2	107.6	104.6	YH_2	435.0	433.4	433.1
W	1.0000	0.9979	0.9980	$TAXH_2$	77.1	76.8	76.8
$HPFMAX$	637.3	635.1	635.0	SAV_2	0.0	0.0	1.9
$K^a/KMIN^p$	1.000	1.003	1.000	CG	3.6	-7.5	-2.3
$HPFMAX/MH^p$	1.000	1.004	1.001	YH_1	463.2	458.6	460.6
MH_4^p	0.0	0.0	0.0	$TAXH_1$	90.3	87.2	88.6
$HPHUN_1$	323.0	321.8	322.4	SAV_1	-0.8	-2.2	-1.0
$XHUN_1$	373.8	374.4	373.9	SD	1012.5	1010.4	1009.4
$HPHUN_2$	435.0	434.6	434.9	CGB	0.5	-0.1	-0.1
$XHUN_2$	321.7	321.8	321.5	ΠB	17.6	17.1	16.8
$LHUN$	482.1	482.6	482.1	$TAXB$	8.8	8.6	8.4
$HPHMAX_1$	323.0	321.5	321.7	$DIVB$	8.8	8.6	8.4
$HPHMAX_2$	435.0	434.3	434.0	DIV	74.4	72.3	74.1
HPH_1	323.0	321.5	321.7	TAX	241.9	236.3	239.5
XH_1	373.8	374.3	373.6	BR	54.5	53.9	55.2
SD^p	1013.3	1010.7	1008.9	$BR**$	55.5	55.5	55.0
HPH_2	435.0	434.3	434.0	$V/(\beta_1 X)$	1.049	1.005	0.998
XH_2	321.7	321.1	319.0	HPF/MH	1.000	1.004	1.001
LH	482.1	481.9	479.7	$K^a/KMIN$	1.001	1.003	1.000
XUN	837.0	841.6	842.2	$EXBB$	-5.0	0.8	1.2

Table 6-6.   (continued)

Experiment 6 (XG_t:+5.0, $VBILLG_t$:+5.0)

	t	$t+1$	$t+2$		t	$t+1$	$t+2$
Real GNP	962.1	964.1	962.8	X	847.0	842.1	839.1
UR	0.0000	0.0000	0.0000	LUN	810.2	804.2	810.4
Surplus (+)	-6.8	0.9	1.0	L	810.2	804.2	806.9
or Deficit (-)				$HPUN$	758.0	759.5	758.3
r	0.06500	0.06522	0.06518	HP	758.0	759.5	758.3
PS	1146.4	1141.2	1143.0	HPF	637.3	638.8	637.6
$FUNDS^e$	1150.2	1151.4	1150.9	MH_4	0.4	0.4	0.1
RL	0.07500	0.07507	0.07495	Y	841.4	843.4	842.1
VBB	340.0	340.4	340.2	V	99.7	101.0	104.0
$LBMAX$	810.2	811.0	810.7	ΠF	129.5	131.4	131.8
$LHMAX$	482.1	482.6	485.6	$TAXF$	64.8	65.7	65.9
$LFMAX$	328.1	328.4	325.1	$\overline{CF}$	5.6	-3.0	-2.0
$LFUN$	328.1	322.5	328.5	DDF	55.9	47.3	47.7
PUN	1.0000	1.0027	1.0027	$VBILLB$	190.0	185.0	185.0
$INVUN$	50.0	51.4	50.2	$BONDB$	9.75	10.13	10.12
Y^pUN	842.0	844.4	844.7	$BONDD$	2.28	1.89	1.91
WUN	1.0000	1.0023	1.0026	ΠD	2.16	1.91	1.92
$HPFMAXUN$	637.3	639.2	639.3	$TAXD$	1.08	0.96	0.96
LF	328.1	322.5	325.0	CGD	-0.12	0.02	0.01
P	1.0000	1.0027	1.0032	DDD	25.1	31.0	30.7
INV	50.0	51.4	48.8	DDH_1	60.1	60.2	60.1
Y^p	842.0	844.4	842.4	DDH_2	51.8	51.8	51.8
X^e	842.0	846.3	842.0	DDB	192.9	190.3	190.4
V^p	105.2	97.7	101.4	YH_2	435.0	436.2	435.3
W	1.0000	1.0023	1.0017	$TAXH_2$	77.1	77.4	77.2
$HPFMAX$	637.3	639.2	637.6	SAV_2	0.0	0.5	-0.3
$K^a/KMIN^p$	1.000	1.000	1.000	CG	-5.2	1.8	2.3
$HPFMAX/MH^p$	1.000	1.000	1.000	YH_1	463.0	466.1	465.6
MH_4^p	0.0	0.0	0.0	$TAXH_1$	88.5	90.5	90.5
$HPHUN_1$	323.0	324.3	323.7	SAV_1	0.7	1.7	1.4
$XHUN_1$	373.8	372.9	372.6	SD	1014.0	1015.7	1017.1
$HPHUN_2$	435.0	435.2	434.6	CGB	-0.5	0.1	0.1
$XHUN_2$	321.7	321.3	321.2	ΠB	16.4	16.4	16.4
$LHUN$	482.1	481.7	481.9	$TAXB$	8.2	8.2	8.2
$HPHMAX_1$	323.0	324.4	323.7	$DIVB$	8.2	8.2	8.2
$HPHMAX_2$	435.0	435.5	434.6	DIV	74.1	74.8	75.1
HPH_1	323.0	324.3	323.7	TAX	239.7	242.7	242.8
XH_1	373.8	372.9	372.6	BR	57.2	61.4	60.4
SD^p	1013.3	1015.8	1017.1	$BR**$	55.5	55.1	55.1
HPH_2	435.0	435.2	434.6	$V/(\beta_1 X)$	0.942	0.959	0.992
XH_2	321.7	321.3	321.2	HPF/MH	1.000	1.000	1.000
LH	482.1	481.7	481.9	$K^a/KMIN$	1.001	1.001	1.000
XUN	847.0	842.1	840.5	$EXBB$	5.0	-1.0	-0.7

Table 6-6. (continued)

	Experiment 7 (d_3:+0.00554)						
	t	$t+1$	$t+2$		t	$t+1$	$t+2$
Real GNP	955.6	958.4	959.2	X	837.0	838.2	839.5
UR	-0.0015	0.0058	0.0041	LUN	812.9	806.2	806.2
Surplus (+)	2.0	-2.5	-0.5	L	810.2	806.5	806.8
or Deficit (-)				$HPUN$	751.9	759.5	758.5
r	0.06500	0.06500	0.06503	HP	753.0	755.1	755.4
PS	1146.4	1143.5	1139.8	HPF	632.3	634.4	634.7
$FUNDS^e$	1150.2	1147.9	1146.2	MH_4	0.4	0.0	0.0
RL	0.07500	0.07511	0.07504	Y	834.9	837.7	838.5
VBB	340.0	339.3	338.8	V	103.1	102.6	101.6
$LBMAX$	810.2	808.6	807.4	ΠF	128.0	128.0	130.6
$LHMAX$	482.1	482.2	482.7	$TAXF$	64.0	64.0	65.3
$LFMAX$	328.1	326.4	324.7	$\overline{CF}$	2.2	2.7	0.3
$LFUN$	328.1	324.2	324.1	DDF	52.5	51.3	51.5
PUN	1.0000	1.0000	1.0003	$VBILLB$	185.0	185.0	185.0
$INVUN$	50.0	47.5	50.5	$BONDB$	10.07	10.03	10.00
$Y^p UN$	842.0	837.7	838.5	$BONDD$	1.95	1.99	2.02
WUN	1.0000	1.0019	0.9990	ΠD	1.95	1.98	2.00
$HPFMAXUN$	637.3	634.4	634.7	$TAXD$	0.98	0.99	1.00
LF	328.1	324.2	324.1	CGD	0.00	-0.01	-0.02
P	1.0000	1.0000	1.0003	DDD	30.0	29.3	28.9
INV	50.0	47.5	50.5	DDH_1	59.8	60.1	59.9
Y^p	842.0	837.7	838.5	DDH_2	51.3	51.6	51.5
X^e	842.0	837.0	838.1	DDB	193.6	192.3	191.9
V^p	105.2	103.8	103.1	YH_2	433.4	434.0	432.8
W	1.0000	1.0019	0.9990	$TAXH_2$	79.0	76.9	76.7
$HPFMAX$	637.3	634.4	634.7	SAV_2	-0.5	0.2	-0.5
$K^a/KMIN^p$	1.000	1.000	1.000	CG	-2.9	-3.7	-0.3
$HPFMAX/MH^p$	1.000	1.000	1.000	YH_1	458.8	461.6	462.2
MH_4^p	0.0	0.0	0.0	$TAXH_1$	90.7	88.6	89.3
$HPHUN_1$	319.6	323.8	323.4	SAV_1	-3.7	-0.4	0.5
$XHUN_1$	371.8	374.5	372.9	SD	1010.0	1009.3	1010.0
$HPHUN_2$	432.3	435.7	435.1	CGB	0.0	-0.1	-0.1
$XHUN_2$	320.2	322.2	321.0	ΠB	17.2	17.0	16.8
$LHUN$	484.8	482.0	482.1	$TAXB$	8.6	8.5	8.4
$HPHMAX_1$	322.2	321.9	322.1	$DIVB$	8.6	8.5	8.4
$HPHMAX_2$	435.8	433.1	433.3	DIV	73.6	73.5	74.7
HPH_1	319.6	321.9	322.1	TAX	243.3	239.0	240.7
XH_1	371.8	373.5	372.2	BR	53.4	55.9	56.3
SD^p	1010.2	1009.2	1009.4	$BR**$	55.6	55.4	55.3
HPH_2	433.4	433.1	433.3	$V/(\beta_1 X)$	0.985	0.980	0.968
XH_2	318.7	320.7	320.3	HPF/MH	1.000	1.000	1.000
LH	482.1	482.2	482.7	$K^a/KMIN$	1.009	1.000	1.000
XUN	838.5	840.7	840.9	$EXBB$	0.0	0.7	1.1

Table 6-6.   (continued)

	t	$t+1$	$t+2$		t	$t+1$	$t+2$
		Experiment 8 (d_3:-0.00554)					
Real GNP	962.7	960.1	960.4	X	842.9	839.9	840.9
UR	0.0083	0.0000	0.0000	LUN	807.4	808.4	809.3
Surplus (+)	−5.0	0.8	−0.1	L	808.8	808.4	809.3
or Deficit (−)				$HPUN$	764.4	756.2	756.4
r	0.06500	0.06500	0.06496	HP	758.0	756.2	756.4
PS	1146.4	1146.0	1148.6	HPF	637.3	635.5	635.7
$FUNDS^e$	1150.2	1153.6	1153.5	MH_4	0.0	0.1	0.0
RL	0.07500	0.07487	0.07481	Y	842.0	839.4	839.7
VBB	340.0	341.0	341.0	V	104.3	103.8	102.7
$LBMAX$	810.2	812.6	812.5	ΠF	130.1	131.6	130.3
$LHMAX$	482.1	482.4	483.9	$TAXF$	65.0	65.8	65.2
$LFMAX$	328.1	330.2	328.7	$\overline{CF}$	0.9	0.3	2.1
$LFUN$	328.1	327.0	326.5	DDF	51.2	50.4	52.0
PUN	1.0000	1.0003	1.0000	$VBILLB$	185.0	185.0	185.0
$INVUN$	50.0	50.3	49.0	$BONDB$	10.07	10.14	10.13
Y^pUN	842.0	842.4	840.7	$BONDD$	1.95	1.88	1.89
WUN	1.0000	0.9970	0.9990	ΠD	1.95	1.90	1.91
$HPFMAXUN$	637.3	637.6	636.4	$TAXD$	0.98	0.95	0.95
LF	328.1	327.0	326.5	CGD	0.00	0.02	0.02
P	1.0000	1.0003	1.0000	DDD	30.0	31.0	30.8
INV	50.0	50.3	49.0	DDH_1	60.2	59.9	60.1
Y^p	842.0	842.4	840.7	DDH_2	51.8	51.6	51.8
X^e	842.0	842.8	840.0	DDB	193.2	192.9	194.7
V^p	105.2	104.0	104.5	YH_2	434.1	432.7	433.6
W	1.0000	0.9970	0.9990	$TAXH_2$	74.8	76.7	76.9
$HPFMAX$	637.3	637.6	636.4	SAV_2	1.4	−0.9	−1.2
$K^a/KMIN^p$	1.000	1.000	1.000	CG	−0.4	2.6	0.7
$HPFMAX/MH^p$	1.000	1.000	1.000	YH_1	464.3	462.3	462.5
MH_4^p	0.0	0.0	0.0	$TAXH_1$	87.1	89.9	89.6
$HPHUN_1$	326.6	322.2	322.3	SAV_1	2.7	−0.1	−0.7
$XHUN_1$	375.9	372.4	373.6	SD	1015.9	1016.1	1015.3
$HPHUN_2$	437.8	434.0	434.0	CGB	0.0	0.1	0.1
$XHUN_2$	323.3	320.7	321.8	ΠB	16.7	16.7	16.8
$LHUN$	479.3	481.4	482.8	$TAXB$	8.4	8.4	8.4
$HPHMAX_1$	323.9	323.1	322.6	$DIVB$	8.4	8.4	8.4
$HPHMAX_2$	434.1	435.3	434.4	DIV	74.4	75.1	74.5
HPH_1	323.9	322.2	322.3	TAX	236.3	241.8	241.0
XH_1	374.5	372.4	373.6	BR	60.4	59.5	59.7
SD^p	1016.0	1016.1	1015.5	$BR**$	55.6	55.5	55.8
HPH_2	434.1	434.0	434.0	$V/(\beta_1 X)$	0.990	0.989	0.977
XH_2	321.9	320.7	321.8	HPF/MH	1.000	1.000	1.000
LH	480.7	481.4	482.8	$K^a/KMIN$	1.000	1.004	1.001
XUN	845.7	839.9	840.9	$EXBB$	0.0	−1.0	−0.9

Table 6-6. (continued)

	Experiment 9 (YG:-2.5)						
	t	*t+1*	*t+2*		*t*	*t+1*	*t+2*
Real GNP	962.3	956.5	954.9	X	837.9	835.1	836.2
UR	0.0051	0.0022	0.0047	LUN	810.1	812.1	807.2
Surplus (+)	4.7	-2.8	-4.7	L	810.2	807.2	806.2
or Deficit (-)				$HPUN$	761.9	757.4	758.6
r	0.06500	0.06500	0.06505	HP	758.0	755.7	755.0
PS	1146.4	1145.9	1141.1	HPF	637.3	635.0	634.3
$FUNDS^e$	1150.2	1146.2	1145.0	MH_4	0.3	0.1	0.0
RL	0.07500	0.07507	0.07520	Y	841.6	835.8	834.2
VBB	340.0	338.8	338.4	V	109.0	109.7	107.7
$LBMAX$	810.2	807.4	806.5	ΠF	129.7	127.9	125.8
$LHMAX$	482.1	480.4	478.5	$TAXF$	64.9	63.9	62.9
$LFMAX$	328.1	327.0	328.0	$\overline{CF}$	-3.7	1.6	2.9
$LFUN$	328.1	330.3	327.6	DDF	46.6	46.8	50.5
PUN	1.0000	0.9983	0.9970	$VBILLB$	185.0	185.0	185.0
$INVUN$	50.0	49.1	49.1	$BONDB$	10.07	10.00	9.98
Y^pUN	842.0	838.1	834.2	$BONDD$	1.95	2.03	2.04
WUN	1.0000	0.9969	0.9955	ΠD	1.95	2.00	2.01
$HPFMAXUN$	637.3	636.7	634.3	$TAXD$	0.98	1.00	1.01
LF	328.1	326.8	327.6	CGD	0.00	-0.02	-0.03
P	1.0000	0.9987	0.9970	DDD	30.0	28.8	28.6
INV	50.0	47.7	49.1	DDH_1	59.9	59.8	59.7
Y^p	842.0	835.8	834.2	DDH_2	51.4	51.2	51.1
X^e	842.0	838.2	835.5	DDB	187.8	186.7	189.9
V^p	105.2	106.6	108.4	YH_2	434.7	432.4	431.7
W	1.0000	0.9960	0.9955	$TAXH_2$	79.6	76.6	76.5
$HPFMAX$	637.3	635.0	634.3	SAV_2	-0.4	1.5	1.8
$K^a/KMIN^p$	1.000	1.003	1.003	CG	-0.5	-4.8	-8.1
$HPFMAX/MX^p$	1.000	1.004	1.004	YH_1	463.5	459.4	458.0
MH_4^p	0.0	0.0	0.0	$TAXH_1$	92.0	87.9	87.0
$HPHUN_1$	325.0	322.3	322.9	SAV_1	-0.6	-0.4	-0.1
$XHUN_1$	372.9	372.7	373.0	SD	1013.1	1012.7	1012.7
$HPHUN_2$	436.9	435.1	435.7	CGB	0.0	-0.1	-0.1
$XHUN_2$	320.8	320.4	320.6	ΠB	17.0	16.7	16.6
$LHUN$	482.0	481.8	479.6	$TAXB$	8.5	8.3	8.3
$HPHMAX_1$	323.3	321.6	321.4	$DIVB$	8.5	8.3	8.3
$HPHMAX_2$	434.7	434.1	433.6	DIV	74.3	73.3	72.2
HPH_1	323.3	321.6	321.4	TAX	246.0	237.8	235.8
XH_1	372.1	372.3	372.3	BR	50.7	53.5	58.2
SD^p	1013.1	1012.8	1012.8	$BR**$	54.7	54.5	55.0
HPH_2	434.7	434.1	433.6	$V/(\beta_1 X)$	1.041	1.051	1.031
XH_2	319.3	318.6	318.3	HPF/MH	1.000	1.003	1.004
LH	482.1	480.4	478.5	$K^a/KMIN$	1.000	1.003	1.003
XUN	840.2	838.6	839.2	$EXBB$	0.0	1.2	1.4

Table 6-6.   (continued)

	Experiment 10 (YG:+2.5)						
	t	$t+1$	$t+2$		t	$t+1$	$t+2$
Real GNP	957.4	962.0	960.8	X	843.8	842.1	843.5
UR	0.0000	0.0007	0.0000	LUN	810.2	802.0	808.0
Surplus (+)	−7.0	0.2	−0.2	L	810.2	802.1	807.2
or Deficit (−)				$HPUN$	754.1	758.1	756.8
r	0.06500	0.06500	0.06493	HP	754.1	757.6	756.8
PS	1146.4	1144.3	1145.8	HPF	633.4	636.9	636.1
$FUNDS^e$	1150.2	1155.9	1150.6	MH_4	0.0	0.0	0.0
RL	0.07500	0.07490	0.07471	Y	836.7	841.3	840.1
VBB	340.0	341.7	340.1	V	98.2	97.4	94.0
$LBMAX$	810.2	814.2	810.5	ΠF	128.7	130.7	130.7
$LHMAX$	482.1	484.5	487.9	$TAXF$	64.4	65.4	65.4
$LFMAX$	328.1	329.7	322.6	$\overline{CF}$	7.0	0.9	2.3
$LFUN$	328.1	319.2	323.3	DDF	57.3	49.3	55.0
PUN	1.0000	1.0024	1.0035	$VBILLB$	185.0	185.0	185.0
$INVUN$	50.0	49.6	51.2	$BONDB$	10.07	10.18	10.07
$Y^p UN$	842.0	841.3	843.3	$BONDD$	1.95	1.84	1.95
WUN	1.0000	1.0032	1.0037	ΠD	1.95	1.87	1.95
$HPFMAXUN$	637.3	636.9	638.4	$TAXD$	0.98	0.94	0.98
LF	328.1	319.2	322.6	CGD	0.00	0.03	0.00
P	1.0000	1.0024	1.0036	DDD	30.0	31.7	29.9
INV	50.0	49.6	50.9	DDH_1	60.3	60.3	60.3
Y^p	842.0	841.3	842.8	DDH_2	51.9	52.0	52.1
X^e	842.0	843.2	841.8	DDB	199.5	193.3	197.3
V^p	105.2	96.3	98.4	YH_2	433.1	435.7	435.2
W	1.0000	1.0032	1.0035	$TAXH_2$	74.3	77.3	77.2
$HPFMAX$	637.3	636.9	638.1	SAV_2	0.1	−0.7	−1.7
$K^a/KMIN^p$	1.000	1.000	1.000	CG	−2.1	1.5	0.4
$HPFMAX/MX^p$	1.000	1.000	1.000	YH_1	460.7	464.8	464.6
MH_4^p	0.0	0.0	0.0	$TAXH_1$	86.2	90.2	89.9
$HPHUN_1$	321.0	323.5	323.1	SAV_1	−0.2	−0.1	−0.4
$XHUN_1$	374.7	373.9	373.7	SD	1013.0	1012.9	1012.5
$HPHUN_2$	433.1	434.6	433.7	CGB	0.0	0.2	0.0
$XHUN_2$	322.6	322.3	322.4	ΠB	17.0	16.6	16.6
$LHUN$	482.1	482.8	484.7	$TAXB$	8.5	8.3	8.3
$HPHMAX_1$	322.6	323.3	323.9	$DIVB$	8.5	8.3	8.3
$HPHMAX_2$	435.3	434.3	434.8	DIV	73.8	74.6	74.7
HPH_1	321.0	323.3	323.1	TAX	234.3	242.1	241.8
XH_1	374.7	373.8	373.7	BR	62.4	62.1	62.4
SD^p	1013.2	1013.0	1012.3	$BR**$	56.6	55.6	56.2
HPH_2	433.1	434.3	433.7	$V/(\beta_1 X)$	0.931	0.925	0.891
XH_2	322.6	322.2	322.4	HPF/MH	1.000	1.000	1.000
LH	482.1	482.9	484.7	$K^a/KMIN$	1.006	1.000	1.003
XUN	843.8	842.3	843.8	$EXBB$	0.0	−1.7	0.1

Table 6-6. (continued)

	Experiment 11 (HPG$_t$:-5.0)						
	t	*t+1*	*t+2*		*t*	*t+1*	*t+2*
Real GNP	957.5	958.0	955.6	X	839.0	835.9	836.4
UR	0.0066	0.0013	0.0039	LUN	810.2	811.5	808.2
Surplus (+)	3.9	-1.5	-4.2	L	810.2	807.7	806.6
or Deficit (-)				HPUN	758.0	757.2	758.3
r	0.06500	0.06500	0.06504	HP	753.0	756.2	755.3
PS	1146.4	1146.2	1143.6	HPF	637.3	635.5	634.6
FUNDS^e	1150.2	1146.9	1145.1	MH$_4$	0.1	0.1	0.0
RL	0.07500	0.07506	0.07517	Y	841.8	837.3	834.9
VBB	340.0	339.0	338.5	V	108.1	109.4	107.9
LBMAX	810.2	807.8	806.6	ΠF	129.9	129.1	126.3
LHMAX	482.1	480.7	478.9	TAXF	64.9	64.6	63.2
LFMAX	328.1	327.2	327.7	$\overline{CF}$	-2.8	0.3	2.6
LFUN	328.1	329.7	328.2	DDF	47.5	46.7	50.0
PUN	1.0000	0.9987	0.9974	VBILLB	185.0	185.0	185.0
INVUN	50.0	49.3	49.1	BONDB	10.07	10.01	9.98
Y^{p}UN	842.0	839.1	835.3	BONDD	1.95	2.01	2.04
WUN	1.0000	0.9966	0.9960	ΠD	1.95	1.99	2.01
HPFMAXUN	637.3	636.9	634.9	TAXD	0.98	1.00	1.01
LF	328.1	327.0	327.7	CGD	0.00	-0.02	-0.03
P	1.0000	0.9991	0.9975	DDD	30.0	29.0	28.7
INV	50.0	48.3	48.9	DDH$_1$	60.0	59.8	59.8
Y^p	842.0	837.3	834.9	DDH$_2$	51.4	51.3	51.1
X^e	842.0	839.2	836.3	DDB	188.9	186.9	189.6
V^p	105.2	106.2	108.0	YH$_2$	432.1	432.6	432.0
W	1.0000	0.9959	0.9958	TAXH$_2$	76.6	76.7	76.6
HPFMAX	637.3	635.5	634.6	SAV$_2$	-0.3	1.2	1.6
K^a/KMIN^p	1.000	1.002	1.003	CG	-0.2	-2.6	-7.3
HPFMAX/MH^p	1.000	1.003	1.004	YH$_1$	461.1	460.3	458.5
MH$_4^p$	0.0	0.0	0.0	TAXH$_1$	89.1	88.5	87.3
HPHUN$_1$	323.0	322.2	322.7	SAV$_1$	-0.7	-0.2	-0.2
XHUN$_1$	373.8	372.5	373.0	SD	1012.8	1012.8	1012.6
HPHUN$_2$	435.0	435.0	435.6	CGB	0.0	-0.1	-0.1
XHUN$_2$	321.7	320.2	320.6	ΠB	17.0	16.7	16.6
LHUN	482.1	481.8	479.9	TAXB	8.5	8.4	8.3
HPHMAX$_1$	320.9	321.8	321.5	DIVB	8.5	8.4	8.3
HPHMAX$_2$	432.1	434.4	433.8	DIV	74.4	73.9	72.5
HPH$_1$	320.9	321.8	321.5	TAX	240.2	239.1	236.4
XH$_1$	372.7	372.3	372.4	BR	51.5	53.0	57.2
SD^p	1012.8	1012.7	1012.7	BR **	54.8	54.5	55.0
HPH$_2$	432.1	434.4	433.8	V/(β$_1$X)	1.031	1.047	1.032
XH$_2$	319.7	318.9	318.6	HPF/MH	1.000	1.002	1.004
LH	482.1	480.7	478.9	K^a/KMIN	1.000	1.002	1.003
XUN	842.0	838.5	839.3	EXBB	0.0	1.0	1.4

Table 6-6.   (continued)

	Experiment 12 (HPG_t:+5.0)						
	t	$t+1$	$t+2$		t	$t+1$	$t+2$
Real GNP	961.0	960.7	960.8	X	842.0	841.2	843.8
UR	0.0000	0.0020	0.0000	LUN	810.2	802.0	807.3
Surplus (+)	−6.5	−0.5	−0.3	L	810.2	802.4	807.3
or Deficit (−)				$HPUN$	758.0	758.3	756.9
r	0.06500	0.06500	0.06493	HP	758.0	756.7	756.9
PS	1146.4	1143.9	1144.3	HPF	632.3	636.0	636.2
$FUNDS^e$	1150.2	1155.5	1150.8	MH_4	0.0	0.0	0.1
RL	0.07500	0.07490	0.07471	Y	835.3	840.0	840.1
VBB	340.0	341.6	340.2	V	98.6	97.4	93.7
$LBMAX$	810.2	813.9	810.7	ΠF	128.4	130.1	130.6
$LHMAX$	482.1	484.3	488.0	$TAXF$	64.2	65.0	65.3
$LFMAX$	328.1	329.6	322.6	$\overline{CF}$	6.7	2.0	2.2
$LFUN$	328.1	319.2	322.3	DDF	57.0	50.1	55.4
PUN	1.0000	1.0020	1.0031	$VBILLB$	185.0	185.0	185.0
$INVUN$	50.0	48.8	51.3	$BONDB$	10.07	10.18	10.08
Y^pUN	842.0	840.0	842.1	$BONDD$	1.95	1.85	1.95
WUN	1.0000	1.0032	1.0030	ΠD	1.95	1.88	1.95
$HPFMAXUN$	637.3	636.0	637.5	$TAXD$	0.98	0.94	0.97
LF	328.1	319.2	322.3	CGD	0.00	0.03	0.00
P	1.0000	1.0020	1.0031	DDD	30.0	31.5	30.0
INV	50.0	48.8	51.3	DDH_1	60.1	60.3	60.3
Y^p	842.0	840.0	842.1	DDH_2	51.8	51.9	52.0
X^e	842.0	841.5	840.9	DDB	198.9	193.8	197.7
V^p	105.2	97.1	98.6	YH_2	435.0	435.1	435.0
W	1.0000	1.0032	1.0030	$TAXH_2$	77.1	77.2	77.1
$HPFMAX$	637.3	636.0	637.5	SAV_2	0.0	−1.0	−1.7
$K^a/KMIN^p$	1.000	1.000	1.000	CG	−2.5	0.4	0.3
$HPFMAX/MH^p$	1.000	1.000	1.000	YH_1	462.5	464.1	464.5
MH_4^p	0.0	0.0	0.0	$TAXH_1$	89.0	89.8	89.9
$HPHUN_1$	323.0	323.6	323.2	SAV_1	−0.2	−0.3	−0.3
$XHUN_1$	373.8	374.1	373.7	SD	1013.2	1012.7	1012.4
$HPHUN_2$	435.0	434.6	433.7	CGB	0.0	0.2	0.0
$XHUN_2$	321.7	322.4	322.3	ΠB	17.0	16.6	16.7
$LHUN$	482.1	482.8	485.0	$TAXB$	8.5	8.4	8.3
$HPHMAX_1$	325.1	323.0	323.7	$DIVB$	8.5	8.3	8.3
$HPHMAX_2$	437.9	433.8	434.5	DIV	73.7	74.3	74.6
HPH_1	323.0	323.0	323.2	TAX	239.8	241.3	241.6
XH_1	373.8	373.8	373.7	BR	61.9	62.4	62.7
SD^p	1013.3	1012.9	1012.2	$BR**$	56.5	55.7	56.3
HPH_2	435.0	433.8	433.7	$V/(\beta_1 X)$	0.937	0.926	0.888
XH_2	321.7	322.1	322.3	HPF/MH	1.000	1.000	1.000
LH	482.1	483.2	485.0	$K^a/KMIN$	1.008	1.000	1.002
XUN	842.0	841.9	843.8	$EXBB$	0.0	−1.6	0.0

of course, be greater than $LBMAX$, although LUN can be. Both can be less than $LBMAX$. $FUNDS^e$ in Table 6-6 is the bank sector's expected level of loanable funds. The actual level of loanable funds is $FUNDS^e$ of the previous period.

Y^p is the firm sector's planned output, and Y is the actual output, Y cannot be greater than Y^p, but it can be less if the firm sector gets less labor than it expected or if its worker hour requirements are greater than expected. $HPFMAX$ is the firm sector's expected quantity of labor, and HPF is the actual quantity of labor received. MH_4^p is the number of worker hours needed to meet the expected change in sales, and MH_4 is the number of worker hours needed to meet the actual change in sales. X^e is the expected level of sales, and X is the actual level of sales. $K^a/KMIN^p$ is the planned ratio of excess capital, and $K^a/KMIN$ is the actual ratio. The actual ratio can be greater than the planned ratio if the firm sector is forced to produce less output. $HPFMAX/MH^p$ is the planned ratio of excess labor, and HPF/MH is the actual ratio. The actual ratio can differ from the planned ratio since HPF can be less than $HPFMAX$ and MH can differ from MH^p. SD^p is the planned level of savings deposits of household 1, and SD is the actual level. The planned level is based on household 1's expectation of the dividend level for the period and on its expectation of the value of capital gains or losses. Since both these expectations may be incorrect, SD can differ from SD^p.

The fifth-to-last variable in Table 6-6, BR^{**}, is the bank sector's desired level of reserves. The desired level of reserves is equal to the required level of reserves plus the planned level of excess reserves, the latter being equal to $(1-g_1)EMAXDD + EMAXSD$. The difference between the desired level of reserves and BR, the actual level of reserves, is a measure of the disequilibrium situation of the bank sector. The fourth-to-last variable in Table 6-6, $V/\beta_1 X$, is the ratio of the actual level of inventories to the level corresponding to no inventory adjustment costs. This variable is used in the price equation (Equation (1) in Table 3-4) and is a measure of the inventory situation of the firm sector. The last variable in Table 6-6 is the difference between the supply of bills and bonds from the government ($VBILLG + BONDG/R$) and the sum of the demand for bills and bonds from the bank sector and the desired value of bills and bonds of the bond dealer ($VBB + VBD^*$). This variable is a measure of the excess supply of bills and bonds and is used by the bond dealer in setting the bill rate for the next period. No values for the goods constraints, $XHMAX_1$ and $XHMAX_2$, are presented in Table 6-6 because these constraints were not binding on the households for any of the experiments.

The self-repeating or equilibrium nature of the base run is evident from the results in Table 6-6. The value of each variable is the same for all three periods. Also, the unconstrained demand for loans (LUN) is equal to the maximum allowed ($LBMAX$), and the unconstrained supply of labor ($HPUN$) is equal to the maximum allowed ($HPFMAX + HPG$). BR is equal to BR^{**}, and there is no excess labor, no excess capital, and no excess supply of bills and bonds. All the planned or expected values are equal to the actual values, and all the unconstrained values are equal to the actual values.

The following discussion is a verbal summary of the results of the twelve experiments in Table 6-6. It is obviously not practical to discuss all the results in detail, and many of the results are left to the reader to read from the table. It should be stressed again, as was done in Section 1.3 (Chapter One), that the results in the table are only meant to aid in understanding the properties of the model and are not meant to be a test of the validity of the model. Although in some cases the initial conditions were chosen to be of the same order of magnitude as data that existed for the U.S. economy, none of the parameter values in the model has been estimated from any data.

Experiment 1:   A Decrease in the Number of Goods Purchased by the Government in Period t (XG_t: -5.0)

The results of the first experiment are presented next in Table 6-6. The decision of the government to purchase fewer goods in period t had no effect on the decisions of the behavioral units for period t. When transactions took place in period t, however, the level of sales of the firm sector was less by 5.0 ($X_t = 837.0$). Compared with the values for the base run, the decrease in sales in period t had the following other effects in the period. Worker hour requirements to handle fluctuations in sales (MH_{4t}) increased by 0.4 from the expected level of 0.0, which forced the firm sector to produce 0.5 fewer goods than originally planned ($Y_t = 841.5$ vs. $Y_t^p = 842.0$). The level of inventories increased by 4.5 ($V_t = 109.7$), corresponding to the sales decrease of 5.0 and the production decrease of 0.5. The profits of the firm sector decreased by 0.5 ($\Pi F_t = 129.6$), corresponding to the decrease in production of 0.5.

Since the firm sector pays out all its profits in the form of taxes and dividends and since the profit tax is 0.5, half the decrease in profits took the form of a decrease in taxes of the firm sector and half took the form of a decrease in dividends. The cash flow net of taxes and dividends of the firm sector ($\overline{CF_t}$) was -4.5, which meant that the demand deposits of the firm sector decreased by 4.5 ($DDF_t = 45.8$). Near the end of period t the bond dealer set the same bill and bond rates for period $t+1$ as existed for period t, since the excess supply of bills and bonds in period t was zero, but it lowered the stock price for period $t+1$ by 0.8 as a result of the decrease in dividends in period t. Household 1 thus received less dividend income in period t and also suffered a capital loss. This caused it to have to pay less in taxes in period t.

The net result of the decrease in dividend income and taxes was an unintended dissavings of 0.1 on the part of household 1, which caused its savings deposits to decrease by 0.1 ($SD_t = 1013.3$ vs. $SD_t^p = 1013.4$). The total tax intake of the government decreased by 0.5, causing the surplus to be 4.5 rather than the 5.0 that it would have been had there been no decrease in taxes. Bank reserves then also decreased by 4.5 ($BR_t = 50.9$). The decrease in bank reserves took the form of a decrease in demand deposits of the firm sector of slightly less than 4.5 and a decrease in the savings deposits of household 1 of slightly less than 0.1.[c]

The action of the government in period t thus decreased sales by 5.0 and decreased bank reserves by 4.5. Had the firm sector not been forced to cut production by 0.5 because of the increased worker hour requirements, profits would have remained unchanged, as would have firm taxes and dividends. Had dividends remained unchanged, the stock price for period $t+1$ would not have been changed, and so household 1 would not have been affected in any way. In this case all that would have happened in period t as a result of the decrease in sales would have been a decrease in the demand deposits of the firm sector of 5.0 and a corresponding decrease in bank reserves of 5.0. Although the decrease in taxes of 0.5 in period t for this experiment is small and not too important, it does provide a good indication of how taxes are affected when profits decrease. When profits decrease, capital losses are suffered by household 1, so that household 1 pays less in taxes both because of lower dividend income and because of the capital losses. This decrease in taxes is in addition to the direct decrease in profit taxes of the firm sector.

Another important point to get out of the example so far is that the level of savings deposits of household 1 can turn out to be different from what the household had originally planned. In this example, household 1 had planned to have savings deposits in period t (SD_t^p) of 1013.4, but ended up having savings deposits (SD_t) of 1013.3. Unintended savings or dissavings (net of capital gains and losses) on the part of household 1 occurs whenever the level of dividends and the stock price turn out to be different from what the household expected. An unintended change in dividend income affects savings directly. An unintended change in the stock price does not affect before-tax income net of capital gains and losses, but it does affect after-tax income (and thus savings) through its effect on the taxes of the household.

Turning next to the results for period $t+1$, the bank sector expected in period $t+1$ to have fewer funds at its disposal because of the lower level of demand and savings deposits that existed in period t. This caused it to raise the loan rate, decrease its demand for bills and bonds, and lower the maxumum value of loans that it will make in the period. Unconstrained, the firm sector chose to lower its price, investment, planned production, wage rate, and the maximum number of hours that it will pay for as a result of the sales decrease in period t and the higher loan rate in period $t+1$.

The firm sector also chose, however, to increase its loans to make up for the lower demand deposits in period t ($LFUN_{t+1} = 330.8$), and this amount of money was greater than the maximum amount allowed ($LFMAX_{t+1} = 327.0$). This constraint caused the firm sector to lower even more its investment, planned production, wage rate, and the maximum number of hours. Its price, however, was higher than the price it chose unconstrained ($P_{t+1} = 0.9985$ vs. $PUN_{t+1} = 0.9979$), although still lower than the price it set for period t (1.0000). The firm sector planned to hold some excess capital and excess labor in period $t+1$ ($K^a_{t+1}/KMIN^p_{t+1} = 1.003$ and $HPFMAX_{t+1}/MH^p_{t+1} = 1.004$). Unconstrained, household 1 chose to work less and consume less as a result of the new price, wage rate, and other relevant inputs into its decision process. Household 2 chose to work more and consume less. The hours constraint was, however, binding on both households ($HPHUN_{1t+1} = 322.7$ vs. $HPHMAX_{1t+1} = 321.6$ and $HPHUN_{2t+1} = 435.3$ vs. $HPHMAX_{2t+1} = 433.7$), and the loan constraint was binding on household 2 ($LHUN_{t+1} = 481.5$ vs. $LHMAX_{t+1} = 480.5$). These constraints caused the households to work and consume less.

When transactions took place in period $t+1$, sales were even less than in period t, even though the government increased its purchases back to the original level, because of the decrease in investment and consumption. Near the end of period $t+1$ the bond dealer increased the bill rate for period $t+2$ because of the lower demand for bills and bonds on the part of the bank sector in period $t+1$. The stock price was set lower because of the lower level of dividends and the higher bill rate.

To summarize the results so far: a decrease in government spending in period t has generated a decrease in the price, the wage rate, production, investment, consumption, employment, and loans. The loan rate and the bill rate, on the other hand, are higher initially. The higher initial interest rates are caused by the fact that the bank sector had less money on hand at the end of period t to lend to households and firms and to buy bills and bonds.

It is easy to see from the above outline how a multiplier reaction can take place corresponding to a one-period decrease in government spending. Sales fall; the firm sector lowers investment and the maximum number of hours that it will pay for; households, being constrained in their work effort, lower consumption; investment and consumption fall, causing sales to fall further; the firm sector lowers investment and the maximum number of hours that it will pay for even more; households lower consumption even more; and so it goes. This multiplier effect is also aggravated in the short run by the fact that the decrease in government spending decreases bank reserves, which causes the bank sector to raise the loan rate and make the loan constraint more restrictive.

Experiment 2:   An Increase in the
Value of Bills Issued in Period t
($VBILLG_t$: +5.0)

Consider next the results of the second experiment. The increase in bills had no effect on the decisions of the behavioral units for period t, although it did cause the bond dealer near the end of period t to increase the bill and bond rates for period $t+1$ because of the excess supply of bills and bonds in period t. The higher bond rate caused both the bank sector and the bond dealer to suffer capital losses on their bonds in period t, which caused their taxes and dividends to be lower. The lower level of dividends and the higher bill rate caused the bond dealer to lower the stock price for period $t+1$, which in turn caused household 1 to suffer a capital loss in period t. The capital losses of the bank sector, the bond dealer, and household 1 and the lower dividend income of household 1 in period t caused taxes to decrease.

The government ran a deficit of 1.4 in period t, which was caused by the decrease in taxes and by an increase in government interest payments because of the greater supply of bills. Bank reserves thus decreased by 3.6, the difference between the 5.0 increase in bills and the 1.4 increase in the deficit. This 3.6 decrease took the form of a 4.9 decrease in the demand deposits of the bond dealer, a 0.7 increase in the savings deposits of household 1 (caused by the lower taxes due to the capital losses), and a 0.5 capital loss of the bank sector on its bonds.[d] Capital losses of the bond dealer have a positive effect on the demand deposits of the bond dealer (see Chapter Five), which is why the demand deposits of the bond dealer only decreased by 4.9 even though the bond dealer absorbed the entire 5.0 increase in bills in period t. Likewise, the capital losses of the bank sector have a positive effect on bank reserves (see Chapter Two), which is why the 0.5 capital loss of the bank sector is needed in describing the form in which the decrease in bank reserves took in period t.

The increase in bills in period t thus had no effect on real output in the period, but it did cause bank reserves to decrease by 3.6. Were it not for the effect of the capital losses on the bonds and stock, bank reserves would have decreased by almost the full 5.0 amount. The decrease would not have been quite 5.0 because the government would still have run a slight deficit due to the increased interest payments on the greater supply of bills. Although the decrease in taxes due to the capital losses for this experiment is not too important, it does provide an indication of how capital losses affect the system.

It is the author's feeling that the *quantitative* effects of capital gains and losses are probably exaggerated in the results in Table 6-6, as compared with the actual effects in practice. In practice, capital gains and losses are not recorded and taxed every period and are not taxed at the same rate as other income. Also, long term interest rates are usually much less volatile than short term rates in practice, whereas in the model the bill and bond rates are always equal because of the simple expectational assumptions used. A less volatile bond rate in the model would decrease the quantitative importance of capital gains and losses. Although the quantitative importance of capital gains and losses may be exaggerated in Table 6-6, the exaggeration should have little effect on the qualitative results and should not decrease the usefulness of the results in helping one to understand the properties of the model.

Turning to the results for period $t+1$, the bank sector expected in period $t+1$ to have fewer funds at its disposal because of the decrease in the sum of demand deposits and savings deposits in period t. As was the case in experiment 1, this caused it to raise the loan rate, decrease its demand for bills and bonds, and lower the maximum value of loans that it will make. The increase in the loan rate caused the firm sector, unconstrained, to raise the price and wage rate slightly and decrease investment, planned production, and the maximum number of hours slightly.[e] The loan constraint in period $t+1$ was binding on the firm sector, however, which caused the firm sector to raise its price more and to decrease investment, planned production, and the maximum number of hours more.

Household 1 chose unconstrained to work more, consume less, and thus save more; and household 2 chose unconstrained to work more, consume less, and thus borrow less. The higher bill rate was one cause of household 1's decision to plan to save more, and the higher loan rate was one cause of household 2's decision to plan to borrow less. The loan constraint in period $t+1$ was binding on household 2, however, and the hours constraint was binding on both households. These constraints caused both households to work less and consume even less than in the unconstrained case. Sales in period $t+1$ were thus lower because of the decrease in investment and consumption.

An increase in bills in period t has thus generated an initial increase in interest rates and the price level and a decrease in production, investment, employment, the wage rate, and loans. The difference between this case and the case of a decrease in government spending is that in this case the price level is initially higher. The price level is initially higher because the initial effect on the firm sector is an increase in the loan rate and a more restrictive loan constraint, both of which cause the firm sector to raise the price level. For this experiment, the price level came back down in period $t+2$ because of the lower sales in period $t+1$.

It is also easy to see from this experiment how a multiplier reaction can take place corresponding to a one-period increase in the value of government bills issued. The bank sector raises the loan rate for period $t+1$ and makes the loan constraint more restrictive because of the decrease in bank reserves in period t. This causes the firm sector to lower planned production, investment, and the maximum number of hours. The more restrictive loan and hours constraints then cause the households to consume less. The lower investment and consumption cause sales to fall in period $t+1$, and thus the cycle as described in experiment 1 has started.

Experiment 3: An Increase in the Number of Goods Purchased by the Government in Period t (XG_t: +5.0)

The results for the third experiment are essentially opposite to those for the first experiment, with one important exception. The exception is as follows. Because of the increase in sales in period t, the firm sector planned to increase production in period $t+1$ to 844.4. It was not constrained in doing so by the bank sector, since the loan constraint was less restrictive in period $t+1$ (due to the increase in bank reserves in period t). The firm sector needed to borrow less anyway because of its positive cash flow net of taxes and dividends in period t (which resulted in an increase in its demand deposits in period t). Unconstrained, household 1 chose to work slightly more and consume slightly less in period $t+1$, and household 2 chose to work slightly less and consume slightly more. As a group, the households chose to work slightly less in period $t+1$ than they did in period t ($HPUN_{t+1}$ = 757.8 vs. $HPUN_t$ = 758.0). Neither household was constrained in any way in period $t+1$. What is the case, however, is that the households chose to work less than the firm sector expected them to work ($HPFMAX_{t+1}$ = 639.2 vs. HPF_{t+1} = 637.1).[f] This meant that the firm sector had to cut back its production from the level originally planned (Y_{t+1} = 841.3 vs. Y^p_{t+1} = 844.4). In other words, the system was constrained in this case by the work effort of households. The work effort of the households in period $t+1$ was such as to lead to a slight decrease in real GNP in period $t+1$. Real GNP, in other words, did not increase in experiment 3 corresponding to an increase in government spending, whereas it decreased in experiment 1 corresponding to a decrease in government spending. In period $t+2$ for experiment 3 the system was again constrained by the work effort of households. The households chose to work slightly less in period $t+2$ than they did in period $t+1$. Real GNP was slightly lower in period $t+2$ than in period $t+1$.

The important point to be gained from this experiment is that the economy can be stimulated to produce more output from an initial position of equilibrium only to the extent that households can be induced to work more. In the present model, as was seen in Chapter Four, the price level has a negative effect on work effort and the wage rate has a positive effect. In addition, the bill rate has a positive effect on the work effort of household 1, and the loan rate has a positive effect on the work effort of household 2. The initial level of wealth of household 1 also has a negative effect on household 1's work effort, which means, for example, that capital gains have a negative effect on work effort. Whether the households can be stimulated to work more depends on how the various variables that affect work change in relationship to one another. Of particular importance in this regard is the size of the firm sector's wage rate change relative to its price change. In the case of the decrease in government spending in experiment 1, the unconstrained reactions of the households were not as important in determining how the system would behave because the more restrictive constraints in experiment 1 forced the households to work less and borrow less. In experiment 3 there is nothing equivalent forcing the households to work more.

One other small difference between experiments 1 and 3 should perhaps be pointed out. In both experiments the level of real GNP in period t

was lower than the base-run value. This is because in both cases the change in sales in period t of 5.0 caused worker hour requirements to increase, which in turn forced the firm sector to produce less in both cases.

Experiment 4:   A Decrease in the Value of Bills Issued in Period t ($VBILLG_t$: -5.0)

The results for the fourth experiment are essentially the opposite from those for the second experiment, with the same exception that in experiment 4 the system is constrained by the work effort of households. The firm sector chose to expand slightly in period $t+1$, because of the lower loan rate that the bank sector set for period $t+1$,[9] but the households chose to work less in period $t+1$ than they did in period t and less than the firm sector expected. This forced the firm sector to cut production in period $t+1$ from the level originally planned and to cut it even below the level for period t. Real GNP thus dropped slightly in period $t+1$ as a result of the decrease in bills. This is another good example of the system being constrained by the work effort of households. The unemployment rate was slightly negative in period $t+2$. This was caused by the fact that household 2 was constrained in its borrowing behavior in period $t+2$, but not in its work behavior. The loan constraint caused household 2 to choose to work slightly more than it would have if it had not been constrained in its borrowing behavior. Therefore, the unconstrained supply of labor for household 2 was slightly less than the constrained supply, thus causing the unemployment rate to be negative.

Experiment 5:   A Decrease in the Number of Goods Purchased by the Government in Period t (XG_t: -5.0) and a Decrease in the Value of Bills Issued in Period t ($VBILLG_t$: -5.0)

For the fifth experiment the number of goods purchased by the government and the value of bills issued were both decreased by 5.0. This had the effect of contracting the economy in periods $t+1$ and $t+2$ less than was the case for the first experiment, where only the number of goods purchased was decreased. The government surplus in period t was 5.9, but since there were 5.0 fewer bills in the system in period t, bank reserves were only decreased by 0.9. In experiment 1 bank reserves were decreased by 4.5. The government surplus of 5.9 is the sum of the surplus of 4.5 in experiment 1 and the surplus of 1.4 in experiment 4. The surplus of 1.4 is due to the increased tax collections caused by the capital gains made in period t. Capital gains are made in period t because of the lower bill and bond rates for period $t+1$. The lower bill and bond rates are due to the excess demand for bills and bonds in period t. The 4.5 surplus in experiment 1 instead of a surplus of 5.0 is, as mentioned in the discussion for experiment 1, due to decreased tax collections caused by lower profits and dividends.

Because bank reserves were only decreased by 0.9 in experiment 5, rather than the 4.5 in experiment 1, the bank sector in period $t+1$ set a lower loan rate and a less restrictive loan constraint in experiment 5 than in experiment 1 ($RL_{t+1} = 0.07491$ vs. 0.07507 and $LBMAX_{t+1} = 809.9$ vs. 807.5). In experiment 5 the firm sector and household 2 were still constrained in their borrowing behavior in period $t+1$, but less so than in experiment 1. Output in period $t+1$ was thus larger in experiment 5 than in experiment 1 ($Y_{t+1} = 835.4$ vs. 834.6) and sales were greater ($X_{t+1} = 839.6$ vs 836.1). Output and sales in period $t+2$ were also greater in experiment 5 than in experiment 1.

It is also interesting regarding experiment 5 to consider the following case. Assume for sake of argument that the change in sales in period t did not affect worker hour requirements, so that output and profits were not changed in period t. Assume also that the capital gains due to the lower bill and bond rates for period $t+1$ were not recorded in period t. Assume finally that the government interest payments in period t were not any lower, even though the value of bills issued was less. Under these assumptions all that would have happened in period t regarding the financial variables would have been a decrease in the demand deposits of the firm sector of 5.0 and an increase in the demand deposits of the bond dealer of 5.0. Bank reserves would have remained unchanged. The demand deposits of the firm sector would be lower because of a negative cash flow net of taxes and dividends of 5.0 in period t, and the demand deposits of the bond dealer would be higher because it buys 5.0 fewer bills from the government than it sells to the bank sector.

In this case the main effects for period $t+1$ would be as follows. Because of the lower bill rate for period $t+1$, the bank sector would lower the loan rate for period $t+1$, decrease its demand for bills and bonds, and make the loan constraint less restrictive. The loan constraint would be made less restrictive because of the fact that in this case the bank sector would expect to have the same amount of funds at its disposal for period $t+1$ as it had for period t and would decrease its demand for bills and bonds. Other things being equal, the firm sector would need to borrow 5.0 more in period $t+1$ because of the lower demand deposits in period t. Since sales were lower in period t, however, the firm sector would choose to contract in period $t+1$. (The lower loan rate would, of course, offset this contraction somewhat.) Whether the firm sector contracts to the point where it needs to borrow less than the maximum set by the bank sector depends on the size of the firm sector's response to the sales decrease, as well as on the size of the bank sector's response to the bill rate decrease in terms of substituting out of bills and bonds. The only way the economy would be prevented from contracting in this case would be if the loan rate decrease offset the sales decrease enough to cause the firm sector to produce and invest the same amount as before, and at the same time the bank sector substituted out of bills and bonds sufficiently to allow the firm sector to borrow the extra amount needed to offset the negative cash flow of the previous period.

The case just described is useful in helping to separate the effects of the tax changes from the other effects. In the results for experiment 5 the surplus of the government in period t was 5.9 rather than the 5.0 that it would have been with no tax changes and no change in government interest payments. This decrease of 0.9 in bank reserves in period t caused the bank sector to decrease slightly the maximum loan value in period $t+1$, whereas in the no-tax case it would have increased the maximum loan value slightly. This difference is not large, however, and similar results would have been obtained for experiment 5 had the tax changes been less.

An important point about experiment 5 in relation to experiment 1 is that in experiment 5 the economy contracts even though the decrease in government spending corresponds to an equal decrease in the value of bills issued. The response of the model in period $t+1$ to the sales decrease in period t is greater than is its response to the lower bill and bond rates for period $t+1$, which thus causes the economy to contract in period $t+1$.

Experiment 6:   An Increase in the Number of Goods Purchased by the Government in Period $t(XG_t\!: +5.0)$ and an Increase in the Value of Bills Issued in Period t $(VBILLG_t\!: +5.0)$

For the sixth experiment the increase in the number of goods purchased by the government was assumed to be financed by an equal increase in bills. The government deficit in period t in this case was 6.8, which, aside from rounding, is the sum of the deficit of 1.4 in experiment 2 and the deficit of 5.5 in experiment 3. The deficit of 1.4 is due to the decreased tax collections caused by the capital losses in period t. The deficit of 5.5 rather than of merely 5.0 is due to the lower profits and dividends caused by the increase in worker hour requirements in period t. The level of output for period $t+1$ is actually higher in experiment 6 than it is in experiment 3, where the increased spending in period t was financed by an increase in bank reserves (*Real GNP = 964.1* vs. *962.0*). In both experiments output was constrained in period $t+1$ by the work effort of households, but in experiment 6 the households chose to work somewhat more. The bill and loan rates in period $t+1$ were higher in experiment 6 than in experiment 3, and higher bill and loan rates have a positive effect on the work effort of the households.

The important difference between experiments 3 and 6 is that interest rates in period *t+1* are higher in experiment 6 because of the excess supply of bills and bonds in period *t*. Although bank reserves in period *t* were higher in experiment 3 than in experiment 6 ($BR_t = 60.9$ vs. 57.2), in neither case was the loan constraint binding on the firm sector and household 2 in period *t+1*.

Experiment 7: An Increase in the Personal Income Tax Parameter in Period t(d_3: $+0.00554$ in period *t*)

The increase in the personal tax rate in period *t* caused households to want to work and consume less in period *t*. Household 2 would have liked, unconstrained, to borrow slightly more in period *t*, but it was prevented from doing so by the bank sector. Being constrained by the bank sector, it chose to work slightly more than it otherwise would have, which caused the unemployment rate to be negative in period *t*. Because of the lower labor supply in period *t*, the firm sector was forced to cut production to *834.9* from the planned level of *842.0*. Sales were less in period *t* because of the lower consumption ($X_t = 837.0$ vs. $X_t = 842.0$ for the base run). For the base run the taxable income of the household sector is *862.2* $[YH_{1t} + YH_{2t} - RL_t LH_t]$. Had there been no drop in income in experiment 7, taxes would have increased by *4.8* $[0.00554 \times 862.2]$. Because of the lower income, however, taxes only increased by 3.0. Bank reserves thus decreased by 3.0 in period *t*. In period *t+1* the bank sector raised the loan rate and lowered the maximum value of loans as a result of the decrease in bank reserves in period *t*. The more restrictive loan constraint was not, however, binding on either the firm sector or household 2 in period *t+1*. The firm sector chose to contract in period *t+1* as a result of the sales decrease in period *t*. The households chose, unconstrained, to work and consume more in period *t+1* than they did in period *t*, because the personal tax rate was lowered back to its original level in period *t+1*. The households were constrained in their work effort, however, which forced them to work less and led them to consume less than they had planned to unconstrained. The level of sales was, however, slightly greater in period *t+1* than it was in period *t*, and the level of production was also slightly greater in period *t+1* than it was in period *t*.

An important point about experiment 7 is that an increase in the personal income tax rate causes a decrease in the work effort of households in addition to a decrease in consumption. Output can thus fall in this case without an increase in the unemployment rate. In experiment 7 real GNP fell in period *t*, but the unemployment rate was actually negative. The level of employment was, of course, less, but the lower level of employment was voluntary.

Experiment 8:   A Decrease in the Personal Income Tax Parameter in Period t (d_t: -0.00554 in period t)

The decrease in the personal tax rate in period t caused households to want to work and consume more in period t. They were constrained from working any more by the firm sector, however, but they still chose, constrained, to consume somewhat more. Sales were thus greater in period t, which forced the firm sector to cut production slightly because of the increased worker hour requirements.[h] Taxes were less by 5.0 because of the lower personal tax rate and the slight decrease in profits.[i] Bank reserves thus increased by 5.0. In periods $t+1$ and $t+2$ no constraints were binding on the households, and the system was constrained by the work effort of the households.

Experiment 9:   A Decrease in the Minimum Guaranteed Level of Income in Period t (YG: - 2.5 in period t)

The decrease in YG in period t caused the households to want to work more and consume less. They were, however, constrained from working more by the firm sector. They thus worked the same and chose to consume even less. Sales were less in period t because of the decreased consumption, which caused the economy to begin to contract in period $t+1$. The unemployment rate was higher in period t than in period $t+1$, even though the level of employment (HP) was lower in period $t+1$, because the decrease in YG in period t caused the unconstrained work effort of the households to increase in period t.

Experiment 10:   An Increase in the Minimum Guaranteed Level of Increase in Period t (YG: +2.5 in period t)

The increase in YG in period t caused the households to work less and consume more. The firm sector was forced to decrease production in period t because of the decreased supply of labor. Sales were greater in period t because of the increased consumption. In period $t+1$ the firm sector chose to produce more than it had actually produced in period t ($Y^p_{t+1} = 841.3$ vs. $Y_t = 836.7$), but slightly less than it had *planned* to produce in period t ($Y^p_t = 842.0$). The firm sector actually expected to sell more in period $t+1$ than it had expected it was going to sell in period t ($X^e_{t+1} = 843.2$ vs. $X^e_t = 842.0$). The reason that Y^p_{t+1} is less than Y^p_t has to do in part with the firm sector's reaction to employment adjustment costs. Unconstrained, the households chose to work more in period $t+1$ than they had in period t, because YG was changed back to the original level in period $t+1$. The households were constrained slightly in period $t+1$, which caused the unemployment rate to rise slightly. The system was again constrained in period $t+2$ by the work effort of the households, and the unemployment rate was back to zero.

Experiment 11: A Decrease in the Number of Worker Hours Paid For by the Government in Period t ($HPG_t : -5.0$)

The decrease in HPG_t caused the hours constraint to be binding on the households in period t. The households worked less and consumed less. Sales were lower because of the decreased consumption. The firm sector planned in period t to produce the same amount as was the case for the base run ($Y_t^P = 842.0$), but it was forced to produce slightly less ($Y_t = 841.8$) because of the increase in worker hour requirements caused by the change in sales.

The government ran a surplus of 3.9 in period t, and so bank reserves were less by 3.9. The decrease in bank reserves took the form of a 2.8 decrease in the demand deposits of the firm sector (caused by a negative cash flow net of taxes and dividends of 2.8), a 0.5 decrease in the demand deposits of the two households (due to the lower consumption), and a 0.5 decrease in the savings deposits of household 1.j Another way of looking at the households' portion of the 3.9 decrease in bank reserves is that the households dissaved 1.0 in period t ($SAV_{1t} = -0.7$ and $SAV_{2t} = -0.3$).

The bank sector raised the loan rate and made the loan constraint more restrictive in period $t+1$ as a result of the decrease in bank reserves in period t. Because of the higher loan rate and the decrease in sales, the firm sector chose, unconstrained, to produce and invest less and hire less labor in period $t+1$. The loan constraint was binding on the firm sector, however, which caused it to contract even more. Even though in period $t+1$ the government increased its amount of labor hired back to the original level, the households were still constrained in their work effort because of the more restrictive hours constraints from the firm sector. The unemployment rate was thus still positive in period $t+1$, although it was less than in period t.

Experiment 12: An Increase in the Number of Worker Hours Paid For by the Government in Period t ($HPG_t : +5.0$)

The increase in HPG_t meant that the firm sector got less labor in period t, which forced it to cut production from the planned level ($Y_t = 835.3$ vs. $Y_t^P = 842.0$). Because of employment adjustment costs, the firm sector planned to produce less in period $t+1$ than it had planned to in period t. The firm sector thus also planned to invest less and hire less labor in period $t+1$. The households were constrained in their work effort in period $t+1$ because of the decrease in HPG back to its original level and because of the more restrictive hours constraint from the firm sector. The government ran a large deficit in period t, which caused the loan rate to decrease in period $t+1$ and the bill rate to decrease in period $t+2$. The system was contrained slightly in period $t+2$ by the work effort of the households.

SUMMARY OF THE EXPERIMENTAL RESULTS

Some of the main characteristics of the model that can be gleaned from the above experiments are as follows. A decrease in the number of goods purchased by the government in period t causes sales and bank reserves in period t to decrease. The decrease in bank reserves leads the bank sector to raise the loan rate for period $t+1$ and lower the maximum value of loans that it will make. The decrease in sales and the higher loan rate lead the firm sector in period $t+1$ to lower planned production, investment, and the maximum number of worker hours that it will pay for. The firm sector's unconstrained demand for loans in period $t+1$ may be greater or less than it was in period t. The lower level of demand deposits of the firm sector in period t, do to the negative cash flow net of taxes and dividends in period t, causes the firm sector to increase its demand for loans in period $t+1$. The contraction planned by the firm sector because of the sales decrease, on the other hand, causes it to decrease its demand for loans. The loan constraint, therefore, may or may not be binding on the firm sector in period $t+1$, depending on the size of the various reactions.

Ignoring tax effects, when a decrease in the number of goods purchased by the government in period t corresponds to an equal decrease in the value of bills issued, bank reserves in period t are unchanged. The bill rate for period $t+1$ is lower because of the excess demand for bills in period t. The lower bill rate leads the bank sector in period $t+1$ to lower the loan rate, decrease its demand for bills and bonds, and increase the maximum value of loans that it will make. The lower interest rates have a positive effect on the economy in period $t+1$, but the decrease in sales in period t and the resulting higher level of inventories have a negative effect. In the model the negative effect outweighs the positive effect, and the economy contracts in period $t+1$ as a result of the simultaneous decrease in goods purchased and bills issued.

Tax changes tend to offset somewhat the effects of the various government actions. When profits decrease, both personal taxes and corporate taxes decrease. Personal taxes decrease both because of lower dividend income and capital losses on stocks. The opposite happens when profits increase. When the bill and bond rates increase, taxes decrease because of the capital losses suffered on bonds and stocks, and vice versa when the bill and bond rates decrease.

When from a position of equilibrium the number of goods purchased by the government is increased or the value of bills issued is decreased, the system may be prevented from expanding by the work effort of households. If the number of goods purchased by the government is increased, the firm sector will want to expand in the next period because of the sales increase, and if the value of bills issued is decreased, the firm sector will want to expand in the next period because of the lower loan rate that will be set by the bank sector. Only if the households can be induced to work more, however, will the system actually be able to expand. It should also be noted that in the case of a *decrease* in government spending or an *increase* in the value of bills issued, the firm sector is forced to contract because of the more restrictive loan constraint, whereas in the case of an *increase* in government spending or a *decrease* in the value of bills issued, there is nothing similar forcing the firm sector to expand.

Regarding the price setting behavior of the firm sector, the price level responds positively to a higher loan rate and a more restrictive loan constraint, so that an increase in the value of bills issued results in an initial increase in the price level. This initial increase then reverses itself as sales fall and the firm sector responds by lowering the price level. Likewise, a decrease in the values of bills issued results in an initial decrease in the price level, which then reverses itself as sales rise and the firm sector responds by raising the price level.

The important difference between the government influencing the economy through a change in the number of goods purchased and a change in one of the tax parameters, d_3 and YG, is that the latter change has a direct effect on the work effort of the households, whereas the former change does not. Increasing taxes by increasing d_3 has a negative effect on the work effort of households, which, other things being equal, has a negative effect on the unemployment rate. Increasing taxes by decreasing the minimum guaranteed level of income, on the other hand, has a positive effect on work effort, which, other things being equal, has a positive effect on the unemployment rate. Increasing taxes and decreasing the number of goods purchased do, however, have similar effects on bank reserves. Both changes lead to a smaller deficit or a larger surplus in the government budget and thus to a decrease in bank reserves.

6.3 THE EFFECTS OF POLICY CHANGES
FROM A DISEQUILIBRIUM POSITION

Although the experiments in Table 6-6 were all made from an initial position of equilibrium, the results do help to show how various policy actions would affect an economy that is out of equilibrium. In an economy characterized by binding loan constraints, the need is to increase bank reserves. Increasing government spending with no change in bills and bonds, and decreasing bills and bonds with no change in government spending both increase bank reserves. Which action is more effective in increasing bank reserves depends on the tax response. In experiments 3 and 4, increasing government spending was more effective in increasing bank reserves. Decreasing bills in experiment 4 led to increased tax collections because of the resulting capital gains on bonds and stocks, whereas increasing government spending in experiment 3 actually led to a slight decrease in tax collections because of the decreased production due to the increased worker hour requirement. The quantitative importance of both of these effects may be exaggerated, however, especially the capital gains effects. Nevertheless, the results do highlight the importance of taking into account possible tax responses when considering the effectiveness of various policy actions in increasing bank reserves.

In an economy characterized by binding hours constraints, the need is to induce the firm sector to produce more and hire more labor. Increasing government spending on goods with no change in bills and bonds does this by increasing the sales of the firm sector directly. Decreasing bills and bonds with no change in government spending leads to lower interest rates, which in turn induces the firm sector to invest more and the household sector to save less and consume more. This then leads to increased sales because of the increased investment and consumption. Which action is initially most effective in increasing sales depends on the size of the initial rate changes and the size of the initial responses to the interest rate changes.

In an economy characterized by binding hours constraints, the government can also increase the amount of labor that it hires. For the same expenditure, this policy is likely to be more effective in increasing aggregate employment in the short run than the policy of increasing the number of goods purchased by the government. When the number of goods purchased by the government is increased, the firm sector initially will meet some of this increase by drawing down inventories (because of the adjustment costs) and so will not increase production to the full extent of the increase in sales. Also, if the firm sector is holding excess labor, it will be able to meet at least part of its increased worker hour requirements, due to the increased production, by taking up the slack in its work force. This will, of course, further lessen the initial employment response to the sales increase.

Ignoring possible tax effects, the policy of increasing government spending and the policy of decreasing the value of bills and bonds issued would appear at first glance to be about equally effective (for the same outlay) in an economy characterized by binding loan constraints. The need in this case is to increase bank reserves, and both policies are of about the same effectiveness in doing this. Increasing government spending in this case, however, has the possibly undesirable characteristic of increasing sales directly. In an economy characterized by binding loan constraints, production is constrained by the availability of loanable funds and not by lack of sales, and increasing government purchases of goods directly may just exaberate the problem in the short run. One does not want to increase the sales of firms before the firms realize that they can borrow more money to increase investment and output. If there are information lags from the banks to the firms, increasing the sales of firms at the same time that bank reserves are increased may lead firms to raise prices in order to lower expected sales to the levels that are consistent with the production plans that are based on the old loan constraints. What is needed in the case of binding loan constraints is just more money in the system, and the most direct way of doing this is merely to decrease the value of bills and bonds issued.

If monetary policy is defined as a change in bills and bonds with no change in government purchases of goods and labor, and fiscal policy is defined as a change in government purchases of goods and labor with no change in bills and bonds, then the above argument says that monetary policy is a more direct tool to use in an economy characterized by binding loan constraints than is fiscal policy. In an economy characterized by binding hours constraints, however, fiscal policy would appear to be the more direct tool to use. The need in this case is to increase sales and employment. Fiscal policy does this directly, whereas monetary policy must work through the interest rate responses of the firm and household sectors. Only if the interest rate responses are large and quick will monetary policy be as effective or more effective than fiscal policy in a binding hours constraint situation.

The above discussion thus indicates that it is not just the interest rate responses that are important in determining the effectiveness of monetary policy versus fiscal policy at any given time, but also the kind of disequilibrium situation that the economy is in at the time. In a situation of binding loan constraints, monetary policy would appear to be more effective, and in a situation of binding hours constraints, fiscal policy may be more effective. Also, in a situation of binding hours constraints, fiscal policy in the form of an increase in government purchases of labor would appear to be more effective in increasing the level of employment than fiscal policy in the form of an increase in government purchases of goods.

If the government desires to contract the economy from, say, a situation in which none of the constraints are binding, the results in the previous section indicate that both monetary policy and fiscal policy are likely to be effective in doing this. A contractionary fiscal policy lowers sales directly. A contractionary monetary policy leads to higher interest rates and more restrictive loan constraints, which in turn cause investment and consumption to decrease. However, a contractionary monetary policy may lead, other things being equal, to a higher price level than will a contractionary fiscal policy. Higher interest rates and more restrictive loan constraints have a positive effect on the prices that firms set.

6.4   THE LONG-RUN PROPERTIES OF THE MODEL

The model used for the results in Table 6-6 is not stable in the sense that it does not return to the "equilibrium" self-repeating position once a one-period shock has been inflicted on it. This conclusion was reached from examining numerous runs in which, from a self-repeating position, a parameter or exogenous variable was changed for one period and then returned the next period to its previous value. The model was allowed to run for 100 periods after the particular change. The model definitely had a tendency to meander around near the original self-repeating values, but in no case did it give any indication of returning exactly to the self-repeating position. This conclusion was also verified for other versions of the condensed model—i.e., for versions based on different sets of parameter values.

The lack of stability of the model in the above sense is, of course, not surprising. In fact, it would be surprising if the model did return to the self-repeating position after being shocked, since there is nothing in the model that indicates that it should return. The bank sector when setting its values only has expectations of what the firm and household sectors are going to do in the period, and the firm sector when setting its values only has expectations of what the household sector is going to do. Even if the assumptions regarding the formation of expectation of banks and firms were made more sophisticated than the assumptions used here, it is not reasonable to assume that these expectations are always perfect. This is particularly true in a market share model, where it is not only the expectations regarding the aggregate quantities that would need to be perfect, but also the expectations of the behavior of other banks and firms. Even if a firm's expectations of the aggregate quantities were perfect, the firm may still misestimate what its competitors are going to do. Since expectations are not perfect, there is no reason to expect the banks and firms to set interest rates, prices, and wage rates in such a way that no constraints are ever binding and in such a way that the system gradually approaches a particular state.[k]

There are, of course, reactions in the model that prevent the system from accelerating or decelerating indefinitely. Holding the variables under the control of the government constant, as the system contracts, interest rates fall. Interest rates fall because the firm and household sectors demand fewer funds to borrow. Falling interest rates, on the other hand, induce the firm sector to invest more and the household sector to save less and consume more. Falling interest rates also cause capital gains on stocks, which have a positive effect on household 1's consumption behavior. As the system contracts the price level and the wage rate also fall, but whether this induces households to consume more depends on how the price level and wage rate change relative to one another. There is thus no natural tendency for the price level and the wage rate to bring the economy out of a contracting situation, as there is for the interest rates. Falling prices and wages do, however, decrease the demand deposit needs of the firm and household sectors, which, other things being equal, decrease the demand for loans of the firm sector and household 2 and increase the savings deposits of household 1. A one-dollar switch from demand deposits to savings deposits frees up fraction g_1 of a dollar in loanable funds because of the reserve requirement ratio on demand deposits. Likewise, a one-dollar decrease in demand deposits and loans at the same time frees up fraction g_1 of a dollar in loanable funds.

An interesting question about the long run dynamic properties of the model is whether it is possible to concoct a self-repeating run in which there exists a positive level of unemployment. It is easy to see that this is not possible. Unemployment occurs if the hours constraint is binding on the households. If the hours constraint is binding, then the ratio of the unconstrained supply of labor (*HPUN*) to the constrained supply of labor (*HP*) is not one, and if the ratio is not one, the firm sector will not set the same wage rate each period (see statements [15] and [36] in Table 3-4). In other words, as long as firms are assumed to know last period's unconstrained as well as constrained supply of labor, one cannot concoct a self-repeating run with positive unemployment.

It is possible, however, to concoct a self-repeating run with positive unemployment if it is assumed that firms do not know the unconstrained supply of labor. Consider a self-repeating run with no unemployment. Now change the utility functions of the households in such a way that they desire to work more, consume more, but keep the same level of savings deposits and loans. Assume also that when constrained by the old equilibrium values of hours worked, they choose the same values of hours worked and goods purchased as they did before (and thus the same level of savings deposits and loans as before). The aggregate unconstrained and constrained demands for loans are the same, so the bank sector is unaffected even if it knows the unconstrained as well as the constrained demands. If the firm sector does not know the unconstrained supply of labor, there is no way for the information on the change in the utility functions of households to be communicated to it. It only observes the actual demand for goods and supply of labor, which are the same as before. The firm sector thus makes the same decisions as it did before, households are subject to the same constraints as before (and so make the same decisions as before) and so on. A self-repeating run will thus still exist, but now in a situation where there is unemployment.

Because firms are assumed to observe the unconstrained supply of labor, unemployment arises in the model only because of errors of expectations. It was seen in Chapter Three that each firm sets its price and wage rate with the expectation that it will not turn any workers away and with the expectation that no workers will be turned away in the aggregate. Therefore, any unemployment that arises in the model is due to errors in the firms' expectations of the behavioral responses of the households. It is also the case that binding loan constraints are due only to errors of expectations. It was seen in Chapter Two that a bank sets its loan rate with the expectation that there will be no customers turned away in the aggregate. Therefore, any binding loan constraints are due to errors in the banks' expectations of the responses of the firms and households.

It is important to distinguish between two kinds of errors of expectations on the part of banks and firms: errors of expectations of aggregate quantities and errors of expectations of market share. A bank, for example, can misestimate either the aggregate demand for loans or its share of the aggregate loan market or both. In practice, with many banks and firms in existence, expectations of market share factors are likely to have more of an effect on the behavior of a bank or firm than are expectations of aggregate quantities. If a bank or firm is a small part of the overall economy, then changes in its market share, due to its behavior relative to the behavior of its competitors, are likely to affect it more than are changes in the aggregate quantities. In other words, there is likely to be less payoff to a particular bank or firm from making accurate expectations of aggregate quantities than from making accurate expectations of its market share, and the bank or firm is likely to put more resources into the latter than the former. If in practice each bank and firm is more concerned with what its competitors are going to do than with what the aggregate quantities are going to be like, it is not surprising that errors of expectations are made in the aggregate. There may be little incentive in the system for firms as a group to set price and wages so as to leave households always unconstrained and for banks as a group to set loan rates so as to leave firms and households always unconstrained.

6.5 PRICE AND WAGE RESPONSES

The price and wage setting behavior of a firm was discussed in Chapter Three, and little extra discussion is needed here. The price that a firm sets responds positively to an increase in sales of the previous period and negatively to the existence of excess labor and excess capital in the previous period. The price also responds positively to the loan rate and to a binding loan constraint, so that periods of tight money correspond, other things being equal, to price increases.

The wage rate that a firm sets is equal to the rate that the firm expects is necessary to attract the amount of labor that it wants in the period. The expected supply of labor facing a firm is a positive function of the firm's wage rate and of the expected aggregate supply of labor, and is a negative function of the expected wage rates of other firms. The expected aggregate supply of labor is a positive function of the expected average wage rate in the economy and of the aggregate unconstrained supply of labor in the previous period, and is a negative function of the expected average price level in the economy.

Although the price and wage decisions of a firm are made simultaneously, both resulting from the solution of the firm's optimal control problem, it is possible to talk loosely about the effect of a firm's price decision on its wage decision. An increase in price, other things being equal, has a negative effect on expected sales, planned production, investment, and planned employment. If planned employment is less, then the firm expects to be able to attract the amount of labor that it wants with a lower wage rate than before. So on this score a higher price implies a lower wage rate being set. On the other hand, if a firm increases its price, it expects the average price in the economy to be higher, especially a few periods into the future as other firms are expected to respond to the firm's higher price. A higher expected average price has a negative effect on the expected aggregate supply of labor, which implies a tighter aggregate labor market and thus the need to raise wages to attract the same number of workers. So on this score a higher price implies a higher wage rate being set. The ceteris paribus relationship between the price that a firm sets and the wage rate that it sets is thus ambiguous.

Because of the market share nature of the model, the most important factors affecting a firm's price and wage decisions are its expectations of what its competitors' prices and wages are going to be. The assumptions that are made about how these expectations are formed are thus of crucial importance in determining the price and wage responses in the model. For the most part the specification of these assumptions has been fairly simple, but it should be obvious that more elaborate assumptions could be easily incorporated into the model.

As one final point regarding prices and wages, it should be obvious that there is no simple relationship in the model between the level of the unemployment rate and changes in prices and wages. Each variable is determined each period by a complex set of factors, many factors being expectations of various sorts, and there is nothing in this process that indicates that one should observe any simple or stable relationship between the unemployment rate and price and wage changes.

6.6 THE RELATIONSHIP BETWEEN DEMAND DEPOSITS AND AGGREGATE OUTPUT

Demand deposits serve two main purposes in the model. Demand deposits are needed to carry out transactions, and they also serve as a buffer for firms and the bond dealer to meet unexpected changes in cash flow. The demand deposits of households are proportional to the households' expenditures on goods and have not been assumed to be a direct function of any interest rate. The number of hours worked and the number of goods purchased by the households are, however, functions of the bill rate and the loan rate, which means that the savings behavior of the households is a function of the interest rates. The savings behavior of the households affects their savings deposits and loans. The saving deposits of household 1 also serve as a buffer in the current period in the sense that any unexpected change in dividend income or tax payments takes the form of a change in the level of savings deposits in the period.

The demand deposits of the firms are on average proportional to the firms' wage bills, but they also serve an important purpose in the current period in meeting unexpected changes in cash flow net of taxes and dividends. Actual net cash flow will differ from expected net cash flow for a firm as the actual price of investment goods differs from the expected price and as the actual level of inventories differs from the expected level. The demand deposits of the bond dealer change as its holdings of bills and bonds change. If, for example, the change in the value of bills and bonds issued by the government in a period is less than the change in the demand for bills and bonds from the banks, the bond dealer will sell bills and bonds to the bank out of its inventories, which will have the effect of increasing its demand deposits.

Because of the residual or buffer nature of the demand deposits of the firms and the bond dealer, the short run relationship between the aggregate level of demand deposits and aggregate level of output is likely to be quite erratic. The aggregate level of demand deposits is likely to be a more erratic variable than the aggregate level of output, especially considering the fact that fluctuations in output are generally less than fluctuations in sales because of the buffer nature of goods inventories. Over long periods of time, demand deposits and output will, of course, move together because of the use of demand deposits for transactions purposes.

Although the demand deposits of the firms and households were assumed not to be a direct function of interest rates, relaxing this assumption would have little effect on the overall properties of the model. The important property of the model in this regard is the fact that the savings behavior of the households and the investment behavior of the firms are functions of the interest rates. Higher interest rates imply more savings and less investment and thus, other things being equal, more loanable funds in the system. Lower interest rates have the opposite effect. The only thing that making demand deposits a negative function of interest rates would do would be to lessen slightly the restrictiveness caused by those policies (e.g., experiments 1 and 2 in Table 6-6) that take money out of the system and lead to higher interest rates. In these cases the higher interest rates would imply that less money would be used to meet the same level of transactions, which, because of the reserve requirement on demand deposits, would allow the bank sector to lend slightly more than otherwise.

If, say, the demand deposits of the firm sector were decreased by 1.0, the firm sector would need to take out 1.0 less in loans. Likewise, if the demand deposits of household 2 were decreased by 1.0, household 2 would need to take out 1.0 less in loans. If the demand deposits of household 1 were decreased by 1.0, household 1's savings deposits could be increased by 1.0. Now, a simultaneous decrease in demand deposits of 1.0 and decrease in loans of 1.0 frees up fraction g_1 of this amount for new loans. Likewise, a simultaneous decrease in demand deposits of 1.0 and increase in savings deposits of 1.0 frees up fraction g_1 of this amount for new loans (assuming no reserve requirement on savings deposits). Since g_1 is only $\frac{1}{6}$ in the model, however, the amount of funds freed up by a decrease in demand deposits would be small unless the responsiveness of demand deposits to interest rate changes was extremely high. Therefore, little is lost in the model by not postulating that demand deposits are a direct function of interest rates.

NOTES

[a]See footnote i in Chapter Three for a discussion of this equation. In the notation in Table 6-2, this equation is $Y_t/\lambda_1 + \beta_2(V_{t-1} + Y_t - X_t - \beta_1 X_t)^2 + MH_{4t} + MH_{5t} + MH_{6t} = HPF_t$.

[b]By consistent in this case is meant a set of values that satisfies all the adding-up and other constraints in the model.

[c]Because of rounding, the numbers in Table 6-6 do not always add together properly. Not rounded, the surplus of the government in period t was 4.530, with the level of bank reserves also being less by this amount. The level of demand deposits of the firm sector was lower by 4.472, and the level of savings deposits of household 1 was lower by 0.058.

[d]Not rounded, the figures are 3.628, 4.882, 0.749, and 0.505, respectively.

[e]The decrease in investment, planned production, and the maximum number of hours was not large enough to show up in the rounded numbers in Table 6-6.

[f]Remember that $HPFMAX$ is the firm sector's expected supply of labor.

[g]The increase in investment, planned production, and the maximum number of hours as a result of the lower loan rate was not large enough in this case to show up in the rounded numbers in Table 6-6.

[h]The cut in production of the firm sector was too small to show up in the rounded numbers in Table 6-6.

[i]The decrease in profits of the firm sector was likewise too small to show up in the rounded numbers in Table 6-6.

[j]The numbers are off by 0.1 because of rounding.

[k]As mentioned in the Appendix, the non-condensed model is also not stable in the above sense, even though for the non-condensed model the banks, firms, and bond dealer are allowed to estimate some of the important expectational parameters on the basis of past observations. Even though some parameters are updated each period, there is still too much room for expectation errors to be made for the model to settle back down to the self-repeating position once it is shocked.

Chapter Seven

A Static-Equilibrium Version of the Model

7.1 INTRODUCTION

The methodology of this study has *not* been to develop a static-equilibrium model first and then to construct a dynamic version of it, but rather to specify from the very beginning a dynamic model. It is the author's view that static-equilibrium models are not of much use in providing insights into how an economy actually functions and that too much attention has been devoted in macroeconomic theory to analyzing static-equilibrium models. The static-equilibrium IS-LM model and its various extensions, for example, have come to dominate much of the teaching of macroeconomic theory. Although, as mentioned in Chapter One, it has recently been debated whether this model is an adequate representation of what Keynes actually had in mind, the model continues to be widely used. This model will be called the "textbook" model in the following discussion.

There are two reasons why a static-equilibrium version of the present dynamic model has been developed in this study. One reason is to show explicitly how much is lost in going from a dynamic model to a static-equilibrium model. It will be seen that many of the important characteristics of the dynamic model are lost when the model is converted into a static-equilibrium model. The other reason is to provide a model that is directly comparable to the textbook model. It is easier to compare two static-equilibrium models than it is to compare a dynamic model and a static-equilibrium model. The comparison between the present dynamic model and the textbook model is thus indirect. It will first be seen how the dynamic model compares to its static-equilibrium version, and it will then be seen how the static-equilibrium version compares to the textbook model. Because of the popularity of the textbook model, it was felt that some kind of a comparison between the dynamic model and the textbook model might aid in understanding the characteristics of the dynamic model. The static model is also useful in helping to point out an error in one of Christ's models [7].

7.2   THE STATIC-EQUILIBRIUM VERSION

An "equilibrium state" of a model is defined to be a state in which none of the variables in the model changes over time. The self-repeating run that was concocted for the dynamic model in Chapter Six is a run in which the dynamic model is in equilibrium. A static model is defined to be a model in which there are no time subscripts.

Some of the main differences between the basic dynamic model in this study and a static-equilibrium version of it are the following. First, in equilibrium no constraints can be binding, and so no distinction needs to be made in the static-equilibrium version between unconstrained and constrained quantities. Second, there can be no net savings or dissavings in equilibrium, for otherwise assets would be changing. This means that the net investment of the firm sector must be zero (gross investment equal to depreciation), savings of the households must be zero, and savings of the government must be zero (a balanced budget).

Third, there can be no excess labor and capital in equilibrium, for otherwise the firm sector would, among other things, be changing its price. Fourth, production must equal sales in equilibrium, for otherwise inventories would be changing. Fifth, there can be no capital gains and losses in equilibrium and no excess supply of bills and bonds. Sixth, the actual level of bank reserves must equal the desired level in equilibrium, for otherwise the bank sector would be changing its decisions. Seventh and finally, prices, wage rates, and interest rates must be determined in equilibrium in a way that clears the goods, labor, and financial markets. This condition usually means that prices, wage rates, and interest rates are determined *implicitly* in a static-equilibrium model. The values of these variables are usually determined by equating the quantities demanded to the quantities supplied.

It should be clear already that in the present case many of the important characteristics of the dynamic model will not be present in the static-equilibrium version. The price level and the wage rate cannot be set by the firm sector, but must be determined implicitly so as to clear the goods and labor markets. The loan rate cannot be set by the bank sector and the bill rate cannot be set by the bond dealer, but must be determined implicitly so as to clear the financial markets. No constraints can ever be binding, and no errors of expectations can ever be made. In the present case, in other words, the static-equilibrium version is more than just the dropping of time subscripts from

Table 7-1.   Notation for the Static-Equilibrium Model in Alphabetic Order

BR	= actual bank reserves
$BR*$	= required bank reserves
d_1	= profit tax rate
d_3	= personal tax rate
DDB	= demand deposits of the bank sector
DDF	= demand deposits of the firm sector
DDH	= demand deposits of the household sector
DEP	= depreciation of the firm sector
DIV	= total dividends paid and received in the economy
$DIVB$	= dividends paid by the bank sector
$DIVF$	= dividends paid by the firm sector
$FUNDS$	= loanable funds of the bank sector
g_1	= reserve requirement ratio
$\overline{H}$	= maximum number of hours that each machine can be used each period
HPF	= number of worker hours paid for by the firm sector
HPG	= number of worker hours paid for by the government
HPH	= number of hours that the household sector is paid for
I	= number of machines purchased by the firm sector in a period
INV	= number of goods purchased by the firm sector for investment purposes
K	= total number of machines on hand in the firm sector
L	= total value of loans of the bank sector
LF	= value of loans taken out by the firm sector
LH	= value of loans taken out by the household sector
m	= length of life of one machine
P	= price level
r	= bill rate and loan rate and bond rate
SD	= savings deposits of the household sector (and of the bank sector)
TAX	= total taxes paid
$TAXB$	= taxes paid by the bank sector
$TAXF$	= taxes paid by the firm sector
$TAXH$	= taxes paid by the household sector
VBB	= value of bills and bonds held by the bank sector
VBG	= value of bills and bonds issued by the government
W	= wage rate
X	= total number of goods sold
XG	= number of goods purchased by the government
XH	= number of goods purchased by the household sector
Y	= total number of goods produced
YG	= minimum guaranteed level of income
YH	= before-tax income of the household sector
δ	= number of goods that it takes to create one machine
λ	= amount of output produced per worker hour
μ_1	= amount of output produced per machine hour
ΠB	= before-tax profits of the bank sector
ΠF	= before-tax profits of the firm sector

Table 7-2.   The Equations of the Static-Equilibrium Model

(1) $VBG = VBB$,

(2) $FUNDS = (1-g_1)DDB + SD$,

(3) $HPF = \dfrac{Y}{\lambda}$,

(4) $K = \dfrac{Y}{\mu_1 \bar{H}}$,

(5) $I = \dfrac{1}{m} K$,

(6) $INV = \delta I$,

(7) $\lambda = 1.3212 \delta^{0.3212}$

$$\overline{\Pi F} = (1-d_1) \, [P \cdot Y - W \cdot HPF - (r+\tfrac{1}{m}) \cdot P \cdot \delta \cdot K]$$
$$= (1-d_1) \, [P \cdot Y - W \cdot \dfrac{Y}{\lambda} - (r+\tfrac{1}{m}) \cdot P \cdot \delta \cdot \dfrac{Y}{\mu_1 \bar{H}}] \ ,$$

(8) $\dfrac{\partial \, \overline{\Pi F}}{\partial \, \delta} = 0 \Rightarrow \dfrac{0.3212 \cdot W}{1.3212 \cdot \delta^{1.3212}} - \dfrac{(r+\tfrac{1}{m}) \cdot P}{\mu_1 \bar{H}} = 0$,

(9) $\dfrac{\partial \, \overline{\Pi F}}{\partial \, Y} = 0 \Rightarrow P - \dfrac{W}{\lambda} - \dfrac{(r+\tfrac{1}{m}) \cdot P \cdot \delta}{\mu_1 \bar{H}} = 0$,

(10) $Y = X$

(11) $HPH = e^{8.350} \, P^{-0.40} \, W^{0.40} \, r^{0.77} \, d_3^{-0.30} DIV^{-0.01} \, (SD-LH)^a - 0.78 \, YG$,

(12) $XH = e^{4.398} \, P^{-1.24} \, W^{1.24} \, r^{-0.54} \, d_3^{-0.18} \, DIV^{0.08} \, (SD-LH)^b + 0.36 \, YG$,

(13) $X = XH + INV + XG$,

(14) $L = LF + LH$,

(15) $HPH = HPF + HPG$,

(16) $DEP = P \cdot INV$,

(17) $\Pi F = P \cdot Y - W \cdot HPF - DEP - r \cdot LF$,

(18) $TAXF = d_1 \Pi F$,

(19) $DIVF = \Pi F - TAXF$,

(20) $DDF = \beta_{14} W \cdot HPF$,

(21) $DDH = \gamma_1 \cdot P \cdot XH$,

Table 7-2. (continued)

(22) $DDB = DDF + DDH$,

(23) $YH = W \cdot HPH + DIV + r \cdot SD$,

(24) $TAXH = d_3(YH - r \cdot LH) - YG$,

(25) $YH - TAXH - P \cdot XH = 0$,

(26) $\Pi B = r(L + VBB - SD)$,

(27) $TAXB = d_1 \, \Pi B$,

(28) $DIVB = \Pi B - TAXB$,

(29) $DIV = DIVB + DIVF$,

(30) $TAX = TAXB + TAXF + TAXH$,

(31) $BR = DDB + SD - L - VBB$,

(32) $BR^* = g_1 DDB$,

(33) $BR = BR^* \; [=> FUNDS = L + VBB]$,

(34) $P \cdot XG + W \cdot HPG + r \cdot VBG - TAX = 0$.

Given values of μ_1, $\bar{H}$, m, β_{14}, and γ_1, the above set of equations consists of 34 equations in 42 unknowns. The unknowns are:

1. BR	*15. HPG	29. $TAXH$
2. BR^*	16. HPH	30. VBB
*3. d_1	17. I	*31. VBG
*4. d_3	18. INV	32. W
5. DDB	19. K	33. X
6. DDF	20. L	*34. XG
7. DDH	21. LF	35. XH
8. DEP	22. LH	36. Y
9. DIV	23. P	*37. YG
10. $DIVB$	24. r	38. YH
11. $DIVF$	25. SD	39. δ
12. $FUNDS$	26. TAX	40. λ
*13. g_1	27. $TAXB$	41. ΠB
14. HPF	28. $TAXF$	42. ΠF

*Variable of the government

One of Equations (25) and (34) is redundant, which means that there are 33 independent equations in 42 unknowns. Given values of LF, LH, and SD and given values of 6 of the 7 government variables, the system of equations consists of the same number of independent equations as unknowns.

Note: Since SD and LH are exogenous, it does not matter what the values of a and b are in Equations (11) and (12).

the variables of the dynamic model. The determination of some of the key variables and the interactions among the behavioral units are substantially changed when going from the dynamic model to the static-equilibrium version.

The static-equilibrium version consists of 34 equations and is presented in Table 7-2. The notation for the model is presented in Table 7-1. The variables in Table 7-2 are roughly in the order in which they appear in Table 6-2. Time subscripts have been dropped from all the variables in this chapter. The bond dealer serves no useful purpose in the model, since the bill rate is implicitly determined, and so the bond dealer has been dropped from the model. There is also no reason to have more than one interest rate in the model, and so the loan rate and the bond rate have been dropped. The only interest rate in the model is the bill rate, r, and so this is the rate not only on government debt, but also on private loans and savings deposits.

Equation (1) in Table 7-2 is a market clearing equation, equating the supply of bills and bonds from the government (VBG) to the demand for bills and bonds by the bank sector (VBB). Since there are no capital gains and losses in equilibrium and since the bond rate is always equal to the bill rate, there is no need to distinguish between bills and bonds. The interest payment of the government on VBG, for example, is simply $r \cdot VBG$. Since there is no bond dealer in the static model, the desired value of bills and bonds of the bond dealer in the dynamic model, VBD^*, does not appear in Equation (1). Equation (2) in Table 7-2 defines the level of loanable funds and is the same as Equation (1) in Table 2-4 without the time subscripts and without the $EMAXDD$ and $EMAXSD$ terms. Since there is no uncertainty in the static model, $EMAXDD$ and $EMAXSD$ serve no useful purpose and can be dropped.

Equations (3) through (10) determine the production of the firm sector and its demand for investment goods and employment. Since the price level and the wage rate are not decision variables of the firm sector in the static-equilibrium model, a much different and simpler behavioral model of the firm sector must be considered. No longer can a firm's decisions be assumed to be based on the solution of an optimal control problem in which the price level and the wage rate are among the decision variables. The simpler model of firm behavior in Equations (3)-(10) is as follows.

Since there can be no excess labor and capital in equilibrium, Equations (3) and (4) must hold. Equation (3) states that the number of worker hours that the firm sector pays for must be equal to the number required to produce the output. Equation (4) states that the number of machines on hand must be equal to the minimum number required to produce the output. Since net investment must be zero in equilibrium, Equation (5) must hold. In equilibrium the number of machines wearing out in a period must be $\frac{1}{m}K$, where m is the length of life of a machine. Equation (5) states that the number of machines purchased in a period (I) must be equal to the number wearing out. In Equation (6) the number of machines purchased is translated into the equivalent number of goods purchased.

Equation (7) determines λ as a function of δ. The three important parameters regarding the technology in the firm sector are λ, output per worker hour, μ_1, output per machine hour, and δ, the number of goods required to create one machine. In the non-condensed model two types of machines were postulated, so that λ, μ, and δ each took on two possible values (λ_1 and λ_2, μ_1 and μ_2, δ_1 and δ_2). μ_1 and μ_2 were, however, assumed to be equal, so that the two types of machines differed only in their λ and δ coefficients.

In the condensed model only one type of machine was postulated, so that λ, μ, and δ each took on only one value. In the condensed model investment was still a function of the loan rate because the firm sector's price decision was a function of the loan rate. The price decision had an effect on the investment decision through its effect on expected sales and planned production. In the static-equilibrium model λ and δ are assumed to be continuous variables, and so there are in effect assumed to be an infinite number of different types of machines. The parameter μ_1 is still assumed to be the same for all of the different types of machines. In Equation (7) λ is a positive function of δ: the more expensive a machine is in terms of the number of goods it takes to produce it, the greater is the output per worker hour on the machine. The ratio μ_1/λ is the worker-machine ratio, and with μ_1 fixed, Equation (7) merely states that machines with lower worker-machine ratios cost more.

The choice of the coefficients in Equation (7) is discussed in the next section. The specification of Equation (7) is a way of keeping the putty-clay nature of the technology for the static-equilibrium model. The worker-machine ratio is fixed ex post, but ex ante the firm sector has a choice of which technology to use.

The next equation in Table 7-2 defines after-tax profits of the firm sector. The total revenue is $P \cdot Y$, the total cost of labor is $W \cdot HPF$, and the total cost of capital is $(r + \frac{1}{m}) \cdot P \cdot \delta \cdot K$. Since each machine has a life of m periods and since one machine costs $P \cdot \delta$ to purchase, the cost of capital for one machine is $(r + \frac{1}{m})P \cdot \delta$. Multiply this by K, the total number of machines on hand, and one has the total cost of capital. The second expression for after-tax profits in Table 7-2 replaces HPF and K by their definitions in Equations (3) and (4).

The two decision variables of the firm sector are the choice of the technology, represented by δ, and the level of output Y. The firm sector is assumed to maximize after-tax profits, and so Equations (8) and (9) must hold. The derivation in Equation (8) uses the fact, from Equation (7), that λ is a function of δ. Equation (9) merely states that in equilibrium the price of a unit of output must equal the cost of producing it. The last equation in the production block for the firm sector, Equation (10), states that output must equal sales in equilibrium, for otherwise inventories would be changing.

Equations (11) and (12) determine the two main decision variables of the household sector, the number of hours to work (*HPH*) and the number of goods to purchase (*XH*). The existence of two different households serves no useful purpose in the static-equilibrium model, and so the households have been aggregated into one. Equation (11) is similar to Equations (2) and (1)′ in Table 4-6, and Equation (12) is similar to Equations (3) and (2)′ in Table 4-6. In Equations (2) and (3) in Table 4-6, the level of savings deposits and the stock price were added together, but in Equations (11) and (12) in Table 7-2 the two have been separated. Since the stock price is DIV/r and since r is already included in the equations, the separation of the level of savings deposits and the stock price merely means that DIV is included as a separate variable in Equations (11) and (12) in Table 7-2.

Equation (11) states that *HPH* is a positive function of the wage rate and the interest rate, and a negative function of the price level, the proportional tax rate, the level of dividends, and the minimum guaranteed level of income. Equation (12) states that *XH* is a positive function of the wage rate, the level of dividends, and the minimum guaranteed level of income, and a negative function of the price level, the interest rate, and the proportional tax rate. The choice of the coefficients in the two equations is discussed in the next section. The coefficients are based on the coefficients in Equations (2), (3), (1)′, and (2)′ in Table 4-6.

Equations (13)-(31) in Table 7-2 are very similar to the relevant equations in Table 6-2, appropriately simplified. Equation (13) determines total sales and is similar to Equation (16) in Table 6-2. The equation in the present context is the market clearing equation for goods. Equation (14) determines the total value of loans, and Equation (15) is the market clearing equation for labor. Equations (16)-(20) determine the financial variables of the firm sector: depreciation, before-tax profits, taxes paid, dividends paid, and demand deposits. Depreciation in Equation (16) is merely the value of investment in equilibrium. Equation (17), determining before-tax profits, does not include an inventory valuation term because the term is zero in equilibrium. If *LF* is zero in Equation (17), as it is taken to be for the results in the next section, then the level of before-tax profits as defined in Equation (17) is merely $r \cdot K$ because of Equation (9). If *LF* were set equal to *K*, then profits in Equation (17) would, of course, be zero. The choice for the value of *LF* is discussed in the next section.

Since there is no uncertainty in the static model, the DDF_2 term in the dynamic model serves no useful purpose in the static model, and so it has not been included in Equation (20) in Table 7-2. Equation (21) determines the demand deposits of the household sector, and Equation (22) determines total demand deposits. Equations (23) and (24) determine the income and taxes of the household sector. Equation (25) is an equilibrium condition and states that the savings of the household sector must be zero in equilibrium. Equations (26)-(28) determine the before-tax profits, taxes, and dividends of the bank sector, and Equations (29) and (30) determine total dividends and total taxes. Equation (31) determines actual bank reserves, and Equation (32) determines required bank reserves. Equation (33) is an equilibrium condition and states that actual reserves must equal required reserves in equilibrium. Equation (34) is also an equilibrium condition and states that the savings of the government must be zero in equilibrium.

Aside from the specific coefficients in Equations (7), (11), and (12), there are five parameters in the static model: μ_1, $\bar{H}$, m, β_{14}, and γ_1. Not counting these parameters, the static model consists of 34 equations in 42 unknowns. The unknowns are listed at the end of Table 7-2. Although it may not be immediately obvious from the model, one of Equations (25) and (34) is redundant. Given all the other equations in the model and one of the two equations, the other is automatically satisfied. Consider, for example, Equation (34), which says that government savings are zero. This equation must be redundant, given the rest of the equations in the model, for the following reason. The firm and bank sectors retain no earnings and so are neither net savers nor net dissavers. Equation (25) states that the household sector is neither a net saver nor a net dissaver. Therefore, since all flows of funds are accounted for in the system, zero net savings in the private sector of the economy must imply that the net level of savings of the government is zero, which is Equation (34). If the government were a net saver or a net dissaver, this would show up somewhere in the savings of the private sector. Equation (34) is thus redundant, given the other equations of the model.

The static model thus consists of 33 independent equations in 42 unknowns, so that there are nine more unknowns than equations. There are seven variables of the government: three tax parameters, d_1, d_3, and YG; the reserve requirement ratio, g_1; the value of bills and bonds issued, VBG; the number of goods purchased, XG; and the number of worker hours paid for, HPG. There are also three stock variables in the model for which there are no explicit equations: the value of savings deposits of the household sector, SD; the value of loans of the household sector, LH; and the value of loans of the firm sector, LF. If these three variables are treated as exogenous, then there are six more unknowns than equations, and so the government can choose six of its seven values. In this case, because of the requirement that the government budget be balanced in equilibrium, given six of the seven government values, the other value is automatically determined.

It seems reasonable in the present context to treat SD, LH, and LF as exogenous. Consider, for example, SD-LH-LF, and denote this variable as A, which is the stock of assets of the private, nonbank sector (not counting common stocks and demand deposits). Let A_{-1} denote the stock of assets of the previous period. Then A is determined as A_{-1} plus the level of savings. Therefore, given

Table 7–3.   Equations of the Static-Equilibrium Model by Blocks (*LF, LH, SD,* and all government values except *VBG* are assumed to be exogenous)

Block 1: 12 equations, 14 endogenous variables: *DIV, HPF, HPH, I, INV, K, P, r, W, X, XH, Y, δ, λ*

Equation Can Be Used to Compute:	Equation No. in Table 7–2
Y	(3) $HPF = \dfrac{Y}{\lambda}$,
K	(4) $K = \dfrac{Y}{\mu_1 \bar{H}}$,
I	(5) $I = \dfrac{1}{m} K$,
INV	(6) $INV = \delta I,$
λ	(7) $\lambda = 1.3212 \cdot \delta^{0.3212},$
δ	(8) $\delta = [\dfrac{\mu_1 \bar{H} \cdot 0.3212}{(r + \frac{1}{m}) \cdot 1.3212} \dfrac{W}{P}]^{\frac{1}{1.3212}},$
W, P, W/P, or r	(9) $\dfrac{W}{P} = \lambda [1 - (r + \frac{1}{m}) \dfrac{\delta}{\mu_1 \bar{H}}]$,
X	(10) $Y = X,$
HPH	(11) $HPH = e^{8.350} P^{-0.40} W^{0.40} r^{0.77} d_3^{-0.30} DIV^{-0.01} (SD-LH)^a$ $- 0.78YG,$
W, P, W/P, or r	(12) $XH = e^{4.398} P^{-1.24} W^{1.24} r^{-0.54} d_3^{-0.18} DIV^{0.08} (SD-LH)^b$ $+ 0.36YG,$
XH	(13) $X = XH + INV + XG,$
HPF	(15) $HPH = HPF + HPG.$

Block 2:	
L	(14) $L = LH + LF,$
DDF	(20) $DDF = \beta_{14} \cdot W \cdot HPF,$
DDH	(21) $DDH = \gamma_1 \cdot P \cdot XH,$
DDB	(22) $DDB = DDF + DDH,$

Table 7-3. (continued)

FUNDS	(2)	$FUNDS = (1 - g_1)DDB + SD,$
VBB	(33)	$FUNDS = L + VBB,$
VBG	(1)	$VBG = VBB,$
DEP	(16)	$DEP = P{\cdot}INV,$
ΠF	(17)	$\Pi F = P{\cdot}Y - W{\cdot}HPF - DEP - r{\cdot}LF,$
TAXF	(18)	$TAXF = d_1\,\Pi F,$
DIVF	(19)	$DIVF = \Pi F - TAXF,$
ΠB	(26)	$\Pi B = r(L + VBB - SD),$
TAXB	(27)	$TAXB = d_1\,\Pi B,$
DIVB	(28)	$DIVB = \Pi B - TAXB,$
DIV	(29)	$DIV = DIVB + DIVF,$
YH	(23)	$YH = W{\cdot}HPH + DIV + r{\cdot}SD,$
TAXH	(24)	$TAXH = d_3(YH - r{\cdot}LH) - YG,$
TAX	(30)	$TAX = TAXB + TAXF + TAXH,$
W, P, or r	(34)	$P{\cdot}XG + W{\cdot}HPG + r{\cdot}VBG - TAX = 0.$

A_{-1}, A must be equal to it in the static model because savings must be zero in equilibrium. Since the model has no way of determining A_{-1} endogenously, it likewise has no way of determining A. Therefore, it is reasonable to treat A as exogenous. If, say, SD were not treated as exogenous (but LH and LF were), there would be seven more unknowns than equations, and so the government could choose all seven of its values. The requirement of a balanced budget for the government in equilibrium would not lead in this case to one of the government values being automatically determined, given the other six. This would, however, only be because of the unreasonable treatment of SD as endogenous.[a]

This completes the specification of the static-equilibrium model. The solution of the model is discussed in the next section, and some results are presented of solving the model for alternative values of the government variables. As was the case for the dynamic model, the results in the next section are meant only to aid in understanding the properties of the static model and are not meant to be a "test" of the model in any sense. The static model is compared to the textbook model in Section 7.4 below.

7.3   THE SOLUTION OF THE STATIC MODEL

Given values of SD, LH, and LF and given six of the seven government values, the model consists of the same number of independent equations as endogenous variables. The model is nonlinear in the variables and so must be solved by some iterative technique. For the results in this section the model was solved using the Gauss-Seidel technique. Before this technique was applied, however, the model was broken up into two blocks, and it will be useful to consider this breakdown. The two blocks are presented in Table 7-3. The first block corresponds to the real sector of the model, and the second block corresponds to the financial sector. The equations in Table 7-3 are in the same form as they appear in Table 7-2 except for Equations (8) and (9), which have been rearranged. The zero-savings equation of the government (Equation (34)) has been included in Table 7-3, and so the zero-savings equation of the household sector (Equation (25)) has not been included.

If VBG is taken to be the one endogenous government variable, then the real block consists of 12 equations in 14 endogenous variables. The model was solved in the endogenous VBG case in the following way. Given values of two of the 14 endogenous variables in block 1, block 1 was solved for the other 12 variables using Gauss-Seidel. Block 2 was then solved for the other variables in the model, including the two variables taken as given for the solution of block 1. Block 1 was then resolved using the new values of the two variables. and block 2 was resolved again. This process was repeated until overall convergence was reached. There are clearly other ways that the model could be solved using Gauss-Seidel, but the way just described converged fairly quickly and so no further experimentation with ways of solving the model was carried out. In addition to its computational convenience, breaking the model up into the two blocks has the advantage of indicating clearly the links between the real and financial sectors.

It was decided for purposes of the static model to make HPH and XH a function of the real wage, W/P. The coefficients for W and P in Equation (11) were taken to be of opposite sign and equal in absolute value, as were the coefficients for W and P in Equation (12). The 0.40 coefficient for W/P in Equation (11) is the average of the absolute values of the coefficients for W and P in Equations (2) and (1)$'$ in Table 4-6 $[(0.41 + 0.71 + 0.25 + 0.22)/4 = 0.40]$. Likewise, the 1.24 coefficient for W/P in Equation (12) is the average of the absolute values of the coefficients for W and P in Equations (3) and (2)$'$ in Table 4-6. The other coefficients in Equations (11) and (12) are similarly averages of the relevant coefficients in Equations (2), (3), (1)$'$, and (2)$'$ in Table 4-6. It makes no difference what coefficients are used for SD-LH in Equations (11) and (12) because SD and LH are both treated as exogenous and thus never change. When SD_{t-1} and PS_t are split up in Equations (2) and (3), the coefficients for PS_t change from -0.38 and 0.14 to -0.22 and 0.08 because of the change of the base from $SD_{t-1} + PS_t$ to SD_{t-1} and PS_t separately. The one change that was made in going from Equation (2) in Table 4-6 to Equation (11) in Table 7-2 was to make the coefficient for DIV smaller in absolute value, from -0.22 to -0.01. (Remember that DIV/r is merely PS in the static model.) This was done to make the solution values in the real block somewhat less sensitive to the values determined in the financial block.

The parameter values, government values, and values of LF, LH, and SD that were used for the basic solution of the model are presented in Table 7-4. These values and the values for the constant terms in Equations (11) and (12) were chosen to make the basic set of solution values come out to be roughly the same as the base run values for the dynamic model in Chapter Six. The values for LF and LH were, however, taken to be zero, and the value for SD was taken to be 203.2. The value 203.2 is the difference between the base run value for SD_t in Chapter Six (1013.4) and the sum of the base run values for LF_t and LH_t (*328.1 + 482.1*). The firm sector was also assumed to hold no demand deposits, so that β_{14} was taken to be zero. These changes have very little effect on the final properties of the model.

Table 7-4.   Parameter Values, Government Values, and Values of
LF, LH, and SD for the Base Run in Table 7-5

Parameter Values	*Government Values*	*Values of LF, LH, SD*
$\bar{H} = 1.0$	$d_1 = 0.5$	$LF = 0.0$
$m = 10$	$d_3 = 0.2391$	$LH = 0.0$
$\beta_{14} = 0.0$	$g_1 = 0.1667$	$SD = 203.2$
$\gamma_1 = 0.32044$	$HPG = 124.7$	
$\mu_1 = 0.6787$	$XG = 93.3$	
	$YG = 0.0$	

Note: The two constant terms were chosen in Equations (11) and (12) under the assumption that the values of a and b were zero.

The two coefficients in Equation (7) (1.3212 and 0.3212) were chosen as follows. The solution value for λ for the basic run was first chosen to be 1.3212, the same as the value of λ_1 in the condensed, dynamic model; and the solution value for δ was taken to be 1.0, also the same as in the condensed, dynamic model. This meant that the first coefficient in Equation (7) had to be 1.3212. Given values for λ, δ, W, P, r, m, and $\bar{H}$, Equation (9) was then solved for μ_1. Finally, given values for W, P, r, m, $\bar{H}$, μ_1, and the 1.3212 coefficient already determined, Equation (8) was solved for the remaining coefficient, which turned out to be 0.3212.

Regarding the solution of the model using Gauss-Seidel, it is somewhat arbitrary as to which two of the 14 variables in block 1 are taken as given for purposes of solving the block. The main choice in the overall model is which equations to use to compute W, P, and r. Note that if the coefficients for W and P in Equations (11) and (12) are of opposite sign and equal in absolute value, as they are specified here to be, then W and P always enter as W/P in block 1. It is not important for purposes of solving the model, however, whether W and P enter separately in Equations (11) and (12) or only as W/P. It should also be noted that it is not important for purposes of solving the model whether r is included in the demand deposit equations, (20) and (21). There is, in other words, nothing in the model that requires that demand deposits be a function of the rate of interest in order to solve the model.

The results of solving the model are presented in Table 7-5. For all the runs in Table 7-5, VBG was taken to be the endogenous government variable. The first set of results in the table is based on the values in Table 7-4. For each of the other runs in the table, one of the six exogenous government values was changed. For all of these results the model was solved by using Equation (9) to compute r, Equation (12) to compute W/P, and Equation (34) to compute P. W was computed as W/P times P. This meant that the two variables taken as given for purposes of solving block 1 were DIV and the breakdown of W/P into W and P. The advantage of solving the model in this way is that block 2 becomes linear in the unknown variables in the block and so can be solved without having to use the Gauss-Seidel technique. Only values for the most important variables in the model are presented in Table 7-5. Real GNP in the table, $GNPR$, is the sum of Y and HPG.

For the first experiment in Table 7-5, the number of goods purchased by the government (XG), was increased by 2.5. This caused output, Y, to rise by 4.77, from 842.03 to 846.80. The price level, the wage rate, and the interest rate were all higher, and the real wage was slightly lower. The values for δ and λ decreased, which meant that the firm sector switched to a cheaper type of machine with a higher worker-machine ratio. Both a higher interest rate and a lower real wage induce the firm sector to switch to a more labor intensive type of machine. The price level and the wage rate each rose by about 12 percent corresponding to the increase in XG of about 2.7 percent. The higher price level corresponded to larger values for the financial variables. Demand deposits increased by about 12 percent, from 200.35 to 225.25, and VBG increased from 370.16 to 390.91. The aggregate level of dividends increased from 45.79 to 51.91, and the aggregate level of taxes increased from 242.26 to 272.80.

Because the model is fully simultaneous, it is not possible to talk about one endogenous variable *causing* another endogenous variable to behave in a certain way. Nevertheless, it is possible to speak loosely about the relationship between one endogenous variable and another. Consider, for example, why the

Table 7-5. Results of Solving the Static-Equilibrium Model for the Endogenous *VBG* Case

	Base Run	1 XG: +2.5	2 XG: -2.5	3 d₃: -0.00304	4 d₃: +0.00304	5 YG: +2.5	6 YG: -2.5	7 HPG: +2.5	8 HPG: -2.5	9 g₁: -0.10	10 g₁: +0.10
GNPR	966.73	971.50	962.12	972.49	961.20	969.60	963.01	971.06	962.58	967.70	965.77
P	1.0009	1.1216	0.8980	1.1131	0.9047	1.1371	0.8551	1.1325	0.8902	1.0221	0.9807
W	1.0009	1.1202	0.8990	1.1124	0.9052	1.1355	0.8565	1.1310	0.8913	1.0218	0.9809
W/P	1.0000	0.9988	1.0011	0.9994	1.0006	0.9986	1.0016	0.9987	1.0012	0.9997	1.0002
r	0.06500	0.06564	0.06439	0.06533	0.06471	0.06573	0.06416	0.06569	0.06435	0.06515	0.06486
Y	842.03	846.80	837.42	847.79	836.50	844.90	838.31	843.86	840.38	843.00	841.07
λ	1.3213	1.3196	1.3238	1.3204	1.3220	1.3193	1.3234	1.3194	1.3229	1.3208	1.3216
δ	1.0000	0.9961	1.0037	0.9980	1.0018	0.9956	1.0051	0.9959	1.0040	0.9991	1.0008
I	124.06	124.77	123.39	124.91	123.25	124.49	123.52	124.33	123.82	124.21	123.92
INV	124.06	124.28	123.84	124.67	123.47	123.94	124.15	123.82	124.31	124.10	124.03
HPF	637.32	641.73	633.08	642.09	632.77	640.40	633.47	639.56	635.26	638.23	636.42
HPH	762.02	766.43	757.78	766.79	757.47	765.10	758.17	766.76	757.46	762.93	761.12
XH	624.67	626.72	622.78	629.83	619.73	627.66	620.86	626.74	622.77	625.60	623.74
DDB	200.35	225.25	179.20	224.65	179.67	228.70	170.13	227.45	177.65	204.90	196.01
VBG	370.16	390.91	352.53	390.41	352.92	393.78	344.97	392.74	351.24	394.44	346.94
DIV	45.79	51.91	40.61	51.44	40.98	52.58	38.61	52.28	40.37	47.55	44.11
TAX	242.26	272.80	216.34	268.07	220.13	273.56	208.72	275.32	214.58	248.48	236.32

price level is higher in experiment 1 than it is in the base run. When the government increases XG without increasing tax rates, some way must be found for satisfying the zero savings equation of the government, Equation (34). Now, a rising price level increases both the money expenditures of the government and taxes, but the relationships in the model are such that taxes rise more than money expenditures as the price level increases. Therefore, speaking loosely, Equation (34) can be met by having the price level rise. The government is, in other words, financing the increase in XG by an increase in the price level.

Regarding the increase in VBG in experiment 1, consider how VBG is determined. From Equations (1), (2), and (33), VBG equals $(1-g_1)DDB + SD-L$. Since SD and L are exogenous, the only endogenous variable on the right-hand side of this equation is the level of demand deposits, DDB. Since DDB is proportional to the price level, VBG increases as the price level increases. Another way of looking at this is as follows. From Equations (2) and (33) the demand for bills and bonds by the bank sector, VBB, is $(1-g_1)DDB + SD - L$. Since SD and L are exogenous, VBB increases as DDB increases. From Equation (1) VBG must equal VBB, so that VBG must increase as DDB increases to meet the increased demand for bills and bonds from the bank sector.

Consider finally the behavior of the household sector. In order to increase the level of output, the household sector has to be induced to work more. The savings of the household sector must be zero, so that if the sector works more, it must also consume more. One way of inducing the sector to work more is for the interest rate to increase, and for the results in Table 7-5 the interest rate is an important factor in inducing the sector to work more. The higher interest rate in experiment 1 also had, however, a negative effect on the number of goods purchased by the household sector, but this was more than offset by the higher level of dividends. The zero savings constraint of the household sector was also met in part by the fact that the price level increased slightly more than did the wage rate. Holding HPH, XH, r, and DIV constant, an increase in P, holding W constant, has a negative effect on the savings of the household sector, and an increase in W, holding P constant, has a positive effect. An increase in P relative to W thus has a negative effect on savings. It is also the case, however, given the coefficients used in Equations (11) and (12), that a decrease in W/P decreases HPH less than XH, so that on this score a decrease in W/P has a positive effect on savings. Overall, of course, the solution values are such that the zero savings constraint is satisfied, and all that can be done here is to give a rough indication of how this comes about.

For the second experiment, the value of XG was decreased by 2.5. The results in Table 7-5 are almost exactly opposite, even quantitatively, to those for the first experiment, and so require no further discussion. Even though the model is nonlinear, the response of the model is quite symmetrical for the size of the changes considered here.

For the third experiment, the personal income tax parameter, d_3, was decreased by 0.00304. With no other changes, this corresponds to an aggregate tax decrease of 2.5. This change had similar effects to the increase in XG in experiment 1. The interest rate rose, although it rose less than it did in experiment 1. A decrease in d_3 has a positive effect on the work effort of the household sector, so that, again speaking loosely, the interest rate needed to rise less in experiment 3 than it did in experiment 1 in order to have the household sector work more. The number of goods purchased by the household sector was greater in experiment 3 than in experiment 1 because the induced increase in output in experiment 3 did not correspond to any increase in the number of goods purchased by the government. The total level of output was also somewhat greater in experiment 3 than in experiment 1. It is interesting to note that even though d_3 was decreased in experiment 3, the aggregate level of tax collections in money terms (TAX) rose substantially because of the increase in the price level. The results for the fourth experiment, an increase in d_3 of 0.00304, are again almost exactly opposite to those for the third experiment.

For the fifth experiment, the minimum guaranteed level of income, YG, was increased by 2.5. This change had similar effects to the increase in XG in experiment 1 and to the decrease in d_3 in experiment 3. In this case, however, the interest rate was higher than it was in experiment 1, and the total level of output was somewhat lower. In contrast to the case in experiment 3, where a decrease in d_3 has a positive effect on the work effort of the household sector, an increase in YG has a negative effect on work effort. Therefore, the increase in output was somewhat less in experiment 5 than in experiment 3, and the interest rate was somewhat greater in order to induce the household sector to work more. In other words, decreasing taxes by decreasing the proportional tax rate has more of an effect on output than does decreasing taxes by increasing the minimum guaranteed level of income because of the work response of the household sector. The results for the sixth experiment, a decrease in YG of 2.5, are opposite to those for the fifth experiment.

For the seventh experiment, the number of worker hours paid for by the government (HPG) was increased by 2.5. Real GNP was about the same in this case as in experiment 1, although in this case 2.5 of the increase in real GNP was due to the increase in HPG. The number of goods produced, Y, was less in experiment 7 than in experiment 1. Overall, however, the results for experiments 1 and 7 are quite similar. The results for the eighth experiment, a decrease in HPG of 2.5, are opposite to those for the seventh experiment.

For the ninth experiment, the reserve requirement ratio, g_1, was decreased from 0.1667 to 0.0667. This change had a stimulative effect on the economy and led, for example, to an increase in output, the price level, the wage rate, the interest rate, and the level of employment. The reason the decrease in g_1 had a positive effect on the economy is roughly as follows. Since SD and L are exogenous, it can be seen from Equations (2) and (33) that a decrease in g_1 leads, other things being equal, to an increase in *VBB*. In other words, more funds are now available for the bank sector to buy bills and bonds. From Equation (1), *VBG* must then increase to meet the increase in the demand for bills and bonds.

An increase in *VBG* means that the level of interest payments from the government to the bank sector is increased, which in turn means that the level of dividends is increased. A higher aggregate dividend level then has a positive effect on the number of goods purchased by the household sector. An expansion in the economy thus takes place when g_1 is decreased because government spending is increased. Government spending is increased because of the increase in interest payments. It may seem puzzling at first glance as to why the interest rate would increase when g_1 is decreased, since a decrease in g_1 frees up more funds, but one of the reasons this happens is because a higher interest rate is needed to induce the household sector to work more. In a loose sense one might say that the interest rate is tied more to the equations in the real block than it is to the equations in the financial block. The results for the tenth experiment, an increase in g_1 to 0.2667, are opposite to those for the ninth experiment.

The results in Table 7-5 are all based on the treatment of *VBG* as the one endogenous variable of the government. *VBG* can be made exogenous if one of the other seven government variables is made endogenous. For the results in Table 7-6, *VBG* was treated as exogenous and d_3 was taken to be the endogenous variable of the government. When d_3 is endogenous, the equations in Table 7-3 can be solved as follows.

The solution in block 1 can remain the same. In block 2, Equation (1) can be used to solve for *VBB*, given the now exogenous value for *VBG*. Equation (33) can be used to solve for *FUNDS*, and Equation (2) can be used to solve for *DDB*. When *VBG* is exogenous, *DDB* is in effect also exogenous. Given *DDB* and *DDF* (which is actually zero since β_{14} is zero), *DDH* is *DDB* – *DDF* from Equation (22). Given *DDH*, *P* can then be determined from Equation (21). *W* is then *W/P* times *P*, where *W/P* is available from block 1. Given *P* and *W*, *TAX* can be computed from Equation (34), the zero savings equation of the government. *TAXF* and *TAXB* can be computed in the usual way, and then given these two values and given *TAX*, *TAXH* can be computed from Equation (30). Given *TAXH*, d_3 can then be computed from Equation (24).

The value chosen for *VBG* for the results in Table 7-6 is the solution value of *VBG* for the base run in Table 7-5. All the other exogenous values for the base run in Table 7-6 were taken to be the same as the values used for the base run in Table 7-5. The base run in Table 7-6 is thus exactly the same as the base run in Table 7-5. For the first experiment in Table 7-6, *XG* was increased by 2.5. This had a positive effect on the price level, the wage rate, and the interest rate, but a negative effect on the level of output. In the endogenous d_3

Table 7-6. Results of Solving the Static-Equilibrium Model for the Endogenous d_3 Case

		Experiment			
	Base Run	*1 XG: +2.5*	*2 XG: -2.5*	*3 g_1: -0.10*	*4 g_1: +0.10*
GNPR	966.73	965.67	967.83	960.83	973.30
P	1.0009	1.0060	0.9958	0.9012	1.1269
W	1.0009	1.0054	0.9964	0.9016	1.1263
W/P	1.0000	0.9994	1.0006	1.0004	0.9995
r	0.06500	0.06531	0.06470	0.06477	0.06528
Y	842.03	840.97	843.13	836.13	848.60
λ	1.3212	1.3204	1.3220	1.3217	1.3205
δ	1.0000	0.9981	1.0018	1.0014	0.9983
I	124.06	123.91	124.23	123.20	125.03
INV	124.06	123.68	124.46	123.37	124.82
HPF	637.32	636.90	637.78	637.58	642.64
HPH	762.02	761.60	762.48	757.28	767.34
XH	624.67	621.50	627.88	619.47	630.48
DDB	200.35	200.35	200.35	178.89	227.67
DIV	45.79	46.08	45.49	41.41	51.36
d_3	0.2391	0.2422	0.2360	0.2429	0.2351
TAX	242.26	245.93	238.61	220.48	269.75

Note: Value used for VBG was 370.16 for all of the runs in this table.

case the increase in XG is financed by an increase in d_3, and an increase in d_3 has a negative effect on the work effort of the household sector. This effect was such in experiment 1 as to lead to a lower value of hours worked by the household sector and a lower value of output. The value for d_3 increased from 0.2391 to 0.2422. The price level and wage rate rose much less in experiment 1 in Table 7-6 than they did in experiment 1 in Table 7-5, since in Table 7-6 the increase in XG was in effect financed by an increase in d_3 rather than an increase in the price level. The results for the second experiment in Table 7-6, a decrease in XG of 2.5, are again the opposite to those for the first experiment.

For the third experiment in Table 7-6, g_1 was decreased to 0.0667. This change had a significant contractionary effect on the economy. The reason for the large contractionary effect can be seen roughly as follows. Given VBG, L, and SD, a decrease in g_1 means from Equations (1), (2), and (33) that DDB must decrease. Given DDF from Equation (20), this means from Equation (22) that DDH must decrease. Given the decrease in DDH, P must then decrease from Equation (21). W, being determined as W/P times P, must then decrease. The decrease in P leads, among other things, to a lower level of dividends and turns out to have a contractionary effect on the economy. The results for the fourth experiment in Table 7-6, an increase in g_1 to 0.26667, are opposite to those for the third experiment.

This concludes the presentation of results for the static model. Although the results of treating other government variables as endogenous could be presented, enough evidence has been presented to give a good indication of the properties of the model.

A few general remarks about the model will be made to conclude this section. First, it should be obvious that it makes an important difference regarding the response of the model to a change in an exogenous variable as to which government variable is made endogenous. When, for example, *VBG* is endogenous, an increase in *XG* leads to an increase in output and a much higher price level, whereas when d_3 is endogenous, an increase in *XG* leads to a slight decrease in output but only a slightly higher price level. It also should be obvious that when *VBG* is endogenous, the multiplier effect of an increase in *XG* on output is not one over the marginal tax rate. In Christ's model [8] the multiplier is over the marginal tax rate, but his model is much simpler than the present model. Christ's model, for example, does not have a labor sector and does not endogenously determine the price level. When a more complicated model than Christ's is considered, there is no reason to expect that his result regarding the multiplier will generalize, and in the present case it clearly does not.

It was mentioned above that it makes no difference from the point of view of solving the model whether the level of demand deposits is a function of the rate of interest or not. It also turns out to make little quantitative difference as to whether this is true or not. The experiments in Tables 7-5 and 7-6 were carried out under the assumption that *DDH* is a function of *r:*

$$DDH = e^{-2.733} \gamma_1 P \cdot XH \cdot r^{1.00} \quad . \tag{21$'$}$$

The constant term in Equation $(21)'$ is such as to make the base run value of *DDH* unchanged. The results of replacing Equation (21) with Equation $(21)'$ were little changed from the results in Tables 7-5 and 7-6. For the first experiment in Table 7-5, for example, the new solution value of *r* was 0.06563 compared to 0.06564. The new level of output was 846.72 compared to 846.80. For the third experiment in Table 7-6, the new solution value of *r* was the same to four significant digits, and the new level of output was 836.04 compared to 836.13. For none of the experiments were the results in the two cases noticeably different. As mentioned above, the interest rate is, in a loose sense, more influenced by the equations in the real block than by the equations in the financial block, and so making *DDH* a function of *r* has very little effect on the quantitative properties of the model.

Two of the equations that are quite important in .nfluencing the properties of the model are the two main equations of the household sector,

Equations (11) and (12). Equation (11) in particular is quite important because, holding the technology constant, the level of output in the economy is constrained by the work effort of the household sector. The coefficients in Equations (11) and (12) were chosen to be consistent with the coefficients in the condensed model, which were in turn chosen to be consistent with the results obtained by solving the optimal control problems of the households in Chapter Four. Although it might be of interest to examine the properties of the static model under different choices for the coefficients in Equations (11) and (12), this will not be done here.

7.4 A COMPARISON OF THE STATIC MODEL TO THE TEXTBOOK MODEL

A version of the standard macroeconomic textbook model is presented in Table 7-7. This version is taken from a textbook by Branson [6], one of the more advanced textbooks in the field. The notation for the most part is Branson's, and the model is what Branson calls "the extended model."[b]

The model in Table 7-7 consists of (1) a consumption function in disposable income and assets, (2) an investment function in the rate of interest and income, (3) an income identity, (4) a real money demand function in the rate of interest and income, (5) a money supply function in the rate of interest, (6) an equilibrium condition equating money supply to money demand, (7) a production function in employment (with the capital stock held fixed), (8) a demand for labor equation equating the marginal product of labor to the real wage rate, (9) a labor supply function in either the money wage or the real wage,[c] and (10) an equilibrium condition equating the supply of labor to the demand for labor. Taking A and $\bar{K}$ to be exogenous and taking the government variables (g, $\bar{M}$, and the parameters in the tax function, $t(y)$) to be exogenous, the model consists of ten equations in ten unknowns (c, i, y, M^D, M^S, N^D, N^S, P, W, and r). The following are some of the differences between the textbook model and the static model in this chapter.

Consumption in the textbook model is a function of after-tax income and the real value of assets, and the supply of labor is a function of the wage rate and perhaps the price level. In the present model both consumption and the supply of labor are functions of the same variables, since they are both decision variables of the household sector and are thus jointly determined by the maximization processes of the households. The explanatory variables in the equations are the price level, the wage rate, the interest rate, the level of savings deposits and loans, the level of dividends, and the two tax parameters, d_3 and YG.

In the textbook model investment is a function of the rate of interest and income, and the demand for labor is a function of the real wage and the shape of the production function. The price level and the wage rate are

Table 7-7. The Equations of the Textbook Model

(1)	$c = c(y - t(y), \frac{A}{P})$,	[consumption function]
(2)	$i = i(r,y)$,	[investment function]
(3)	$y = c + i + g$,	[income identity: equilibrium condition for the goods market]
(4)	$\frac{M^D}{P} = l(r) + k(y)$,	[demand for money function]
(5)	$M^S = \overline{M}$ or $M^S = M(r)$,	[supply of money function]
(6)	$M^S = M^D$,	[equilibrium condition for the money market]
(7)	$y = f(N^D, \overline{K})$,	[production function]
(8)	$f'(N^D) = \frac{W}{P}$,	[demand for labor function]
(9)	$N^S = h(W \text{ or } \frac{W}{P})$,	[supply of labor function]
(10)	$N^S = N^D$.	[equilibrium condition for the labor market]

Given values for A, $\overline{K}$, g, and $\overline{M}$, the model consists of 10 equations in 10 unknowns: c, i, y, M^D, M^S, N^D, N^S, W, P, r.

Notation in alphabetic order:

A = value of assets in money terms

c = value of consumption in real terms

g = value of government purchases of goods in real terms

i = value of investment in real terms

$\overline{K}$ = value of $\digamma$ capital stock

M^D = quantity of money demanded

M^S = quantity of money supplied

$\overline{M}$ = quantity of money supplied by the government

N^D = quantity of labor demanded

N^S = quantity of labor supplied

P = price level

r = interest rate

W = wage rate

y = value of output in real terms

implicitly determined in the textbook model, being determined essentially by the market clearing equations for goods and labor (Equations (3) and (10)). In the present model the firm sector chooses the technology and the level of output so as to maximize after-tax profits. The net result of this is that both the demand for investment and the demand for labor are a function of the real wage rate and the interest rate. The price level and the wage rate are also implicitly determined in the present static model.

In the textbook model there are no government bills or bonds in existence, and no zero savings constraint is postulated.[d] It is thus somewhat difficult to compare the financial sector of the textbook model to the financial sector of the present model. In both models the interest rate is determined implicitly. In the textbook model this comes about by equating the demand for money to the supply of money. In the present model this comes about by equating the demand for bills and bonds (VBB) to the supply (VBG), and by equating actual bank reserves (BR) to required reserves ($BR*$). In the present model, unlike in the textbook model, the interest rate has a direct effect on the demand for labor, the supply of labor, and the consumption demand of the household sector. The interest rate actually affects the supply of labor and consumption in two ways, one directly and one through its effect on the aggregate stock price (DIV/r). The interest rate is thus in some sense a more integral part of the present model than it is of the textbook model.

It is well known that the demand for money equation in the textbook model is an important equation in influencing the properties of the model, and much empirical work has to be done on estimating the interest rate sensitivity of the demand for money. In the present model, as was seen above, it is not very important whether the level of demand deposits is or is not a function of the rate of interest. The interest rate is more influenced by the equations in the real block. This appears to be a significant difference between the present model and the textbook model, and puts the importance of empirical studies of the demand for money in a somewhat different light.

The main differences between the present model and the textbook model can be summarized as follows. In the present model the demand for investment and the demand for labor are joint decision variables of the firm sector and are determined jointly through a maximization process. Likewise, the supply of labor and the demand for consumption are joint decision variables of the household sector and can be considered to be determined jointly through a maximization process. Neither of these characteristics is true of the textbook model. The present model also accounts explicitly for all flows of funds in the model and for the zero-savings constraints, which the textbook model does not.

While these are important differences and while the present model does appear to be an improvement over the textbook model, it is still the author's opinion that the most significant weakness of both models is their static-equilibrium nature. What is hoped this chapter has demonstrated is how many important characteristics of the dynamic model are lost when the model is converted into a static-equilibrium model.

NOTES

[a]Christ's model [7] is actually in error in this regard. His model consists of 11 equations (counting the zero-savings equation of the government) in 14 unknowns. Four of the unknowns are government values, and one of the unknowns is real private wealth (w in his notation). w is similar to the variable A in the above discussion. Christ treats w as endogenous and argues that the government can choose only three of its four values. If w were treated as exogenous, as it is argued here it should be, then Christ's model would seem to imply that the government could choose all four of its values. The error in Christ's model, however, is the treatment of two interest rates (r, the yield on bonds, and r', the yield on physical capital) as endogenous. In equilibrium these two rates should be equal, and yet Christ does not impose any restrictions on the two rates. If one of the two rates were dropped, or an equation was added equating the two rates, w could be treated as exogenous and the government would still be able to choose only three of its four values.

[b]See in particular Chapter 14 in Branson [6].

[c]Usually in textbooks the "classical" model is the version in which the supply of labor is a function of the real wage, while the "Keynesian" model is the version in which the supply of labor is a function of the money wage.

[d]This latter point has been emphasized by Christ [8], among others. As mentioned above, both of Christ's models, [7] and [8], incorporate a zero savings constraint, but neither model has a labor sector, and in both models the price level is exogenous.

Chapter Eight

Conclusion

8.1 SUMMARY

The purpose of this study has been to develop a theoretical model of macroeconomic activity with the characteristics outlined at the beginning of Chapter One. The model should be general, should be based on solid microeconomic foundations, should not be based on the assumption of perfect foresight, and should not be based on the postulation of tâtonnement processes that clear markets every period.

The model is general in the sense that the goods market, the labor market, and the financial markets are all treated endogenously. The model also accounts for wealth effects, capital gains effects, all flow-of-funds constraints, and the government budget constraint. The model is based on solid micro-economic foundations in the sense that the decisions of the main behavioral units in the model—banks, firms, and households—are assumed to be based on the solutions of optimal control problems. Before the behavioral units solve these problems, they are assumed to form expectations of future values, and these expectations are used in the solutions of the problems. Much of the specification of the model is concerned with how these expectations are formed. None of the behavioral units in the model is assumed to have perfect foresight. The model is recursive in the sense that information flows in one direction, and no tâtonnement processes, in which information flows back and forth between behavioral units before transactions take place, are postulated.

In a nontâtonnement model, where the quantity demanded of something may not always equal the quantity supplied, one must specify carefully how the actual quantities traded are determined. In the present model the actual quantities traded are the quantities determined from the *constrained* maximization processes of the firms and households. Firms solve their optimal control problems knowing the loan constraints, and households solve their optimal control problems knowing the loan, hours, and goods constraints. Because of this, the aggregate demand for loans that results from the solutions of the constrained problems of the firms and households is always less than the aggregate amount that the bank sector is willing to supply, and the aggregate supply of labor that results from the solutions of the constrained problems of the households is always less than the aggregate amount that the firm sector and the government are willing to hire. Also, the demand for goods that results from the solutions of the constrained problems of the households is always less than the amount the firm sector is willing to sell to the households after meeting the demand from the government and from itself.

There is thus an important distinction in the model between unconstrained and constrained quantities. While the unconstrained demand for loans, supply of labor, and demand for goods can be greater than the supply of loans, demand for labor, and supply of goods, respectively, the constrained quantities are guaranteed from the way they are determined to be less. The bond dealer also serves a useful purpose in the model in determining the actual quantities of bills and bonds traded. The bond dealer absorbs each period the difference between the supply of bills and bonds from the government and the demand for bills and bonds from the bank sector.

In a nontâtonnement model some mechanism must also be postulated as to how prices, wages, and interest rates are determined, since these can no longer be assumed to be set by an auctioneer. In the present model each firm is assumed to set its own price and wage rate and each bank is assumed to set its own loan rate. The bond dealer is assumed to set the bill and bond rates and the stock price. The rates set by the firms and banks result, of course, along with the values of the other decision variables, from the solutions of the optimal control problems. Market share considerations play an important role in influencing the rates set by the firms and banks. A firm is assumed to expect, for example, that its market share of goods sold is a function of its price relative to the expected prices of the other firms. This assumption is common to a number of recent studies, in particular, Mortensen [39], Phelps [40], Phelps and Winter [47], and Maccini [36]. In the present case, however, the firm is also assumed to expect that the prices of other firms are in part a function of its own past prices.

The main factors that influence the decisions of the behavioral units have been discussed in a summary fashion at the beginning of Chapter Six, and this discussion will not be repeated here. The behavioral model for firms is clearly the most complicated of the behavioral models because of the treatment of the price, production, investment, and employment decisions as joint decision variables of a firm. (The employment decision corresponds to a firm's wage rate decision and its decision on the maximum amount of labor to hire.) In previous studies no more than two of these decisions have been considered simultaneously. Two important characteristics of the present behavioral model of a firm are the postulation of a putty-clay technology and the assumption that there are costs of adjustment in changing the size of the work force and the size of the capital stock. Because of these characteristics, it may at times be optimal for a firm to hold excess labor and/or excess capital.

The way in which the complete model is put together is presented in Tables 6-2 and A-2 and discussed in Section 6.1, and this discussion will also not be repeated here. Once all the decisions have been made at the beginning of the period, the determination of the transactions that take place throughout the rest of the period is quite straightforward. Although for the non-condensed model time paths of the decision variables are computed each period, only the values for the current period are used in computing the transactions that take place. Each period the behavioral units reoptimize, and so the optimal values of the decision variables for periods other than the current one never get used in computing the transactions that take place.

The properties of the complete model have been discussed in Chapter Six. The loan constraints are an important channel through which government actions that take money out of the system affect the behavior of the private sector. The hours constraints are an important channel through which a decrease in the sales of the firm sector affects the household sector. The goods constraints are not an important part of the model because of the fact that the firm sector holds inventories of goods.

In an economy characterized by binding loan constraints, an argument can be made for the use of monetary policy rather than fiscal policy to stimulate the economy. Monetary policy is defined as a change in the value of bills and bonds with no change in government purchases of goods and labor, and fiscal policy is defined as a change in government purchases of goods and labor with no change in bills and bonds. Both policies have about the same effect in the model in increasing bank reserves, an increase in bank reserves being what is needed in a situation of binding loan constraints, but an expansionary fiscal policy also increases sales of goods directly. As discussed in Chapter Six, one does not want to increase the sales of firms before the firms realize that they can borrow more money to increase investment and output.

In an economy characterized by binding hours constraints, an argument can be made for the use of fiscal policy rather than monetary policy, unless the interest rate responses of the firm and household sectors are large and quick. Fiscal policy, by increasing the sales of the firm sector directly, leads the firm sector in general to want to increase output and employment and thus to make the hours constraints less restrictive. Monetary policy, by not increasing the sales of the firm sector directly, must rely on increasing sales by stimulating the investment and consumption demand of the firm and household sectors through the lower interest rates that an expansionary monetary policy produces.

When trying to expand the economy in any way, consideration must be given to the work effort of the household sector. If, for example, the hours constraints are not binding (no unemployment) and the firm sector is not holding any excess labor, then output can be increased only if the household sector can be induced to work more (or the firm sector induced to purchase less labor-intensive machines). In the model the work effort of the household sector is a positive function of the wage rate and the interest rates, and a negative function of the price level, the value of assets, the proportional tax parameter, and the minimum guaranteed level of income (transfer payments). The response of the household sector to the tax parameters is important. If taxes are raised by increasing the proportional tax parameter, this has a negative effect on work effort. If there was unemployment before the increase, there will be less unemployment after the increase, other things being equal, because of the decrease in the unconstrained supply of labor. If taxes are raised by lowering the minimum guaranteed level of income (decreasing transfer payments), this has a positive effect on work effort. This change will cause more unemployment, other things being equal, because of the increase in the unconstrained supply of labor. Also, a contractionary monetary policy that increases interest rates will cause more unemployment, other things being equal, because of the increase in the unconstrained supply of labor due to the higher interest rates.

Unemployment arises in the model because of errors of expectations on the part of the firms. Firms choose the values of their decision variables with the expectation that there will be no unemployment in the current period and in the future. Therefore, any unemployment that arises in the model is due to errors in the firms' expectations of the behavioral responses of the households. As discussed in Section 6.4, it is not possible for there to exist unemployment in equilibrium if firms observe the unconstrained supply of labor as well as the constrained supply.

Equilibrium is defined to be a situation in which the value of each variable in the model is the same from period to period—a self-repeating run. If firms are assumed *not* to observe the unconstrained supply of labor, then it is possible, as discussed in Section 6.4, to concoct a self-repeating run in which there does exist unemployment. There is no frictional unemployment in the model because search is not treated as a decision variable of the households. "Full employment" corresponds to a zero unemployment rate.

Errors of expectations are also an important factor in causing the model not to return to a self-repeating position once a one-period shock has been inflicted in it—i.e., in causing the model not to be stable. The lack of stability of the model does not appear to be an unreasonable property of the model. The decision processes of the banks, firms, and households are complicated enough that it would seem to be unrealistic to assume that the bond dealer learns over time exactly what the responses of the banks are, that the banks learn over time exactly what the responses of the firms and households are, and that the firms learn over time exactly what the responses of the households are. This is especially true in a market share context, where banks and firms are likely to put more resources into finding out what their competitors are going to do than in finding out what the aggregate quantities are going to be. There is, in short, too much room in the model for errors of expectations to be made in the model to expect that the model will settle back down to the self-repeating position once it is shocked.

Because of the lack of perfect foresight in the model, and because of the way the constraints operate, it was seen in Chapter Six that it is easy to generate multiplier reactions in the model. If, for example, firms make the hours constraints more restrictive, this causes the households to consume less, which in turn causes the sales of the firms to be less. Lower sales, other things being equal, will cause the firms to plan to produce less and make the hours constraints even more restrictive, which causes the households to consume even less, and so on. In an expansion the opposite can happen. Firms make the hours constraints less restrictive, households consume more, sales of firms rise, firms make the hours constraints even less restrictive, households consume even more, and so on.

Three of the most important variables in the model that prevent the model from accelerating or decelerating indefinitely are the three interest rates. Holding the variables under the control of the government constant, as the system contracts, interest rates fall, and falling interest rates have a positive effect on investment and consumption demand. Conversely, as the system expands, interest rates rise, and rising interest rates have a negative effect on investment and consumption demand. Falling interest rates also cause capital gains on stocks, and capital gains have a positive effect on consumption demand. Conversely, rising interest rates cause capital losses on stocks, which have a negative effect on consumption demand. There is no natural tendency for the price level and wage rate to bring the economy out of, for example, a contracting situation. Whether the price level and the wage rate help in this regard depends on how the firm sector changes the two relative to one another and how the household sector responds to such changes.

The price decision of a firm is heavily influenced by what it expects other firms' prices to be. The specification of how these expectations are formed has been kept fairly simple in this study, but it would be easy to incorporate more complicated assumptions into the model. Because these expectations are so important in influencing a firm's price decision and since these expectations need not be tied to aggregate demand factors, it is quite possible within this basic theoretical framework for there to be rising prices during periods of falling aggregate demand and vice versa. There is also no reason to expect within the general structure of the model for there to be any simple or stable relationship between the unemployment rate and changes in prices and wages.

Demand deposits serve two main purposes in the model. They are needed for transactions purposes, and they serve as a buffer for firms and the bond dealer to meet unexpected changes in cash flow. Because of the residual nature of part of demand deposits, there is no reason to expect in the model a close short run relationship between the aggregate level of demand deposits and the aggregate level of output. It also makes little difference in the model, as discussed in Section 6.6, whether or not demand deposits are assumed to be an explicit function of interest rates. Relaxing the assumption that they are not an explicit function of interest rates would have little effect on the final properties of the model.

The static-equilibrium version of the model in Chapter Seven is meant to show how much is lost in going from a dynamic model to a static model and to provide something to compare to the standard, textbook model. Some of the main characteristics lost in going from the dynamic model to the static model are the treatment of prices and wages as decision variables of the firms, the treatment of loan rates as decision variables of the banks, the treatment of the bill and bond rates as decision variables of the bond dealer, any treatment of loan, hours, and goods constraints, any treatment of excess labor and excess capital, and any treatment of errors of expectations. Regarding the comparison to the textbook model, the static model appeared to be an improvement over the textbook model in its joint treatment of the consumption and labor supply decisions of the household sector, in its joint treatment of the investment and labor demand decisions of the firm sector, and in its accounting for all flows of funds in the system and for the zero savings constraints. It was also seen in the static model that it makes little difference to the properties of the model whether or not demand deposits are made a function of the rate of interest.

8.2 POSSIBLE EXTENSIONS OF THE MODEL

There are a number of ways in which the model developed in this study might be extended or changed. One obvious change is that different expectational assumptions could be made. The model is structured in such a way that it would be quite easy to replace the particular expectational assumptions made in this study with other assumptions. The expectational assumptions have for the most part been kept relatively simple in this study, so that the properties of the model could be more easily examined, but there is no reason why more complicated assumptions could not be used. One might want, for example, to postulate that a behavioral unit's expectations of the future values of a particular variable are a function of more than just the immediate past value of the variable. In practice, these expectations are likely to be a function of other past values of the variable and of past values of other variables.

Another way in which the expectational assumptions might be modified has to do with the possible effects of "cost push" factors on the level of prices. Consider, for example, a case in which for some reason a firm observes that it has to pay a higher wage rate than before to attract the same amount of labor as before—i.e., that the firm observes a shift in the labor supply curve facing it. Given the present expectational assumptions in the model, this shift has no effect on the firm's expectations of other firms' prices. The shift will, of course, still affect the firm's price decision through its general effect on the optimal control problem of the firm.

One might want, however, to postulate that the shift affects directly the firm's expectations of other firms' prices. In other words, it may be reasonable to assume that the firm expects that other firms are observing similar shifts in the labor supply curves facing them and will respond to these shifts by raising their own prices. Certainly in the case in which an industry-wide union obtains a large settlement from all of the firms in the industry or in the case in which the cost of any common input to the industry rises, it seems reasonable to assume that this will affect firms' expectations of other firms' prices. While this type of an assumption has not been built into the model, it would be easy to do so. The more are a firm's expectations of other firms' prices influenced by "cost push" factors, the more will cost push factors influence the determination of the level of prices.

Another way in which the model might be changed is to postulate a different order of the flow of information. As mentioned in Chapter One, the particular order chosen here was designed to try to capture possible credit rationing effects from the financial sector to the real sector and possible employment constraints from the business sector to the household sector. Other orders could obviously be postulated. Another important assumption of the model in this regard is the assumption that the frequency with which decisions are modified is the same for all of the behavioral units, namely one period. Households, for example, are not allowed to modify their decisions or reoptimize more often than are the firms and banks.

It is also the case that no future commitments are allowed in the model. Although, for example, firms plan how much they are going to invest in the future, they are always free to change their plans in the next period as new information becomes available. There are also no delivery lags in the model and no lags between the time a firm buys a machine and the time the machine is ready for use. The properties of any nontâtonnement model may be sensitive to the assumptions regarding the order and frequency of the flow of information among the behavioral units and to the assumptions regarding the lags between the time decisions are made and the time that they are carried out. In the present case it would be interesting to see how the properties of the model change when different assumptions along these lines are made.

An important extension of the model might be to make search a decision variable of households and possibly firms. Treating search as a decision variable, however, would enormously complicate the model, since distributional issues could then no longer be ignored, and it is not clear whether the possible gains from such a project are worth the cost. It may be best in a macroeconomic context to continue to ignore distributional issues and not try to specify a model in which one needs to keep track of the trades between each pair of behavioral units in the model.

Another important assumption of the model, which is related to the ignoring of distributional issues, is the assumption that bills and bonds are perfect substitutes from the point of view of the banks, and that savings deposits and stocks are perfect substitutes from the point of view of the households. In order to justify these assumptions it had to be assumed that capital gains and losses were recorded each period and taxed as regular income. It also had to be assumed that banks and households were indifferent to the fact that the rate of return on bills and savings deposits is certain, while the rate of return on bonds and stocks is not. All the behavioral units in the model deal only with expected values and are not concerned with variances or other measures of risk. Another possible extension of the model thus might be to relax the assumptions that are necessary to insure that bills and bonds are perfect substitutes and that savings deposits and stocks are perfect substitutes.

This is again not a trivial extension, for relaxing such assumptions would greatly complicate the model. The model has essentially ignored the financial portfolio choices of the asset holders, and this has, of course, greatly simplified matters. What appeared to be most important to account for in the model were the aggregate flows of funds, and it seemed less important to consider the question of how asset holders divide their funds among alternative securities. Nevertheless, it might be of interest to consider more types of securities in the model and to treat the portfolio choices of asset holders in a more detailed way. If this were done, it would probably be desirable at the same time to bring risk considerations into the model.

No price, wage, or interest rate rigidities have been postulated in the model, but it would be easy to do so. For example, price and wage ceilings could easily be incorporated into the optimal control problem of the firm as just another constraint on the firm's behavior. The firm would solve its control problem subject not only to constraints like the loan constraint, but also to constraints that said that it could not set its price above a certain value and could not set its wage rate above a certain value. Likewise, a loan rate ceiling could be handled by having a bank solve its control problem subject to a constraint that said that it could not set its loan rate above a certain value. Costs of *changing* prices, wages, and interest rates could also be incorporated into the control problems in the same way that costs of changing employment, investment, and sales were incorporated into the control problem of the firm. Each bank and firm would solve its control problem incorporating these costs as well.[a]

The way the model is currently specified, unemployment and other disequilibrium phenomena arise only because of errors of expectations. Incorporating various price, wage, and interest rate rigidities into the model would obviously mean that disequilibrium could arise even if there were no expectation errors. One reason for not incorporating these rigidities into the model in this study was to show that disequilibrium phenomena can easily arise without such rigidities. It might be of interest, however, to incorporate some of these rigidities into the model, since rigidities of various sorts obviously exist in practice.

Three other potentially important extensions of the model would be: (1) to consider consumer durables explicitly, (2) to add a foreign sector, and (3) to incorporate population growth and technical progress into the model. Adding consumer durables would require changing the utility function and the optimal control problem of the households to incorporate the fact that goods could be purchased that render utility over more than one period. Adding a foreign sector would require keeping track of the flows of funds between the domestic economy and the rest of the world and keeping track of the other transactions (in goods and labor) that occur between the two. Adding population growth and technical progress would require, among other things, changing the definition of an equilibrium run in Chapter Six from a self-repeating run to a run in which variables either self-repeat or grow at constant rates.

Consideration might also be given to examining the effects on the economy of changing depreciation laws and investment tax credits. In this study depreciation has been assumed to be straight line and there have been assumed to be no investment tax credits, but it would be easy to change these assumptions. One could examine the effects of changing these policy variables in the same way that the effects of changing other policy variables have already been examined. In future simulation work of this sort it would be desirable to consider more than just two types of machines to give the firms more flexibility in their investment decisions.

Making demand deposits a function of the rate of interest would not, as mentioned above, have much effect on the properties of the model, and it is probably not worth spending much time on this issue.

It might also be of interest to solve the optimal control problems of the banks, firms, and households using different parameter values and under different specifications of the equations to see how sensitive the results are to these changes. As mentioned in the Appendix, there are some aspects of the optimal control problem of the firm that might be desirable to change. There are clearly other ways in which the control problems of the behavioral units could be specified, and one hope of this study is that it will stimulate further work in analyzing the decisions of economic agents by the numerical solutions of optimal control problems.

A final possible extension to consider is the treatment of the government decisions as endogenous. One could either postulate certain reaction functions of the government or, more formally, postulate that the government behaves by maximizing a welfare function. Consider the latter case, and assume that the horizon of the government is M periods, so that at any one time the welfare function is a function of the values of the relevant endogenous variables for the current period and for the next $M-1$ periods. The government, in solving its maximization problem, would have to compute optimal *time paths* of its decision variables. For any given set of time paths of the government values, a value of the welfare function could be computed. One computation of the welfare function would correspond to solving the model M times. Each of the M solutions requires, of course, that the optimal control problem of each behavioral unit in the model be solved. The solution of the maximization or optimal control problem of the government would require choosing in some way that set of time paths of the government values that maximizes the welfare function.

Although it would not be feasible to solve this problem for the non-condensed model, it would probably be feasible to do so for the condensed model using the method described in Fair [15]. As long as one can compute the value of the welfare function fairly cheaply, given a set of time paths of the government values, the method in [15] should be feasible to use.[b] For the non-condensed model, it is not cheap to compute the value of the welfare function because each computation requires the solution of M optimal control problems of each behavioral unit. For the condensed model, however, it is fairly cheap to compute the value of the welfare function because no optimal control problems need to be solved for the solution of the condensed model.

It is important to realize that in solving its optimal control problem the government would be maximizing its welfare function *subject to* the constraint that the behavioral units in the model are each maximizing their own objective functions. When one is solving the control problem of the government, one is also solving separate optimal control problems within the overall optimal control problem. This is, of course, the way things should be, since the government must take into account the responses of the private sector of the economy in determining the optimal values of its own decision variables.

8.3   EMPIRICAL IMPLICATIONS OF THE MODEL

Since the purpose of Volume II of this study is to specify an econometric model that is based on the present theoretical model, only a brief discussion is presented here of the empirical implications of the theoretical model. Consider first the behavior of the firm. Since a firm's price, production, investment, employment, and wage rate decisions all come out of the same maximization process, one should probably consider these decision variables together in empirical work. One should in particular be wary of including the current value of a decision variable on the right-hand side of an equation explaining the current value of another decision variable.

In some cases one may be able to consider the decisions of the firm as being made sequentially and specify, for example, that the current level of production is a function of the current level of sales and that the current levels of employment and investment are functions of the current level of production. In general, however, one should probably use only nondecision variables or lagged values of decision variables as explanatory variables. In particular, the common practice[c] of specifying a simultaneous equations model determining prices and wages, in which the current price variable appears in the wage equation and the current wage variable appears in the price equation, is questionable in the present context. If both these variables are decision variables of firms and thus affected by the same factors, their current values are likely to be highly correlated, but this does not mean that the current values ought to be explanatory variables of each other.

It is also the case, regarding the decision variables of a firm in the model, that inventory investment is not a direct decision variable, but a consequence of the other decisions. It is thus questionable whether one ought to treat inventory investment as a decision variable, as is done in most macroeconometric models.

The results in Chapter Three indicate that the reactions of the firm are not symmetrical to increases and decreases in particular variables. Although asymmetricies are difficult to deal with econometrically, more consideration should probably be given in econometric work to possible asymmetrical reactions. Since (as discussed in Chapter Three) the ability of firms to hold excess labor and excess capital during contractions may be an important cause of asymmetrical behavior, more consideration should probably be given to accounting for the existence of excess labor and excess capital than has been done previously.

Regarding the behavior of a household, a household's decision on the number of hours to work and its decision on the number of goods to purchase also both come out of the same maximization process. In empirical work these decisions should thus probably be considered together. Again, one should be wary of including the current value of one of these decision variables on the right hand side of an equation explaining the current value of the other. The Keynesian consumption function does, of course, by having current income as an explanatory variable, treat the current number of hours worked as an explanatory variable. This procedure can be justified if it is assumed that the hours constraints are always binding on the households. If the constraints are always binding, then the number of hours worked is in effect not a decision variable of the households, and so there is no harm in including it as an explanatory variable in the consumption function. If the constraints are not binding all of the time, then one would presumably want to try to determine when they are and are not binding and specify the consumption function differently in the two cases. One would also presumably want to specify the equation determining the number of hours worked differently in the two cases. In the binding constraint case the number of hours worked is determined by the firms, and in the nonbinding case the number is determined by the households.

The situation in which constraints are binding at certain times and not at others is difficult to deal with econometrically. One must somehow decide or estimate when the constraints are binding and when they are not and then proceed accordingly. In estimating the behavior of the firm sector there is only one important constraint to consider, the loan constraint; but in estimating the behavior of the household sector there are two important constraints to consider, the loan constraint and the hours constraint.

Some recent work in econometric theory has been concerned with the problem of estimating supply and demand schedules in markets that are not always in equilibium.[d] It is usually postulated that the actual quantity observed in the market at any one time is the minimum of the quantity demanded and the quantity supplied. Two regimes then exist in this case, one in which the quantity demanded is observed and one in which the quantity supplied is observed. The basic idea of much of this work is to use information on price changes to help in the choice of which regime is in effect at any one time. Price changes are assumed to be a positive function of excess demand, so that when prices are rising, the quantity supplied is assumed to be observed, and when prices are falling, the quantity demanded is assumed to be observed. Rising prices, for example, correspond to positive excess demand (the quantity demanded being greater than the quantity supplied), so that if the minimum of the quantity demanded and the quantity supplied is what is observed, then rising prices correspond to the quantity supplied being observed.

This recent work in econometric theory is, unfortunately, of somewhat limited use in the present context. In the household case, for example, there are at least two constraints to be concerned about, so that more than two different regimes can exist. Also, if prices, wage rates, and interest rates are set in a market share context, in which expectations are not only important but may not always turn out to be correct, then one may not always be able to rely on changes in prices, wage rates, and interest rates to determine which regime is in effect at any one time. In other words, prices may be rising even if there is not excess demand, and vice versa, so that one may not, for example, be able to postulate that the quantity supplied is what is always observed when prices are rising.

The present case does have the advantage, however, that disequilibrium takes the form of one sector constraining another sector, so that one may be able to use information on one sector to help determine which regime is in effect in another sector. In other words, in the estimation of a multisector, macroeconometric model, there may be more information available on the status of any particular sector than there is when the estimation of only a single market is considered. Because of the links among the various sectors, there are likely to be a number of variables, other than changes in prices, wage rates, and interest rates, that one might attempt to use to help determine when the various regimes are in effect. In particular, the flow of funds data may be helpful in this regard. Otherwise, it is difficult to know in general what data will be useful without knowing the particular data base in question and the particular specification of the empirical model.

Since expectations play such an important role in the theoretical model, any empirical model that is based on it must be concerned with estimating or accounting for these expectations in some way. For example, any variable that is likely to influence a firm's expectations of other firms' prices is a possible candidate for inclusion as an explanatory variable in equations determining price behavior. The importance of expectations in the theoretical model also provides an explanation for why lagged endogenous variables are important explanatory variables in most macroeconometric models. When there is not perfect foresight and when decisions are made on the basis of expectations, it is likely that what has happened in the past will have an important effect on expectations of the future and thus on current decisions.

This is not the place to dwell on how each equation in an empirical model that is based on the theoretical model might be specified, but three specific points about the empirical implications of the model will be made. First, the model implies that excess labor should have a negative effect on employment and that excess capital should have a negative effect on investment. The negative effect of excess labor on employment is confirmed by the results in Fair [14]. Second, the model indicates that excess labor and capital should have a negative effect on prices and that the loan rate and the loan constraints should have a positive effect on prices. Finally, as mentioned in Chapter Three, the model indicates that the loan rate and other aspects of the cost of capital may have effects on investment that have nothing to do with capital-labor substitution in the sense of the firm purchasing different types of machines.

It would be of interest to test for the effects of excess labor and excess capital on prices and also for the effects of the loan rate and loan constraints on prices. It would also seem to be important in empirical work to be aware of the different ways in which the costs of labor and capital can affect employment and investment. One should not necessarily attribute all of the estimated cost effects to the existence of capital-labor substitution.

It should be clear by now that the theoretical model implies that econometric models ought to be specified differently than they now are. The model implies that the four or five main decisions of the firm sector should be considered together, that the two main decisions of the household sector should be considered together, and that the possibility of different regimes existing at different times should be considered. In addition, the model indicates that it is likely to be important to account for all of the flows of funds in the model. The model also, of course, implies that the specification of many individual equations should be different from currently existing specifications. The fact that the model does imply that econometric models ought to be specified differently means that it should be possible, according to the philosophy expounded in Chapter One, to determine if the model is more useful than currently existing theoretical models.

8.4   CONCLUDING REMARKS

It is hoped that this study will stimulate further work, both on extending the theoretical model and on developing empirical versions of it. It is also hoped that this study has demonstrated some of the advantages of using computer simulation techniques over standard analytic methods to analyze theoretical models. By the use of such techniques it appears feasible to consider a macroeconomic model that is dynamic, general, and based on solid micro-economic foundations. It appears feasible, in other words, to break away from the standard static-equilibrium model found in most macroeconomic textbooks to a more satisfactory model.

NOTES

[a]Barro [4] has considered a model of monopoly behavior in which there are lump-sum costs of adjusting the price that the monopolist sets.

[b]The method in Fair [15] converts an optimal control problem into an unconstrained maximization problem, and then uses standard algorithms for maximizing unconstrained functions of variables to solve the problem. This method could have been tried in this study to solve the optimal control problems of the banks, firms, and households. It seemed best in these three cases, however, to write separate algorithms for each problem in order to take more advantage of the structure of each individual problem. For the optimal control problem of the government, on the other hand, it may not be as important to take advantage of the structure of the problem, and one may be able to rely on the method in [15].

[c]For two recent empirical studies see Eckstein and Brinner [13] and Gordon [23].

[d]See, for example, Fair and Jaffee [16], Fair and Kelejian [17], Goldfeld and Quandt [21], Maddala and Nelson [37], Amemiya [2], and Quandt [48].

Appendix

The Non-Condensed Version of the Model

The complete notation for the non-condensed model is presented in alphabetic order in Table A-1, and the complete set of equations for the non-condensed model is presented in Table A-2. The specification in Table A-2 is based on the assumption of two identical banks, two identical firms, one creditor household, and one debtor household. However, some remarks are presented in the table on how the model can be generalized. For ease of reference, the numbering of the equations or statements in Table A-2 corresponds to the numbering in Table 6-2 for the condensed model. Table A-2 should be self-explanatory, given the remarks in the table and the discussion of Table 6-2 in Chapter Six. In Table A-3 the flow-of-funds accounts for the non-condensed model are presented, and in Table A-4 the national income accounts for the non-condensed model are presented. Tables A-3 and A-4 are analogous to Tables 6-3 and 6-4 for the condensed model.

Table A-1. The Complete Notation for the Non-Condensed Model in Alphabetic Order

Subscript t denotes variable for period t. A p superscript in the text denotes a planned value of the variable, and an e superscript denotes an expected value of the variable.

A_{it}	= value of non-demand-deposit assets or liabilities of household i
$BONDB_{it}$	= number of bonds held by bank i
$BONDD_t$	= number of bonds held by the bond dealer
$BONDG_t$	= number of bonds issued by the government
BR_{it}	= actual reserves of bank i
BR_{it}^*	= required reserves of bank i $[g_1 DDB_{it}]$
BR_{it}^{**}	= desired reserves of bank i $[g_1(DDB_{it}-EMAXDD_i) + EMAXDD_i$ $+ EMAXSD_i]$

Table A-1.   (continued)

CF_{it}	= cash flow before taxes and dividends of firm i
$\overline{CF}_{it}$	= cash flow net of taxes and dividends of firm i
CG_{it}	= capital gains or losses on stocks of household i
CGB_{it}	= capital gains or losses on bonds of bank i $[BONDB_{it}/R_{t+1} - BONDB_{it}/R_t]$
CGD_t	= capital gains or losses on bonds of the bond dealer
	$[BONDD_t/R_{t+1} - BONDD_t/R_t]$
d_1	= profit tax rate
d_2	= penalty rate on the composition of banks' portfolios
d_3	= personal tax rate
DDB_{it}	= demand deposits of bank i
DDD_t	= demand deposits of the bond dealer
DDF_{it}	= actual demand deposits of firm i
DDF_{1it}	= demand deposits set aside by firm i for transactions purposes
DDF_{2i}	= demand deposits set aside by firm i to be used as a buffer to meet unexpected decreases in cash flow
DDH_{it}	= demand deposits of household i
DEP_{it}	= depreciation of firm i
DIV_t	= total dividends paid and received in the economy
$DIVB_{it}$	= dividends paid by bank i
$DIVD_t$	= dividends paid by the bond dealer
$DIVF_{it}$	= dividends paid by firm i
$DIVH_{it}$	= dividends received by household i
$EMAXDD_i$	= largest error bank i expects to make in overestimating its demand deposits for any period
$EMAXHP_i$	= largest error firm i expects to make in overestimating the supply of labor available to it for any period
$EMAXMH_i$	= largest error firm i expects to make in underestimating its worker hour requirements for any period
$EMAXSD_i$	= largest error bank i expects to make in overestimating its savings deposits for any period
$EXBB_t$	= excess supply of bills and bonds $[(VBILLG_t + BONDG_t/R_t) - (\sum_{i=1}^{NB} VBB_{it} + VBB^*)]$
$FUNDS_{it}^e$	= amount that bank i knows it will have available to lend to households and firms and to buy bills and bonds even if it overestimates its demand and savings deposits by the maximum amounts
g_1	= reserve requirement ratio
g_2	= no-tax proportion of banks' portfolios held in bills and bonds
$\bar{\bar{H}}$	= maximum number of hours that each machine can be used each period
HP_t	= total number of worker hours paid for in the economy
HPF_{it}	= number of worker hours paid for by firm i
$HPFMAX_{it}$	= maximum number of worker hours that firm i will pay for
$HPFMAXUN_{it}$	= maximum number of worker hours that firm i would pay for if it were not constrained
HPG_t	= number of worker hours paid for by the government
HPH_{it}	= number of hours that household i is paid for

Table A-1. (continued)

$HPHMAX_{it}$	= maximum number of hours that household i can be paid for
$HPHUN_{it}$	= unconstrained supply of hours of household i
$HPUN_t$	= total unconstrained supply of hours in the economy
I_{nit}	= number of machines of type n purchased by firm i ($n=1,2$)
INV_{it}	= number of goods purchased by firm i for investment purposes
$INVUN_{it}$	= unconstrained demand of firm i for goods for investment purposes
IUN_{nit}	= unconstrained demand of firm i for machines of type n ($n=1,2$)
K^a_{nit}	= actual number of machines of type n held by firm i ($n=1,2$)
KH_{nit}	= number of machine hours worked on machines of type n in firm i ($n=1,2$)
$KMIN_{nit}$	= minimum number of machines of type n required to produce Y_{nit} ($n=1,2$)
L_t	= total value of loans
LB_{it}	= value of loans of bank i
$LBMAX_{it}$	= maximum value of loans that bank i will make
LF_{it}	= value of loans taken out by firm i
$LFMAX_{it}$	= maximum value of loans that firm i can take out
$LFUN_{it}$	= unconstrained demand for loans of firm i
LH_{it}	= value of loans taken out by household i
$LHMAX_{it}$	= maximum value of loans that household i can take out
$LHUN_{it}$	= unconstrained demand for loans of household i
LUN_t	= total unconstrained demand for loans
m	= length of life of one machine
MH_{nit}	= number of worker hours worked on machines of type n in firm i ($n=1,2$)
MH_{3it}	= number of worker hours required to handle deviations of inventories from β_1 times sales in firm i
MH_{4it}	= number of worker hours required to handle fluctuations in sales in firm i
MH_{5it}	= number of worker hours required to handle fluctuations in worker hours paid for in firm i
MH_{6it}	= number of worker hours required to handle fluctuations in net investment in firm i
MH_{it}	= total number of worker hours required by firm i
PF_{it}	= price set by firm i
$\overline{PF}_t$	= average price level in the economy
PFF_{it}	= price paid for investment goods by firm i
$PFUN_{it}$	= price that firm i would set if it were not constrained
PG_t	= price paid by the government
PH_{it}	= price paid by household i
PS_t	= price of the aggregate share of stock
r_t	= bill rate
R_t	= bond rate
RB_{it}	= loan rate set by bank i
$\overline{RB}_t$	= average loan rate in the economy
RF_{it}	= loan rate paid by firm i

Table A-1.   (continued)

RH_{it}	= loan rate paid by household i
S_{it}	= fraction of the aggregate share of stock held by household i
SAV_{it}	= savings net of capital gains or losses of household i
SDB_{it}	= savings deposits of bank i
SDH_{it}	= savings deposits of household i
TAX_t	= total taxes paid
$TAXB_{it}$	= taxes paid by bank i
$TAXD_t$	= taxes paid by the bond dealer
$TAXF_{it}$	= taxes paid by firm i
$TAXH_{it}$	= taxes paid by household i
V_{it}	= stock of inventories of firm i
VBB_{it}	= value of bills and bonds that bank i chooses to purchase $[VBILLB_t + BONDB_t/R_t]$
VBD^*	= value of bills and bonds that the bond dealer desires to hold
$VBILLB_{it}$	= value of bills held by bank i
$VBILLD_t$	= value of bills held by the bond dealer
$VBILLG_t$	= value of bills issued by the government
WF_{it}	= wage rate set by firm i
$\overline{WF}_t$	= average wage rate in the economy
$WFUN_{it}$	= wage rate that firm i would set if it were not constrained
WG_t	= wage rate paid by the government
WH_{it}	= wage rate received by household i
X_t	= total number of goods sold in the economy
XF_{it}	= number of goods sold by firm i
$XFMAX_{it}$	= maximum number of goods that firm i will sell
XG_t	= number of goods purchased by the government
XH_{it}	= number of goods purchased by household i
$XHMAX_{it}$	= maximum number of goods that household i can purchase
$XHUN_{it}$	= unconstrained demand for goods of household i
XUN_t	= total unconstrained demand for goods
Y_{nit}	= number of goods produced on machines of type n by firm i ($n=1,2$)
Y_{it}	= total number of goods produced by firm i
YG	= minimum guaranteed level of income
YH_{it}	= before-tax income excluding capital gains or losses of household i
Y^pUN_{it}	= number of goods that firm i would plan to produce if it were not constrained
δ_n	= number of goods it takes to create a machine of type n ($n=1,2$)
λ_n	= amount of output produced per worker hour on machines of type n ($n=1,2$)
μ_n	= amount of output produced per machine hour on machines of type n ($n=1,2$)
ΠB_{it}	= before-tax profits of bank i
ΠD_{it}	= before-tax profits of the bond dealer
ΠF_{it}	= before-tax profits of firm i

Table A-2. The Complete Set of Equations for the Non-Condensed Model

Under the assumption of two identical banks, two identical firms, one creditor household, and one debtor household. Remarks are also presented on how the model can be generalized to include NB banks, NF firms, and NH households.

(1) r_t, R_t, and PS_t are determined by the bond dealer at the end of period $t-1$. See (42) and (62) below for the determination of the values for period $t+1$.

(2) The government sets d_1, d_2, d_3, YG, g_1, g_2, XG_t, HPG_t, $VBILLG_t$, $BONDG_t$.

(3) The banks determine RB_{it}, VBB_{it}, and $LBMAX_{it}$ ($i=1,2$) as described in Chapter Two.

(3)′ Since the banks are identical, $RB_{1t} = RB_{2t}$. Therefore, set $RF_{1t} = RF_{2t} = RH_{2t} = RB_{1t}$. In general, with NB nonidentical banks, NF nonidentical firms, and NH households, the values of RF_{it} ($i=1,\ldots,NF$) and RH_{it} ($i=1,\ldots,NH$) must satisfy, given RB_{it} ($i=1,\ldots,NB$):

$$\sum_{i=1}^{NB} RB_{it}LB_{it} = \sum_{i=1}^{NF} RF_{it}LF_{it} + \sum_{i=1}^{NH} RH_{it}LH_{it},$$

i.e., the total interest revenue of banks must equal the total interest payments of firms and households.

(4) $$LHMAX_{2t} = \left(\frac{LHUN_{2t-1}}{LHUN_{2t-1}+LFUN_{1t-1}+LFUN_{2t-1}}\right)(LBMAX_{1t}+LBMAX_{2t}).$$

(5) $$LFMAX_{1t} = LFMAX_{2t} = \frac{1}{2}(LBMAX_{1t}+LBMAX_{2t}-LHMAX_{2t}).$$

In general, the values of $LFMAX_{it}$ ($i=1,\ldots,NF$) and $LHMAX_{it}$ ($i=1,\ldots,NH$) must satisfy, given $LBMAX_{it}$ ($i=1,\ldots,NB$):

$$\sum_{i=1}^{NF} LFMAX_{it} + \sum_{i=1}^{NH} LHMAX_{it} \leq \sum_{i=1}^{NB} LBMAX_{it},$$

i.e., the allocation of the loan constraints among firms and households must not exceed the total loan constraint from banks.

(6) The firms determine PF_{it}, I_{1it}, I_{2it}, Y^p_{1it}, Y^p_{2it}, WF_{it}, LF_{it}, $HPFMAX_{it}$, $XFMAX_{it}$, IUN_{1it}, IUN_{2it}, and $LFUN_{it}$ ($i=1,2$) as described in Chapter Three.

(6)′ $INV_{it} = \delta_1 I_{1it} + \delta_2 I_{2it}$, ($i=1,2$).

(6)″ $INVUN_{it} = \delta_1 IUN_{1it} + \delta_2 IUN_{2it}$, ($i=1,2$).

(6)‴ Since the firms are identical, $PF_{1t} = PF_{2t}$ and $WF_{1t} = WF_{2t}$. Therefore, set $PH_{1t} = PH_{2t} = PFF_{1t} = PFF_{2t} = PG_t = PF_{1t}$ and $WH_{1t} = WH_{2t} = WG_t = WF_{1t}$.

Table A-2.   (continued)

In general, the values of PH_{it} $(i=1,\ldots,NH)$, PFF_{it} $(i=1,\ldots,NF)$, and PG_t must satisfy, given PF_{it} $(i=1,\ldots,NF)$:

$$\sum_{i=1}^{NF} PF_{it}XF_{it} = \sum_{i=1}^{NF} PFF_{it}INV_{it} + \sum_{i=1}^{NH} PH_{it}XH_{it} + PG_tXG_t,$$

i.e., the total revenue of firms from the sale of goods must equal the total amount paid by firms, households, and the government for goods.

Also, in general, the values of WH_{it} $(i=1,\ldots,NH)$ and WG_t must satisfy, given WF_{it} $(i=1,\ldots,NF)$:

$$\sum_{i=1}^{NH} WH_{it}HPH_{it} = \sum_{i=1}^{NF} WF_{it}HPF_{it} + WG_tHPG_t,$$

i.e., the total wages of households must equal the total wages paid by firms and the government.

(7)   The households determine $HPHUN_{1t}$, $XHUN_{1t}$, $HPHUN_{2t}$, $XHUN_{2t}$, and $LHUN_{2t}$ as described in Chapter Four.

(8) $HPHMAX_{1t} = (\dfrac{HPHUN_{1t}}{HPHUN_{1t}+HPHUN_{2t}}) (HPFMAX_{1t}+HPFMAX_{2t}+HPG_t).$

(9) $HPHMAX_{2t} = (HPFMAX_{1t}+HPFMAX_{2t}+HPG_t) - HPHMAX_{1t}.$

In general, the values of $HPHMAX_{it}$ $(i=1,\ldots,NH)$ must satisfy, given $HPFMAX_{it}$ $(i=1,\ldots,NF)$ and HPG_t:

$$\sum_{i=1}^{NH} HPHMAX_{it} \leqslant \sum_{i=1}^{NF} HPFMAX_{it}+HPG_t,$$

i.e., the allocation of the hours constraints among households must not exceed the total hours constraint from the firms and the government.

(10) $XHMAX_{1t} = (\dfrac{XHUN_{1t}}{XHUN_{1t}+XHUN_{2t}}) (XFMAX_{1t} + XFMAX_{2t} - INV_{1t}$
$- INV_{2t} - XG_t) .$

(11) $XHMAX_{2t} = (XFMAX_{1t} + XFMAX_{2t} - INV_{1t} - INV_{2t} - XG_t) - XHMAX_{1t}.$

In general, the values of $XHMAX_{it}$ $(i=1,\ldots,NH)$ must satisfy, given $XFMAX_{it}$ $(i=1,\ldots,NF)$, INV_{it} $(i=1,\ldots,NF)$, and XG_t:

$$\sum_{i=1}^{NH} XHMAX_{it} \leqslant \sum_{i=1}^{NF} XFMAX_{it} - \sum_{i=1}^{NF} INV_{it} - XG_t,$$

i.e., the allocation of the goods constraints among households must not exceed the total goods constraint from firms after meeting investment and government demand.

Table A–2. (continued)

(12) The households determine HPH_{1t}, XH_{1t}, HPH_{2t}, XH_{2t}, and LH_{2t} as described in Chapter Four.

(13) $XUN_t = XHUN_{1t} + XHUN_{2t} + INVUN_{1t} + INVUN_{2t} + XG_t$.

(14) $LUN_t = LFUN_{1t} + LFUN_{2t} + LHUN_{2t}$

(15) $HPUN_t = HPHUN_{1t} + HPHUN_{2t}$.

(16) $X_t = XH_{1t} + XH_{2t} + INV_{1t} + INV_{2t} + XG_t$.

(16)' $XF_{1t} = XF_{2t} = \frac{1}{2}X_t$.

In general, XF_{it} $(i=1,\ldots,NF)$ would be determined according to the relationship between firm i's price and the other firms' prices, subject to the restrictions that:

$$\sum_{i=1}^{NF} XF_{it} = X_t \text{ and } XF_{it} \leqslant XFMAX_{it}, (i=1,\ldots,NF).$$

(17) $L_t = LF_{1t} + LF_{2t} + LH_{2t}$.

(17)' $LB_{1t} = LB_{2t} = \frac{1}{2}L_t$.

In general, LB_{it} $(i=1,\ldots,NB)$ would be determined according to the relationship between bank i's loan rate and the other banks' loan rates, subject to the restrictions that:

$$\sum_{i=1}^{NB} LB_{it} = L_t \text{ and } LB_{it} \leqslant LBMAX_{it}, (i=1,\ldots,NB).$$

(18) $HP_t = HPH_{1t} + HPH_{2t}$.

(19) $HPF_{1t} = HPF_{2t} = \frac{1}{2}(HP_t - HPG_t)$.

In general, HPF_{it} $(i=1,\ldots,NF)$ would be determined according to the relationship between firm i's wage rate and other firms' wage rates, subject to the restrictions that:

$$\sum_{i=1}^{NF} HPF_{it} = HP_t - HPG_t \text{ and } HPF_{it} \leqslant HPFMAX_{it}, (i=1,\ldots,NF).$$

(20) $K^a_{nit} = K^a_{nit-1} + I_{nit} - I_{nit-m}$, $(n=1,2; i=1,2)$.

(21) $V^p_{it} = V_{it-1} + Y^p_{1it} + Y^p_{2it} - XF_{it}$, $(i=1,2)$.

(22) $MH^p_{nit} = \dfrac{Y^p_{nit}}{\lambda_n}$, $(n=1,2; i=1,2)$.

Table A-2. (continued)

(23) $MH^p_{3it} = \beta_2(V^p_{it} - \beta_1 XF_{it})^2$, $(i=1,2)$.

(24) $MH_{4it} = \beta_3(XF_{it} - XF_{it})^2$, $(i=1,2)$.

(25) $MH_{5it} = \beta_4(HPF_{it-1} - HPF_{it-2})^2$, $(i=1,2)$.

(26) $MH_{6it} = \beta_5(K^a_{1it} + K^a_{2it} - K^a_{1it-1} - K^a_{2it-1})^2$, $(i=1,2)$.

(27) $MH^p_{it} = MH^p_{1it} + MH^p_{2it} + MH^p_{3it} + MH_{4it} + MH_{5it} + MH_{6it}$, $(i=1,2)$.

(28) If $MH^p_{it} \leqslant HPF_{it}$, then $Y_{1it} = Y^p_{1it}$, $Y_{2it} = Y^p_{2it}$, $V_{it} = V^p_{it}$, and $MH_{it} = MH^p_{it}$, $(i=1,2)$.

(29) If $MH^p_{it} > HPF_{it}$, then $MH_{it} = HPF_{it}$; $Y_{it} =$ maximum amount that can be produced given K^a_{1it}, K^a_{2it}, XF_{it}, and MH_{it};

  $Y_{1it} = \min \left\{ Y_{it}, \text{ maximum amount that can be produced on machines of type 1 } (\mu_1 K^a_{1it} \bar{H}) \right\}$;

  $Y_{2it} = Y_{it} - Y_{1it}$; $V_{it} = V_{it-1} + Y_{1it} + Y_{2it} - XF_{it}$, $(i=1,2)$.

(30) $KMIN_{nit} = \dfrac{Y_{nit}}{\mu_n \bar{H}}$, $(n=1,2; i=1,2)$.

(31) $DEP_{it} = \dfrac{1}{m}(PFF_{it}INV_{it} + \ldots + PFF_{it-m+1}INV_{it-m+1})$, $(i=1,2)$.

(32) $\Pi F_{it} = PF_{it}(Y_{1it} + Y_{2it}) - WF_{it}HPF_{it} - DEP_{it} - RF_{it}LF_{it}$
  $+ (PF_{it} - PF_{it-1})V_{it-1}$, $(i=1,2)$.

(33) $TAXF_{it} = d_1 \Pi F_{it}$, $(i=1,2)$.

(34) $DIVF_{it} = \Pi F_{it} - TAXF_{it}$, $(i=1,2)$.

(35) $CF_{it} = PF_{it}XF_{it} - WF_{it}HPF_{it} - PFF_{it}INV_{it} - RF_{it}LF_{it}$, $(i=1,2)$.

(36) $\overline{CF}_{it} = CF_{it} - TAXF_{it} - DIVF_{it}$
  $= DEP_{it} - PFF_{it}INV_{it} + PF_{it-1}V_{it-1} - PF_{it}V_{it}$, $(i=1,2)$.

(37) $DDF_{it} = DDF_{it-1} + LF_{it} - LF_{it-1} + \overline{CF}_{it}$.

(38) $VBILLD_t = 0$.

(39) $VBILLB_{1t} = VBILLB_{2t} = \dfrac{1}{2}VBILLG_t$.

(40) $BONDB_{it} = R_t(VBB_{it} - VBILLB_{it})$, $(i=1,2)$.

Table A-2. (continued)

In general, $VBILLB_{it}(i=1,\ldots,NB)$ would be determined according to the relationship between the value of VBB_{it} and the other banks' values of this variable, subject to the restriction that

$$\sum_{i=1}^{NB} VBILLB_{it} = VBILLG_t.$$

(41) $BONDD_t = BONDG_t - BONDB_{1t} - BONDB_{2t}.$

(42) The bond dealer determines r_{t+1} and R_{t+1} as described in Chapter Five.

(43) $\Pi D_t = BONDD_t + (\dfrac{BONDD_t}{R_{t+1}} - \dfrac{BONDD_t}{R_t}).$

(44) $TAXD_t = d_1 \Pi D_t.$

(45) $DIVD_t = \Pi D_t - TAXD_t.$

(46) $DDD_t = DDD_{t-1} - (\dfrac{BONDD_t}{R_{t+1}} - \dfrac{BONDD_t}{R_t}).$

(47) $DDH_{1t} = \gamma_1 PH_{1t} XH_{1t}.$

(48) $DDH_{2t} = \gamma_1 PH_{2t} XH_{2t}.$

(49) $DDB_{1t} = DDB_{2t} = \dfrac{1}{2}(DDF_{1t} + DDF_{2t} + DDD_t + DDH_{1t} + DDH_{2t}).$

In general, DDB_{it} ($i=1,\ldots,NB$) could be determined in other ways, subject to the restriction that:

$$\sum_{i=1}^{NB} DDB_{it} = \sum_{i=1}^{NF} DDF_{it} + DDD_t + \sum_{i=1}^{NH} DDH_{it}.$$

(50) $YH_{2t} = WH_{2t} HPH_{2t}.$

(51) $TAXH_{2t} = d_3(YH_{2t} - RH_{2t} LH_{2t}) - YG.$

(52) $SAV_{2t} = YH_{2t} - TAXH_{2t} - PH_{2t} XH_{2t} - RH_{2t} LH_{2t}.$

Table A-2.   (continued)

(53)′ $S_{1t} = 1$.

In general, with more than one creditor household, S_{it} $(i=1,\ldots,NH)$ would have to be determined in some way, subject to the restriction that

$\sum_{i=1}^{NH} S_{it} = 1$. For each fraction of the aggregate share transferred from one household to another, the household receiving the fraction would pay the other household the fraction times PS_t.

(53) $CG_{1t} = (PS_{t+1} - PS_t)S_{1t}$. [Equations (53)-(62) are solved simultaneously]

(54) $YH_{1t} = WH_{1t}HPH_{1t} + r_t SDH_{1t} + DIVH_{1t}$.

(55) $TAXH_{1t} = d_3(YH_{1t} + CG_{1t} - YG)$.

(56) $SAV_{1t} = YH_{1t} - TAXH_{1t} - PH_{1t}XH_{1t}$.

(57) $SDH_{1t} = SDH_{1t-1} - (DDH_{1t} - DDH_{1t-1}) + SAV_{1t} - PS_t(S_{1t} - S_{1t-1})$.

(57)′ $SDB_{1t} = SDB_{2t} = \frac{1}{2}SDH_{1t}$.

(58) $\Pi B_{it} = RB_{it}LB_{it} + r_t VBILLB_{it} + BONDB_{it} - r_t SDB_{it}$

   $+ (\dfrac{BONDB_{it}}{R_{t+1}} - \dfrac{BONDB_{it}}{R_t})$, $(i=1,2)$.

(59) $TAXB_{it} = d_1\Pi B_{it} + d_2 [VBB_{it} - g_2(VBB_{it} + LB_{it})]^2$, $(i=1,2)$.

(60) $DIVB_{it} = \Pi B_{it} - TAXB_{it}$, $(i=1,2)$.

(61) $DIV_t = DIVF_{1t} + DIVF_{2t} + DIVD_t + DIVB_{1t} + DIVB_{2t}$.

(61)′ $DIVH_{1t} = DIV_t$.

(62) $PS_{t+1} = \dfrac{\frac{1}{5}(DIV_t + DIV_{t-1} + DIV_{t-2} + DIV_{t-3} + DIV_{t-4})}{r_{t+1}}$

In general, with more than one creditor household, $DIVH_{it}$ $(i=1,\ldots,NH)$ would be allocated according to households' ownership of stock, S_{it} $(i=1,\ldots,NH)$, with the property that $\sum_{i=1}^{NH} DIVH_{it} = DIV_t$.

Also, in general, SDB_{it} $(i=1,\ldots,NB)$ could be determined in other ways, subject to the restriction that

$\sum_{i=1}^{NB} SDB_{it} = \sum_{i=1}^{NH} SDH_{it}$.

Table A-2.   (continued)

(63) $TAX_t = TAXH_{1t} + TAXH_{2t} + TAXF_{1t} + TAXF_{2t} + TAXD_t + TAXB_{1t}$
$+ TAXB_{2t}$.

(64) $BR_{it} = DDB_{it} + SDB_{it} - LB_{it} - VBILLB_{it} - \dfrac{BONDB_{it}}{R_{t+1}}$, $(i=1,2)$

and

$BR_{1t} + BR_{2t} = BR_{1t-1} + BR_{2t-1} + PG_t XG_t + WG_t HPG_t + r_t VBILLG_t + BONDG_t - TAX$

$- (VBILLG_t - VBILLG_{t-1}) - (\dfrac{BONDG_t - BONDG_{t-1}}{R_t})$.

The one item that does need to be discussed for the non-condensed model is the assumption that the banks, the firms, and the bond dealer reestimate some of the parameters each period. Consider first, Equation (2.11) for banks:

$$LUN_t^e = LUN_{t-1}\left(\frac{\overline{RB}_{t-1}}{\overline{RB}_t^e}\right)^{\alpha_3}, \alpha_3 > 0.$$

(2.11)

In the programming of the non-condensed model for the results in this Appendix, each bank was assumed to estimate α_3 on the basis of its past observations of the correlation between changes in the aggregate unconstrained demand for loans and changes in the average loan rate. Given observations on, for example, LUN_{t-1}, LUN_{t-2}, $\overline{RB}_{t-1}$, and $\overline{RB}_{t-2}$, an estimate of α_3 can be obtained as $[log(LUN_{t-1}/LUN_{t-2})]/[(log(\overline{RB}_{t-2}/\overline{RB}_{t-1})]$. At the beginning of period t, each bank was assumed to make estimates of α_3 in this way for the five periods, $t-1,\ldots,t-5$. The bank was also assumed, however, to have a prior view regarding the minimum and maximum values of α_3, a view that was assumed not to be subject to change based on further information. Therefore, if an estimate of α_3 for a particular past period fell below the minimum value, the bank was assumed to set the estimate at the minimum value. Likewise, if an estimate fell above the maximum value, the bank was assumed to set the estimate at the maximum value. The estimate of α_3 used for the decisions made at the beginning of period t was assumed to be the simple average of the five estimates. This procedure of estimating α_3 allows the program some flexibility in determining a value for α_3, while at the same time insuring that extreme values for α_3 are not chosen.

Table A-3.   Flow-of-Funds Accounts for the Non-Condensed Model: Stocks of Assets and Liabilities

NB = number of banks
NF = number of firms
NH = number of households

	Households A	Households L	Firms A	Firms L	Banks A	Banks L	Bond Dealer A	Bond Dealer L	Government A	Government L
1. Demand Deposits	$\sum_{i=1}^{NH} DDH_{it}$	—	$\sum_{i=1}^{NF} DDF_{it}$	—	—	$\sum_{i=1}^{NB} DDB_{it}$	DDD_t	—	—	—
2. Bank Reserves	—	—	—	—	$\sum_{i=1}^{NB} BR_{it}$	—	—	—	—	$\sum_{i=1}^{NB} BR_{it}$
3. Savings Deposits	$\sum_{i=1}^{NH} SDH_{it}$	—	—	—	—	$\sum_{i=1}^{NB} SDB_{it}$	—	—	—	—
4. Bank Loans	—	$\sum_{i=1}^{NH} LH_{it}$	—	$\sum_{i=1}^{NF} LF_{it}$	$\sum_{i=1}^{NB} LB_{it}$	—	—	—	—	—
5. Government Bills	—	—	—	—	$\sum_{i=1}^{NB} VBILLB_{it}$	—	$VBILLD_t$	—	—	$VBILLG_t$
6. Government Bonds	—	—	—	—	$\sum_{i=1}^{NB} VBONDB_{it}$	—	$VBONDD_t$	—	—	$VBONDG_t$
7. Common Stocks	$\sum_{i=1}^{NH} PS_t S_{it}$	$\sum_{i=1}^{NH} PS_t S_{it}$	—	—	—	—	—	—	—	—

Notes: Total Assets $- \sum_{i=1}^{NH} PS_t S_{it}$ = Total Liabilities

Table A-4. National Income Accounts for the Non-Condensed Model

NB = *number of banks*
NF = *number of firms*
NH = *number of households*

Expenditure Side

(1)   Consumption (real) = $\sum\limits_{i=1}^{NH} XH_{it}$

(2)   Consumption (money) = $\sum\limits_{i=1}^{NH} PH_{it} XH_{it}$

(3)   Fixed Investment (real) = $\sum\limits_{i=1}^{NF} INV_{it}$

(4)   Fixed Investment (money) = $\sum\limits_{i=1}^{NF} PFF_{it} INV_{it}$

(5)   Government Expenditures on Goods (real) = XG_t

(6)   Government Expenditures on Goods (money) = $PG_t XG_t$

(7)   Government Expenditures on Labor (real) = HPG_t

(8)   Government Expenditures on Labor (money) = $WG_t HPG_t$

(9)   Inventory Investment (real) = $\sum\limits_{i=1}^{NF} (V_{it} - V_{it-1})$

(10)   Inventory Investment (money) = $\sum\limits_{i=1}^{NF} PF_{it} (V_{it} - V_{it-1})$

Gross National Product (real) = (1) + (3) + (5) + (7) + (9)
Gross National Product (money) = (2) + (4) + (6) + (8) + (10)

Income Side

(1)   Wages = $\sum\limits_{i=1}^{NH} WH_{it} HPH_{it}$

(2)   Before-Tax Profits Net of Capital Gains and Losses =

$$\sum_{i=1}^{NB} \left[\Pi B_{it} - \left(\frac{BONDB_{it}}{R_{t+1}} - \frac{BONDB_{it}}{R_t} \right) \right] + \sum_{i=1}^{NF} \Pi F_{it} + \left[\Pi D_t - \left(\frac{BONDD_t}{R_{t+1}} - \frac{BONDD_t}{R_t} \right) \right]$$

(3)   Inventory Valuation Adjustment = $- \sum\limits_{i=1}^{NF} [(PF_{it} - PF_{it-1}) V_{it-1}]$

Table A-4.   (continued)

(4)   Profits and Inventory Valuation Adjustment = (2) + (3)

(5)   Capital Consumption Allowances = $\sum\limits_{i=1}^{NF} DEP_{it}$

(6)   Net Interest = $\sum\limits_{i=1}^{NH} r_t\, SDH_{it} - \sum\limits_{i=1}^{NH} RH_{it}\, LH_{it} - BONDG_t - r_t\, VBILLG_t$

Gross National Product (money) = (1) + (4) + (5) + (6)

Production Side

(1)   Production of Goods (real) = $\sum\limits_{i=1}^{NF} (Y_{1it} + Y_{2it})$

(2)   Production of Goods (money) = $\sum\limits_{i=1}^{NF} PF_{it}\, (Y_{1it} + Y_{2it})$

(3)   Government Expenditures on Labor (real) = HPG_t

(4)   Government Expenditures on Labor (money) = $WG_t\, HPG_t$
       Gross National Product (real) = (1) + (3)
       Gross National Product (money) = (2) + (4)

Consider next Equations (3.26) and (3.33) for firms:

$$X_t^e = X_{t-1} \left(\frac{\overline{PF}_t^e}{\overline{PF}_{t-1}} \right)^{\beta_8}, \beta_8 < 0, \tag{3.26}$$

$$HPUN_t^e = HPUN_{t-1} \left(\frac{\overline{WF}_t^e}{\overline{WF}_{t-1}} \right)^{\beta_{11}} \left(\frac{\overline{PF}_t^e}{\overline{PF}_{t-1}} \right)^{\beta_{12}}, \beta_{11} > 0, \beta_{12} < 0. \tag{3.33}$$

In the programming of the non-condensed model, each firm was assumed to estimate β_8 in the same way that the banks were assumed to estimate α_3. For Equation (3.33) the constraint that β_{11} be equal to β_{12} in absolute value was imposed, and each firm was assumed to estimate the absolute value in the same way that the banks were assumed to estimate α_3.

Consider finally Equation (5.8) for the bond dealer:

$$\frac{r_t - r_{t-1}}{r_{t-1}} = \lambda \left[\frac{(VBILLG_{t-1} + \dfrac{BONDG_{t-1}}{R_{t-1}} - (\sum_{i=1}^{NB} VBB_{it-1} + VBD^*)}{\sum_{i=1}^{NB} VBB_{it-1} + VBD^*} \right], \lambda > 0.$$

$$(5.8)$$

In the programming of the non-condensed model, the bond dealer was assumed to estimate λ in a similar way that banks were assumed to estimate α_3, by observing the past correlation between percentage changes in the bill rate and percentage changes in the demand for bills and bonds from banks. In period $t-1$, for example, the bond dealer can compute

$$\left. \frac{\sum_{i=1}^{NB} VBB_{it-1} - \sum_{i=1}^{NB} VBB_{it-2}}{\sum_{i=1}^{NB} VBB_{it-2}} \right/ \frac{r_{t-1} - r_{t-2}}{r_{t-2}} ,$$

which is an estimate of the elasticity of the demand for bills and bonds with respect to the bill rate. The bond dealer was assumed to compute this estimate for each of the previous five periods, with, however, prior bounds on each of the estimates. The five estimates were then averaged, and the value of λ used in determining r_t was taken to be the inverse of this average.

The parameter values, initial conditions, and government values that were used for the base run are presented in Table A-5. The values for the government and the bond dealer are the same as for the base run for the condensed model in Chapter Six. The values for the banks, firms, and households are the same as those used for the base run solutions of the optimal control problems in Chapters Two, Three, and Four, with one minor exception for the firms. In Table 3-2 the lagged values of the aggregate unconstrained and constrained supplies of labor were taken to be 637.3, whereas here they are taken to be 758.0. This difference of 120.7 is the number of worker hours paid for by the government. The values referred to in Table A-5 were chosen so that the base run for the non-condensed model would be a self-repeating run. The choice of the initial values must, of course, meet certain consistency re-

Table A-5.   Parameter Values, Initial Conditions, and Government Values for the Base Run in Table A-6

The Government
>   Same as in Table 6-5 for the Condensed Model.

The Bond Dealer
>   Same as in Table 6-5 for the Condensed Model.

The Banks
>   Same as in Table 2-2. Values are relevant for both banks.

The Firms
>   Same as in Table 3-2 except:

$$HP_{t-1} = 758.0,$$

$$HPUN_{t-1} = 758.0.$$

>   Values in Table 3-2 are relevant for both firms.

The Households
>   Same as in Table 4-2.

---

quirements, since there are important links among all the sectors, and all these requirements have been met for the values referred to in Table A-5.

It should be remembered that the values of α_3, β_8, β_{11}, β_{12}, and λ change over time as the banks, firms, and bond dealer re-estimate the values each period. The values referred to in Table A-5 are the values used for the first period (period t) of the run. Values of the estimates of each of these parameters for periods $t-3$, $t-2$, and $t-1$ are also needed to compute the estimates of the parameters for period $t+1$, and in each case these lagged values were taken to be the same as the value for period t.

It should also be noted that when the non-condensed model was solved for successive periods, the length of the decision horizon of banks and firms, $T+1$, was always taken to be 30. In other words, when the model was solved for period t, banks and firms were assumed to look ahead to period $t+30$, whereas when the model was solved for period $t+1$, banks and firms were assumed to look ahead to period $t+31$. The length of the expected remaining lifetime of households, $N+1$, was also always taken to be 30 for the runs. Without these assumptions, it would not be possible to concoct a self-repeating run, which would make it somewhat more difficult to compare the experimental runs to the base run.

It should finally be noted that when Y_{it} had to be computed in Equation (29) in Table A-2, the inventory cost parameter β_2 was taken to be 0.010 rather than 0.075. In the discussion of Equation (29) for the condensed model in Chapter Six, it was mentioned that computing the level of output in Equation (29) requires solving a quadratic equation in output. The quadratic equation for the condensed model is presented in footnote a in Chapter Six, and the quadratic equation for the non-condensed model is the same with the appropriate change of notation. The parameter β_2 is part of this equation. The higher is β_2, the more does output have to be lowered when worker hour requirements exceed the number of worker hours allocated to the firm. The value of β_2 was lowered for the computations in Equation (29) to make the decrease in output less for a given difference between worker hour requirements and worker hours on hand.

The value of β_2 used for the condensed model was 0.001, and so the 0.010 value used here is more in line with the value used for the condensed model. The value of 0.075 was, however, still used in the solution of the optimal control problem of the firms, since this was the value used for the results in Chapter Four. This procedure means that it had to be assumed that the firms *expect* that the value of β_2 is 0.075 when solving their control problems, while in fact the actual value is only 0.010. This assumption is not, however, a very important assumption of the model, and it was made so that the results between the condensed and non-condensed models would be somewhat more comparable.

The results for the base run are presented in Table A-6 for periods *t,* *t+1,* and *t+2.* The same variables are presented in Table A-6 as were presented in Table 6-6, and the discussion of the variables in Table 6-6 in Chapter Six is relevant here also. Since there are two identical banks and two identical firms, the optimal control problem of each bank and firm only had to be solved once each period. The appropriate bank and firm variables have been multiplied by 2 in Table A-6 to put them on an aggregative basis and to make them directly comparable to the variables in Table 6-6. The variables in Table 6-6 that have *"UN"* for the last two letters are unconstrained quantities. The unconstrained quantities for the firms are the quantities that result from solving the optimal control problems of the firms under the assumption of no loan constraints. Similarly, the unconstrained quantities for the households are the quantities that result from solving the optimal control problems of the households under the assumption of no loan, hours, and goods constraints. The results for the base run in Table A-6 are identical to the results for the base run in Table 6-6 except, in a few cases, for the last digit of the number. In these few cases the last digits differ by 1.

The first four experiments that were carried out in Chapter Six for the condensed model were also carried out for the non-condensed model: a decrease in XG_t of 5.0, an increase in $VBILLG_t$ of 5.0, an increase in XG_t of 5.0, and a decrease in $VBILLG_t$ of 5.0. The results for these four experiments are presented in Table A-6. The results for these four experiments in Table A-6 are so similar to the results in Table 6-6 that they require little further discussion here.

Table A-6. Results of Solving the Non-Condensed Model

| | Base Run | | | | | | |
	t	t+1	t+2		t	t+1	t+2
Real GNP	962.7	962.7	962.7	XUN	842.0	842.0	842.0
UR	0.0000	0.0000	0.0000	X	842.0	842.0	842.0
Surplus (+)	0.0	0.0	0.0	LUN	810.2	810.2	810.2
or Deficit (−)				L	810.2	810.2	810.2
r	0.06500	0.06500	0.06500	$HPUN$	758.0	758.0	758.0
PS	1146.4	1146.4	1146.4	HP	758.0	758.0	758.0
$2 \cdot FUNDS_i^e$	1150.2	1150.2	1150.2	$2 \cdot HPF_i$	637.3	637.3	637.3
RB_i	0.07500	0.07500	0.07500	$2 \cdot MH_{4i}$	0.0	0.0	0.0
$2 \cdot VBB_i$	340.0	340.0	340.0	$2 \cdot Y_i$	842.0	842.0	842.0
$2 \cdot LBMAX_i$	810.2	810.2	810.2	$2 \cdot V_i$	105.3	105.3	105.3
$LHMAX_2$	482.1	482.1	482.1	$2 \cdot \Pi F_i$	130.1	130.1	130.1
$2 \cdot LFMAX_i$	328.1	328.1	328.1	$2 \cdot TAXF_i$	65.0	65.0	65.0
$2 \cdot LFUN_i$	328.1	328.1	328.1	$2 \cdot \overline{CF_i}$	0.0	0.0	0.0
$PFUN_i$	1.0000	1.0000	1.0000	$2 \cdot DDF_i$	50.3	50.3	50.3
$2 \cdot INVUN_i$	50.0	50.0	50.0	$2 \cdot VBILLB_i$	185.0	185.0	185.0
$2 \cdot Y^P UN_i$	842.0	842.0	842.0	$2 \cdot BONDB_i$	10.08	10.08	10.07
$WFUN_i$	1.0000	1.0000	1.0000	$BONDD$	1.95	1.95	1.95
$2 \cdot HPFMAXUN_i$	637.3	637.3	637.3	ΠD	1.95	1.95	1.95
$2 \cdot LF_i$	328.1	328.1	328.1	$TAXD$	0.97	0.97	0.97
PF_i	1.0000	1.0000	1.0000	CGD	0.00	0.00	0.00
$2 \cdot INV_i$	50.0	50.0	50.0	DDD	30.0	30.0	30.0
$2 \cdot Y_i^P$	842.0	842.0	842.0	DDH_1	60.1	60.1	60.1
$2 \cdot X_i^e$	842.0	842.0	842.0	DDH_2	51.8	51.8	51.8
$2 \cdot V_i^P$	105.3	105.2	105.2	$2 \cdot DDB_i$	192.2	192.2	192.1
WF_i	1.0000	1.0000	1.0000	YH_2	435.0	435.0	435.0
$2 \cdot HPFMAX_i$	637.3	637.3	637.3	$TAXH_2$	77.1	77.1	77.1
a	1.000	1.000	1.000	SAV_2	0.0	0.0	0.0
$HPFMAX_i/MH_i^P$	1.000	1.000	1.000	CG_1	0.0	0.0	0.0
$2 \cdot MH_{4i}^P$	0.0	0.0	0.0	YH_1	463.4	463.4	463.4
$HPHUN_1$	323.0	323.0	323.0	$TAXH_1$	89.6	89.6	89.6
$XHUN_1$	373.8	373.8	373.8	SAV_1	0.0	0.0	0.0
$HPHUN_2$	435.0	435.0	435.0	SDH_1	1013.4	1013.4	1013.4
$XHUN_2$	321.7	321.7	321.7	$2 \cdot CGB_i$	0.0	0.0	0.0
$LHUN_2$	482.1	482.1	482.1	$2 \cdot \Pi B_i$	17.0	17.0	17.0
$HPHMAX_1$	323.0	323.0	323.0	$2 \cdot TAXB_i$	8.5	8.5	8.5
$HPHMAX_2$	435.0	435.0	435.0	$2 \cdot DIVB_i$	8.5	8.5	8.5
HPH_1	323.0	323.0	323.0	DIV	74.5	74.5	74.5
XH_1	373.8	373.8	373.8	TAX	241.3	241.3	241.3
SDH_1^P	1013.4	1013.4	1013.4	$2 \cdot BR_i$	55.4	55.4	55.4
HPH_2	435.0	435.0	435.0	$2 \cdot BR_i^{**}$	55.4	55.4	55.4
XH_2	321.7	321.7	321.7	$V_i/(\beta_1 XF_i)$	1.000	1.000	1.000
LH_2	482.1	482.1	482.1	HPF_i/MH_i	1.000	1.000	1.000
$^a(K_{1i}^a+K_{2i}^a)/$				$(K_{1i}^a+K_{2i}^a)/$	1.000	1.000	1.000
$(KMIN_{1i}^P+KMIN_{2i}^P)$				$(KMIN_{1i}+KMIN_{2i})$	1.000	1.000	1.000
				$EXBB$	0.0	0.0	0.0

Table A-6. (continued)

	t	t+1	t+2		t	t+1	t+2
Real GNP	960.6	954.3	948.1	XUN	837.0	839.8	833.9
UR	0.0000	0.0082	0.0097	X	837.0	835.6	830.8
Surplus (+)	3.1	-1.6	-3.0	LUN	810.2	808.6	804.8
or Deficit (−)				L	810.2	807.5	804.8
r	0.06500	0.06500	0.06503	$HPUN$	758.0	758.0	756.8
PS	1146.4	1143.1	1142.0	HP	758.0	751.8	749.4
$2 \cdot FUNDS_i^e$	1150.2	1147.6	1145.8	$2 \cdot HPF_i$	637.3	631.1	628.7
RB_i	0.07500	0.07505	0.07509	$2 \cdot MH_{4i}$	1.6	0.1	1.4
$2 \cdot VBB_i$	340.0	339.2	338.7	$2 \cdot Y_i$	839.8	833.6	827.4
$2 \cdot LBMAX_i$	810.2	808.4	807.1	$2 \cdot V_i$	108.1	106.1	102.6
$LHMAX_2$	482.1	481.0	481.2	$2 \cdot \Pi F_i$	127.9	129.9	129.4
$2 \cdot LFMAX_i$	328.1	327.4	325.9	$2 \cdot TAXF_i$	64.0	65.0	64.7
$2 \cdot LFUN_i$	328.1	326.5	323.7	$2 \cdot \overline{CF_i}$	-2.9	2.4	4.3
$PFUN_i$	1.0000	0.9990	0.9995	$2 \cdot DDF_i$	47.4	48.2	49.7
$2 \cdot INVUN_i$	50.0	49.7	49.1	$2 \cdot VBILLB_i$	185.0	185.0	185.0
$2 \cdot Y^P UN_i$	842.0	833.8	830.0	$2 \cdot BONDB_i$	10.08	10.02	10.00
$WFUN_i$	1.0000	0.9956	0.9917	$BONDD$	1.95	2.00	2.03
$2 \cdot HPFMAXUN_i$	637.3	631.1	629.7	πD	1.95	1.99	2.01
$2 \cdot LF_i$	328.1	326.5	323.7	$TAXD$	0.97	0.99	1.00
PF_i	1.0000	0.9990	0.9995	CGD	0.00	-0.01	-0.02
$2 \cdot INV_i$	50.0	49.7	49.1	DDD	30.0	29.2	28.8
$2 \cdot Y_i^P$	842.0	833.8	830.0	DDH_1	60.1	59.8	59.4
$2 \cdot X_{i_P}^e$	842.0	837.2	833.1	DDH_2	51.8	51.0	50.8
$2 \cdot V_i^P$	105.3	104.7	103.0	$2 \cdot DDB_i$	189.3	188.3	188.8
WF_i	1.0000	0.9956	0.9917	YH_2	435.0	429.5	427.2
$2 \cdot HPFMAX_i$	637.3	631.1	629.7	$TAXH_2$	77.1	76.1	75.6
a	1.000	1.009	1.012	SAV_2	0.0	0.3	-0.2
$HPFMAX_i/MH_i^P$	1.000	1.000	1.000	CG_1	-3.3	-1.1	-2.5
$2 \cdot MH_{4i}^P$	0.0	0.0	0.4	YH_1	462.3	459.1	455.7
$HPHUN_1$	323.0	323.0	322.4	$TAXH_1$	88.8	88.6	87.7
$XHUN_1$	373.8	372.9	370.0	SAV_1	-0.2	-1.2	-1.2
$HPHUN_2$	435.0	435.0	434.4	SDH_1	1013.2	1012.3	1011.5
$XHUN_2$	321.7	320.7	318.4	$2 \cdot CGB_i$	0.0	-0.1	-0.1
$LHUN_2$	482.1	482.1	481.0	$2 \cdot \Pi B_i$	17.0	16.8	16.6
$HPHMAX_1$	323.0	320.4	319.6	$2 \cdot TAXB_i$	8.5	8.4	8.3
$HPHMAX_2$	435.0	431.4	430.8	$2 \cdot DIVB_i$	8.5	8.4	8.3
HPH_1	323.0	320.4	318.6	DIV	73.4	74.3	74.0
XH_1	373.8	372.1	369.4	TAX	239.4	239.0	237.3
SDH_1^P	1013.4	1012.1	1011.3	$2 \cdot BR_i$	52.3	53.9	56.9
HPH_2	435.0	431.4	430.8	$2 \cdot BR_i^{**}$	54.9	54.7	54.8
XH_2	321.7	317.3	315.8	$V_i/(\beta_1 XF_i)$	1.033	1.016	0.988
LH_2	482.1	481.0	481.0	HPF_i/MH_i	1.000	1.000	1.000
$^a(K_{1t}^a+K_{2i}^a)/$				$(K_{1i}^a+K_{2i}^a)/$			
$(KMIN_{1i}^P+KMIN_{2i}^P)$				$(KMIN_{1i}+KMIN_{2i})$	1.003	1.009	1.015
				$EXBB$	0.0	0.8	1.2

Experiment 2 ($VBILLG_t$:+5.0)

	t	$t+1$	$t+2$		t	$t+1$	$t+2$
Real GNP	962.7	961.2	950.0	XUN	842.0	841.2	835.7
UR	0.0000	0.0033	0.0098	X	842.0	838.9	832.5
Surplus (+)	−1.3	−1.1	−2.9	LUN	810.2	809.0	803.9
or Deficit (−)				L	810.2	807.6	805.1
r	0.06500	0.06521	0.06523	$HPUN$	758.0	760.0	758.5
PS	1146.4	1142.2	1140.2	HP	758.0	757.5	751.0
$2 \cdot FUNDS_i^e$	1150.2	1146.9	1149.6	$2 \cdot HPF_i$	637.3	636.8	630.3
RB_i	0.07500	0.07515	0.07514	$2 \cdot MH_{4t}$	0.0	0.6	2.5
$2 \cdot VBB_i$	340.0	339.0	339.8	$2 \cdot Y_i$	842.0	840.5	829.3
$2 \cdot LBMAX_i$	810.2	807.8	809.8	$2 \cdot V_i$	105.3	106.8	103.6
$LHMAX_2$	482.1	480.7	481.4	$2 \cdot \Pi F_i$	130.1	129.4	129.0
$2 \cdot LFMAX_i$	328.1	327.1	328.4	$2 \cdot TAXF_i$	65.0	64.7	64.5
$2 \cdot LFUN_i$	328.1	328.1	324.4	$2 \cdot \overline{CF}_i$	0.0	−1.2	3.9
$PFUN_i$	1.0000	1.0000	1.0004	$2 \cdot DDF_i$	50.3	47.9	49.2
$2 \cdot INVUN_i$	50.0	50.0	49.2	$2 \cdot VBILLB_i$	190.0	185.0	185.0
$2 \cdot Y^P UN_i$	842.0	842.0	831.0	$2 \cdot BONDB_i$	9.75	10.04	10.10
$WFUN_i$	1.0000	1.0000	0.9938	$BONDD$	2.27	1.98	1.93
$2 \cdot HPFMAXUN_i$	637.3	637.3	630.3	ΠD	2.16	1.97	1.93
$2 \cdot LF_i$	328.1	326.9	324.4	$TAXD$	1.08	0.99	0.97
PF_i	1.0000	1.0000	1.0004	CGD	−0.11	−0.01	0.01
$2 \cdot INV_i$	50.0	49.6	49.2	DDD	25.1	29.6	30.5
$2 \cdot Y_i^P$	842.0	841.3	831.0	DDH_1	60.1	60.0	59.5
$2 \cdot X_i^e$	842.0	842.0	834.5	DDH_2	51.8	51.5	51.0
$2 \cdot V_i^P$	105.3	104.5	103.3	$2 \cdot DDB_i$	187.3	189.0	190.3
WF_i	1.0000	0.9997	0.9938	YH_2	435.0	434.4	428.6
$2 \cdot HPFMAX_i$	637.3	636.8	630.3	$TAXH_2$	77.1	77.0	75.9
a	1.000	1.000	1.011	SAV_2	0.0	1.1	−0.5
$HPFMAX_i/MH_i^P$	1.000	1.000	1.000	CG_1	−4.2	−2.0	−2.2
$2 \cdot MH_{4i}^P$	0.0	0.0	1.2	YH_1	463.3	463.0	457.7
$HPHUN_1$	323.0	324.0	322.9	$TAXH_1$	88.8	89.2	88.1
$XHUN_1$	373.8	373.5	371.1	SAV_1	0.7	1.1	−0.4
$HPHUN_2$	435.0	436.0	435.6	SDH_1	1014.1	1015.4	1015.4
$XHUN_2$	321.7	321.3	318.9	$2 \cdot CGB_i$	−0.5	0.0	0.0
$LHUN_2$	482.1	480.9	479.5	$2 \cdot \Pi B_i$	16.5	16.5	16.5
$HPHMAX_1$	323.0	322.9	319.8	$2 \cdot TAXB_i$	8.2	8.3	8.2
$HPHMAX_2$	435.0	434.6	431.3	$2 \cdot DIVB_i$	8.2	8.3	8.2
HPH_1	323.0	322.9	319.8	DIV	74.4	73.9	73.7
XH_1	373.8	372.7	369.9	TAX	240.3	240.1	237.7
SDH_1^P	1013.4	1015.5	1015.6	$2 \cdot BR_i$	51.7	57.8	60.7
HPH_2	435.0	434.6	431.3	$2 \cdot BR_i^{**}$	54.6	54.9	55.1
XH_2	321.7	320.1	317.0	$V_i/(\beta_1 XF_i)$	1.000	1.019	0.996
LH_2	482.1	480.7	480.7	HPF_i/MH_i	1.000	1.000	1.000
$^a(K_{1i}^a + K_{2i}^a)/$				$(K_{1i}^a + K_{2i}^a)/$			
$(KMIN_{1i}^P + KMIN_{2i}^P)$				$(KMIN_{1i} + KMIN_{2i})$	1.000	1.001	1.013
				$EXBB$	5.0	0.4	−0.5

Table A-6. (continued)

Experiment 3 (XG_t:+5.0)

	t	$t+1$	$t+2$		t	$t+1$	$t+2$
Real GNP	960.2	960.7	956.8	XUN	847.0	843.4	847.5
UR	0.0000	0.0000	0.0000	X	847.0	843.4	847.5
Surplus (+)	−7.2	−1.2	−5.0	LUN	810.2	809.6	813.6
or Deficit (−)				L	810.2	809.6	813.6
r	0.06500	0.06500	0.06493	$HPUN$	758.0	758.0	758.0
PS	1146.4	1142.6	1141.8	HP	758.0	758.0	758.0
$2 \cdot FUNDS_i^e$	1150.2	1156.2	1158.2	$2 \cdot HPF_i$	637.3	637.3	637.3
RB_i	0.07500	0.07489	0.07471	$2 \cdot MH_{4i}$	1.6	0.8	1.0
$2 \cdot VBB_i$	340.0	341.8	342.4	$2 \cdot Y_i$	839.5	840.0	836.1
$2 \cdot LBMAX_i$	810.2	814.4	815.9	$2 \cdot V_i$	97.8	94.4	83.0
$LHMAX_2$	482.1	484.6	487.1	$2 \cdot \Pi F_i$	127.6	128.7	124.2
$2 \cdot LFMAX_i$	328.1	329.8	328.8	$2 \cdot TAXF_i$	63.8	64.3	62.1
$2 \cdot LFUN_i$	328.1	326.2	327.8	$2 \cdot \overline{CF}_i$	7.5	2.2	8.6
$PFUN_i$	1.0000	1.0034	1.0067	$2 \cdot DDF_i$	57.8	58.1	68.3
$2 \cdot INVUN_i$	50.0	50.8	52.6	$2 \cdot VBILLB_i$	185.0	185.0	185.0
$2 \cdot Y^P UN_i$	842.0	843.4	847.7	$2 \cdot BONDB_i$	10.08	10.19	10.22
$WFUN_i$	1.0000	1.0043	1.0089	$BONDD$	1.95	1.84	1.81
$2 \cdot HPFMAXUN_i$	637.3	642.3	643.6	ΠD	1.95	1.87	1.84
$2 \cdot LF_i$	328.1	326.2	327.8	$TAXD$	0.97	0.93	0.92
PF_i	1.0000	1.0034	1.0067	CGD	0.00	0.03	0.04
$2 \cdot INV_i$	50.0	50.8	52.6	DDD	30.0	31.7	32.1
$2 \cdot Y_i^P$	842.0	843.4	847.7	DDH_1	60.1	60.4	60.7
$2 \cdot X_i^e$	842.0	839.5	842.1	DDH_2	51.8	52.0	52.4
$2 \cdot V_i^P$	105.3	101.6	100.0	$2 \cdot DDB_i$	199.7	202.2	213.5
WF_i	1.0000	·1.0043	1.0089	YH_2	435.0	435.8	437.8
$HPFMAX$	637.3	642.3	643.6	$TAXH_2$	77.1	77.3	77.7
a	1.000	1.000	1.000	SAV_2	0.0	−1.0	−2.0
$2 \cdot HPFMAX_i$	1.000	1.000	1.000	CG_1	−3.8	−0.8	−6.9
$2 \cdot MH_{4i}^P$	0.0	3.5	0.1	YH_1	462.1	465.1	464.3
$HPHUN_1$	323.0	324.0	324.0	$TAXH_1$	88.6	89.8	88.5
$XHUN_1$	373.8	373.9	374.7	SAV_1	−0.3	0.2	−1.3
$HPHUN_2$	435.0	434.0	434.0	SDH_1	1013.1	1013.1	1011.4
$XHUN_2$	321.7	322.2	323.7	$2 \cdot CGB_i$	0.0	0.2	0.2
$LHUN_2$	482.1	483.3	485.8	$2 \cdot \Pi B_i$	17.0	17.2	17.5
$HPHMAX_1$	323.0	326.1	326.7	$2 \cdot TAXB_i$	8.5	8.6	8.8
$HPHMAX_2$	435.0	436.9	437.6	$2 \cdot DIVB_i$	8.5	8.6	8.8
HPH_1	323.0	324.0	324.0	DIV	73.3	73.9	71.8
XH_1	373.8	373.9	374.7	TAX	239.1	240.9	237.9
SDH_1^P	1013.4	1013.3	1012.0	$2 \cdot BR_i$	62.6	63.8	68.8
HPH_2	435.0	434.0	434.0	$2 \cdot BR_i^{**}$	56.6	57.1	58.9
XH_2	321.7	322.2	323.7	$V_i/(\beta_1 XF_i)$	0.923	0.895	0.783
LH_2	482.1	483.3	485.8	HPF_i/MH_i	1.000	1.000	1.000
$^a(K_{1i}^a+K_{2i}^a)/$				$(K_{1i}^a+K_{2i}^a)/$			
$(KMIN_{1i}^P+KMIN_{2i}^P)$				$(KMIN_{1i}+KMIN_{2i})$	1.003	1.004	1.014
				$EXBB$	0.0	−1.8	−2.2

Table A-6. (continued)

Experiment 4 ($VBILLG_t$: -5.0)

	t	$t+1$	$t+2$
Real GNP	962.7	961.2	961.0
UR	0.0000	0.0000	0.0000
Surplus (+) or Deficit (−)	1.3	−0.3	−0.8
r	0.06500	0.06479	0.06477
PS	1146.4	1150.7	1150.7
$2 \cdot FUNDS_i^e$	1150.2	1153.6	1150.9
RB_i	0.07500	0.07485	0.07486
$2 \cdot VBB_i$	340.0	341.0	340.2
$2 \cdot LBMAX_i$	810.2	812.6	810.7
$LHMAX_2$	482.1	483.5	482.9
$2 \cdot LFMAX_i$	328.1	329.1	327.8
$2 \cdot LFUN_i$	328.1	328.1	326.2
$PFUN_i$	1.0000	1.0000	1.0008
$2 \cdot INVUN_i$	50.0	50.0	50.5
$2 \cdot Y^P UN_i$	842.0	842.0	842.9
$WFUN_i$	1.0000	1.0000	1.0016
$2 \cdot HPFMAXUN_i$	637.3	637.3	638.4
$2 \cdot LF_i$	328.1	328.1	326.2
PF_i	1.0000	1.0000	1.0008
$2 \cdot INV_i$	50.0	50.0	50.5
$2 \cdot Y_i^P$	842.0	842.0	842.9
$2 \cdot X_i^e$	842.0	842.0	842.8
$2 \cdot V_i^P$	105.3	105.2	102.6
WF_i	1.0000	1.0000	1.0016
$2 \cdot HPFMAX_i$	637.3	637.3	638.4
a	1.000	1.000	1.000
$HPFMAX_i/MH_i^P$	1.000	1.000	1.000
$2 \cdot MH_{4i}^P$	0.0	0.0	0.0
$HPHUN_1$	323.0	323.0	322.0
$XHUN_1$	373.8	374.7	375.1
$HPHUN_2$	435.0	434.0	435.0
$XHUN_2$	321.7	322.1	321.9
$LHUN_2$	482.1	483.3	483.3
$HPHMAX_1$	323.0	323.4	322.9
$HPHMAX_2$	435.0	434.6	436.2
HPH_1	323.0	323.0	322.0
XH_1	373.8	374.7	375.1
SDH_1^P	1013.4	1011.3	1008.7
HPH_2	435.0	434.0	435.0
XH_2	321.7	322.1	321.6
LH_2	482.1	483.3	482.9
$^a(K_{1i}^a+K_{2i}^a)/$ $(KMIN_{1i}^P+KMIN_{2i}^P)$			

	t	$t+1$	$t+2$
XUN	842.0	843.3	844.1
X	842.0	843.3	843.7
LUN	810.2	811.4	809.5
L	810.2	811.4	809.1
HPUN	758.0	757.0	757.0
HP	758.0	757.0	757.0
$2 \cdot HPF_i$	637.3	636.3	636.3
$2 \cdot MH_{4i}$	0.0	0.1	0.0
$2 \cdot Y_i$	842.0	840.5	840.3
$2 \cdot V_i$	105.3	102.5	99.1
$2 \cdot \Pi F_i$	130.1	129.6	129.3
$2 \cdot TAXF_i$	65.0	64.8	64.6
$2 \cdot \overline{CF}_i$	0.0	2.8	2.8
$2 \cdot DDF_i$	50.3	53.1	54.0
$2 \cdot VBILLB_i$	180.0	185.0	185.0
$2 \cdot BONDB_i$	10.40	10.11	10.05
BONDD	1.62	1.92	1.97
ΠD	1.71	1.93	1.96
TAXD	0.85	0.96	0.98
CGD	0.08	0.01	−0.01
DDD	34.9	30.4	29.6
DDH_1	60.1	60.3	60.4
DDH_2	51.8	51.8	51.8
$2 \cdot DDB_i$	197.1	195.6	195.7
$-YH_2$	435.0	434.0	435.7
$TAXH_2$	77.1	76.9	77.3
SAV_2	0.0	−1.2	0.4
CG_1	4.2	0.1	−1.2
YH_1	463.5	463.0	462.1
$TAXH_1$	90.5	89.6	89.1
SAV_1	−0.7	−1.3	−2.4
SDH_1	1012.7	1011.2	1008.7
$2 \cdot CGB_i$	0.5	0.0	0.0
$2 \cdot \Pi B_i$	17.6	17.3	17.2
$2 \cdot TAXB_i$	8.8	8.7	8.6
$2 \cdot DIVB_i$	8.8	8.7	8.6
DIV	74.7	74.5	74.2
TAX	242.3	240.9	240.7
$2 \cdot BR_i$	59.1	54.3	55.2
$2 \cdot BR_i^{**}$	56.2	55.9	56.0
$V_i/(\beta_1 XF_i)$	1.000	0.972	0.939
HPF_i/MH_i	1.000	1.000	1.000
$(K_{1i}^a+K_{2i}^a)/$ $(KMIN_{1i}+KMIN_{2i})$	1.000	1.002	1.003
EXBB	−5.0	−0.4	0.5

Quantitatively, the most important difference between the two models is probably the solution of the quadratic equation in Equation (29) in Tables 6-2 and A-2. Even given the adjustment in β_2, the cost parameters are still larger for the non-condensed model, and so the decrease in output due to adjustment costs is greater. In experiment 1, for example, the change in sales in period t caused worker hour requirements in period t to increase by 1.6 for the non-condensed model ($2 \cdot MH_{4it} = 1.6$ in Table A-6), but by only 0.4 for the condensed model ($MH_{4t} = 0.4$ in Table 6-6). For the non-condensed model, aggregate output in period t was forced to decrease from its planned level of 842.0 to 839.8, whereas for the condensed model, aggregate output in period t was only forced to decrease from its planned level of 842.0 to 841.5. This basic quantitative difference between the two models is, however, not very important and has virtually no effect on the qualitative similarities of the two models.

This quantitative difference between the two models does point out a characteristic of the optimal control problem of the firm that the author is not too satisfied with. As mentioned in Chapter Three, the firm had a proclivity, given the parameter values tried, to want to raise its price and thus lower expected sales and planned production. In order to get the optimal path of the price of the firm and the optimal paths of the other decision variables to be flat, the adjustment cost parameters had to be set fairly high, higher than one might want them to be for purposes of solving the overall model as in Table A-6. In future work it would be of interest to do more experimentation on solving the control problem of the firm both under different assumptions about the parameter values and under different specifications of some of the equations.

One other difference between the results in Table A-6 and the results in Table 6-6 that should be pointed out is the following. In experiment 2 in Table 6-6 the higher loan rate and more restrictive loan constraint in period $t+1$ caused the firm sector to raise its price in period $t+1$, whereas in Table A-6 the firms did not change their prices in period $t+1$. The higher loan rate and more restrictive loan constraint were not large enough in Table A-6 to lead the firms to raise their prices. Likewise, the lower loan rate in period $t+1$ in experiment 4 did not lead the firms to lower their prices in period $t+1$ in Table A-6, although the lower loan rate did lead the firm sector to lower its price in period $t+1$ in Table 6-6.

Other results of solving the non-condensed model could be presented, but since the results for the non-condensed and condensed models are so close, there is little point in doing so. The main purpose of this Appendix has been to show how the non-condensed model is solved (Table A-2) and to show that the results are similar to the results for the condensed model in Chapter Six (Table A-6). The non-condensed model is also not stable in the sense that the model did not give any indication of returning to the self-repeating run after having a one-period shock inflicted on it. As mentioned in Chapter Six, this lack of stability is not surprising, given the structure of the model.

References

[1] Alchian, Armen A., "Information Costs, Pricing, and Resource Unemployment," in Phelps et al. [44], 27-52.

[2] Amemiya, Takeshi, "A Note on a Fair and Jaffee Model," *Econometrica*, forthcoming.

[3] Athans, Michael, "The Discrete Time Linear-Quadratic-Gaussian Stochastic Control Problem," *Annals of Economic and Social Measurement*, I (October 1972): 449-491.

[4] Barro, Robert J., "A Theory of Monopolistic Price Adjustment," *Review of Economic Studies*, XXXIX (January 1972): 19-26.

[5] Barro, Robert J., and Herschel I. Grossman, "A General Disequilibrium Model of Income and Employment," *American Economic Review*, LXI (March 1971): 82-93.

[6] Branson, William H., *Macroeconomic Theory and Policy* (New York: Harper & Row, 1972).

[7] Christ, Carl F., "A Short-Run Aggregate-Demand Model of the Interdependence and Effects of Monetary and Fiscal Policies With Keynesian and Classical Interest Elasticities," *American Economic Review*, LVII (May 1967): 434-443.

[8] Christ, Carl F., "A Simple Macroeconomic Model with a Government Budget Restraint," *Journal of Political Economy*, LXXVI (January/February 1968): 53-67.

[9] Clower, Robert W., "Competition, Monopoly, and the Theory of Price," *Pakistan Economic Journal*, V (September 1955): 219-226.

[10] Clower, Robert W., "The Keynesian Counterrevolution: A Theoretical Appraisal," in F. H. Hahn and F. P. R. Brechling, eds., *The Theory of Interest Rates* (London: Macmillan, 1965).

[11]   Coen, Robert M., and Bert G. Hickman, "Constrained Joint Estimation of Factor Demand and Production Functions," *The Review of Economics and Statistics,* LII (August 1970): 287–300.

[12]   Diamond, Peter A., "A Model of Price Adjustment," *Journal of Economic Theory,* III (June 1971): 156–168.

[13]   Eckstein, Otto, and Roger Brinner, "The Inflation Process in the United States," A Study Prepared for the Use of the Joint Economic Committee, 92 Congress, 2nd Session, 1972.

[14]   Fair, Ray C., *The Short-Run Demand for Workers and Hours* (Amsterdam: North-Holland Publishing Co., 1969).

[15]   Fair, Ray C., "On the Solution of Optimal Control Problems as Maximization Problems," *Annals of Economic and Social Measurement,* III (January 1974): 135–154.

[16]   Fair, Ray C., and Dwight M. Jaffee, "Methods of Estimation for Markets in Disequilibrium," *Econometrica,* XL (May 1972): 497–514.

[17]   Fair, Ray C., and Harry H. Kelejian, "Methods of Estimation for Markets in Disequilibrium: A Further Study," *Econometrica,* XLII (January 1974).

[18]   Fisher, Franklin M., "Quasi-Competitive Price Adjustment by Individual Firms: A Preliminary Paper," *Journal of Economic Theory,* II (June 1970): 195–206.

[19]   Fisher, Franklin M., "On Price Adjustment without an Auctioneer," *Review of Economic Studies,* XXXIX (January 1972): 1–15.

[20]   Gepts, S., "Individual Selling Prices in an Exchange Economy," Core Discussion Paper No. 7107, 1970.

[21]   Goldfeld, Stephen M. and Richard E. Quandt, *Nonlinear Econometric Methods* (Amsterdam: North-Holland Publishing Co., 1972).

[22]   Gordon, Donald F. and Allan Hynes, "On the Theory of Price Dynamics," in Phelps et al. [44] , 369–393.

[23]   Gordon, Robert J., "Inflation in Recession and Recovery," *Brookings Papers on Economic Activity,* 1 (1971): 105–158.

[24]   Grossman, Herschel I., "Money, Interest and Prices in Market Disequilibrium," *Journal of Political Economy,* LXXIX (September/October 1971): 943–961.

[25]   Grossman, Herschel I., "Was Keynes a 'Keynesian'? A Review Article," *Journal of Economic Literature,* X (March 1972): 26–30.

[26]   Grossman, Herschel I., "A Choice-Theoretic Model of an Income Investment Accelerator," *American Economic Review,* LXII (September 1972): 630–641.

[27]   Hay, George A., "Production, Price, and Inventory Theory," *American Economic Review,* LX (September 1970), 531–545.

[28]   Henderson, James M., and Richard E. Quandt, *Microeconomic Theory* (New York: McGraw-Hill, 1958).

[29] Holt, Charles C., Franco Modigliani, John F. Muth, and Herbert A. Simon, *Planning Production, Inventories, and Work Force* (Englewood Cliffs, N.J.: Prentice-Hall, 1960).

[30] Keynes, John Maynard, *The General Theory of Employment Interest and Money* (New York: Harcourt, Brace & World, 1935).

[31] Korliras, Panayotis G., "A Disequilibrium Macroeconomic Model," mimeographed, September 1972.

[32] Leijonhufvud, Axel, *On Keynesian Economics and the Economics of Keynes* (New York: Oxford University Press, 1968).

[33] Leijonhufvud, Axel, "Effective Demand Failures," *The Swedish Journal of Economics,* LXXV (March 1973): 27-48.

[34] Lucas, Robert E., Jr., "Optimal Investment Policy and the Flexible Accelerator," *International Economic Review,* VIII (February 1967): 78-85.

[35] Lucas, Robert E., Jr., and Leonard A. Rapping, "Real Wages, Employment, and Inflation," in Phelps et al. [44], 257-305.

[36] Maccini, Louis J., "The Dynamic Behavior of Prices, Output, and Inventories," mimeographed, February 1972.

[37] Maddala, G. S., and Forrest D. Nelson, "Maximum Likelihood Methods for Models of Markets in Disequilibrium," *Econometrica,* forthcoming.

[38] Mills, Edwin S., *Price, Output, and Inventory Policy* (New York: John Wiley, 1962).

[39] Mortensen, Dale T., "A Theory of Wage and Employment Dynamics," in Phelps et al. [44], 167-211.

[40] Mortensen, Dale T., "Job Search, the Duration of Unemployment, and the Phillips Curve," *American Economic Review,* LX (December 1970): 847-862.

[41] Nadiri, M. Ishag, and Sherwin Rosen, "Interrelated Factor Demand Functions," *The American Economic Review,* LIX (September 1969): 457-471.

[42] Nordhaus, William D., "Recent Developments in Price Dynamics," Cowles Foundation Discussion Paper No. 296, August 13, 1970.

[43] Patinkin, Don, *Money, Interest, and Prices* (New York: Harper and Row, 2d ed., 1965).

[44] Phelps, Edmund S., et al., *Microeconomic Foundations of Employment and Inflation Theory* (New York: W. W. Norton, 1970).

[45] Phelps, Edmund S., "Introduction: The New Microeconomics in Employment and Inflation Theory," in Phelps et al. [44], 1-23.

[46] Phelps, Edmund S., "Money Wage Dynamics and Labor Market Equilibrium," in Phelps et al. [44], 124-166.

[47] Phelps, Edmund S. and Sidney S. Winter, Jr., "Optimal Price Policy under Atomistic Competition," in Phelps et al. [44], 309-337.

[48] Quandt, Richard E., "A New Approach to the Estimation of

Switching Regressions," *Journal of American Statistical Association,* LXVII (June 1972): 306–310.

[49] Rothschild, Michael, "Prices Information and Market Structure, mimeographed, 1970.

[50] Rothshild, Michael, "Models of Market Organization with Imperfect Information: A Survey," *Journal of Political Economy,* LXXXI (November/December 1973): 1283–1308.

[51] Solow, Robert M., and Joseph E. Stiglitz, "Output, Employment, and Wages in the Short Run," *Quarterly Journal of Economics,* LXXXII (November 1968), 537–560.

[52] Stigler, George J., "The Economics of Information," *Journal of Political Economy,* LXVIII (June 1961): 213–225.

[53] Tucker, Donald P., "Credit Rationing, Interest Rate Lags, and Monetary Policy Speed," *Quarterly Journal of Economics,* LXXXII (February 1968): 54–84.

[54] Tucker, Donald P., "Macroeconomic Models and the Demand for Money under Market Disequilibrium," *Journal of Money, Credit and Banking,* III (February 1971): 57–83.

[55] Tucker, Donald P., "Expansion-Contraction Asymmetry in Disequilibrium Adjustments to Monetary Policy," Paper presented at Econometric Society summer meetings, Boulder, Colorado, August 23–27, 1971.

[56] Tucker, Donald P., "Discussion of Panayotis G. Korliras, 'A Disequilibrium Macroeconomic Model'," Presented at ASSA Convention, Toronto, December 1972.

Index

223

About the Author

Ray C. Fair was born in 1942 in Fresno, California. He received a B.A. degree in economics from Fresno State College in 1964 and a Ph.D. degree in economics from the Massachusetts Institute of Technology in 1968.

From 1968 to 1974 he was an Assistant Professor of Economics at Princeton University. He is currently an Associate Professor of Economics at Yale University. His primary fields of interest are econometrics, macroeconomics, and income distribution.

Professor Fair is the author of *The Short-Run Demand for Workers and Hours* (North-Holland, 1969), *A Short-Run Forecasting Model of the United States Economy* (D.C. Heath, 1971), *A Model of Macroeconomic Activity Volume II* (Ballinger, 1976), and various journal articles.